Language Style and Social Space

Language Style and Social Space

Stylistic Choice in Suriname Javanese

CLARE WOLFOWITZ

Illinois Studies in Anthropology
No. 18

UNIVERSITY OF ILLINOIS PRESS
Urbana and Chicago

Board of Editors: Janet D. Keller, David C. Grove, Olga Soffer-Bobyshev,
Clark E. Cunningham

© 1991 by the Board of Trustees of the University of Illinois
Manufactured in the United States of America
P 5 4 3 2 1

This book is printed on acid-free paper.

Library of Congress Cataloging-in-Publication Data

Wolfowitz, Clare.
    Language style and social space : stylistic choice in Suriname
Javanese / Clare Wolfowitz.
      p.   cm. — (Illinois studies in anthropology : no. 18)
    Includes bibliographical references and index.
    ISBN 0-252-06160-8 (alk. paper)
    1. Javanese language—Social aspects—Surinam. 2. Javanese
language—Surinam—Style. 3. Javanese language—Surinam—Variation.
4. Speech and social status—Surinam. 5. Javanese—Surinam—Social
life and customs. 6. Sociolinguistics. I. Title. II. Series.
PL5169.W65   1991
306.4′4′095982—dc20   90-45468
                                                                                              CIP

Contents

PART ONE: MODELS

Chapter 1. Introduction	3
Chapter 2. The Style System of Suriname Javanese	36

PART TWO: THE REPERTOIRE

Chapter 3. Expressive Features of Ordinary Style	69
Chapter 4. Domestic Politeness	87
Chapter 5. Speech Levels in Javanese	120
Chapter 6. Individual Styles of Lexical Politeness	139
Chapter 7. Pronoun Selection and Replacement	171

PART THREE: SOCIAL SPACE

Chapter 8. Domestic Space	189
Chapter 9. Functional Adaptation in Suriname-Javanese Households	211
Chapter 10. Stylization and Social Context	236

References 254

Index 260

Preface

A book as long in the making as this one accumulates layer on layer of debts, scholarly and otherwise, until the list of acknowledgments begins to seem absurdly out of proportion to the product. Even so, there will be thanks owed that have been somehow overlooked; of all the errors and omissions that may strike a reader, these are the omissions that weigh most heavily on the author's conscience and for which pardon is most sincerely asked.

Much of the material here was originally presented in my dissertation in anthropology at Johns Hopkins University, which was given initial impetus by Beatriz Lavandera and shepherded to completion particularly by Emily Martin, Kathleen Ryan, and Richard Price. This work also benefited from helpful discussions with Dell Hymes, Alton Becker, Hildred Geertz, Neil Hertz, and John Wolff (who have probably long since forgotten them). Financial support for the fieldwork came from the Johns Hopkins University Program in Atlantic Culture and History, augmented by a grant from the Sigma Chi Foundation.

This version provides a revised framework presented in the first and final chapters; in this I received invaluable guidance and encouragement from various readers and discussants, including Ward Keeler, Parsudi Suparlan, Clark Cunningham, Clifford Geertz, Eugene Galbraith, Suzanne Siskel, Barry Weller, and Grace Goodell. I especially appreciate Janet Keller's insightful reading and editing and Penny Brown's extraordinarily detailed and incisive commentary. I hope, but I hardly expect, that the results will satisfy these mentors and critics.

There is, finally, a broader kind of support that is more difficult to acknowledge properly. My earliest tutors in Javanese culture were the family of Dr. Soetarto of Yogyakarta, Indonesia, in whose home I gathered something of the richly integrated patterns of social life. Their kindness and sensitivity have been a sustaining image over the years. My teachers of Javanese language and Javanese dance also have contributed in intensely personal ways to a deeper understanding of these patterns, and I thank in particular Dra. Sri Kuhns of Washington, D.C., and Sulistyo Kusumatirta of Jakarta. Mbah Duldjalal of Paramaribo provided a philosophical perspective on Suriname-Javanese cultural life. Most essential, of course, has been the encouragement provided by my longtime culture hero, Paul Wolfowitz. To a certain unmeasurable extent, this book is their creation as well.

PART ONE
Models

CHAPTER 1

Introduction

1.1 Context and Paradigm

Speech style is as much an element of social structure as of language, and its study belongs as much to anthropology as to linguistics. From an anthropological perspective, speech style is of special interest as providing insight into the "grammar" of social relations—the participants' model that links "macrolevel" institutional structures with "microlevel" social interaction. This study is essentially anthropological in its approach to observation and interpretation, but it rests on a basic analytic framework coming originally from linguistics, though very widely current in anthropology: the concept of a paradigmatic structure.

Linguistics can be most broadly defined as the study of systematic discriminations pertaining to language. These discriminations are structured as sets (or paradigms) of alternative elements, available for selection and arrangement in meaningful sequences according to rules of syntax, contextual constraints, and speaker intention. Such paradigms exist for elements of sound (phonemes), referential significance (morphemes or lexicon), and—the focus of the present study—stylistic variation.

The field of sociolinguistics has extended the study of systematic linguistic discriminations beyond the framework of the isolated utterance to the broader level of discourse, including such interactional phenomena as turn-taking, terms of address, logical inference, and selection among stylistic options. The definition of relevant context is broadened correspondingly to include social features such as setting, social status and state of knowledge of participants, and topic or task. (Seminal works include Ervin-Tripp 1964; Gumperz and Hymes 1964, 1972; Labov 1970; Gumperz 1970, 1971; Hymes 1974.) The approach presented here further extends the frame of contextual analysis, reflecting an anthropological perspective on social meaning. It is an extension that I hope to demonstrate is compelled by the material itself.

Stylistic meaning has received little scholarly attention, but it too must be understood in terms of a paradigm of alternatives. The meaning of style A is, most simply, that it is *not* style B (or C or D, as the paradigm may provide). The compartmental model presented in chapters 3 and 10 treats style selection as a paradigm of value-loaded alternatives.

1.1.1 Javanese Speech Style

For Javanese language, the paradigmatic structure of stylistic choice is rendered extraordinarily clear by its articulation in obligatory lexical variation. But there are nonlexical stylistic variables as well: close-polite forms of expression (described in chaps. 3 and 4); strategies of pronoun avoidance (chap. 7); respectful intonation patterns and kin terms used as vocatives (chap. 2). Unlike lexical alternation, these elements of style selection have received little scholarly attention, but they nevertheless form an important part of the repertoire of every Javanese speaker.

Sociolinguistic analysis of social context has as its customary focus such broadly predictive factors as social status, social or ethnic group membership, and regional or class identification. I will argue, however, that the selection of speech-style elements in Javanese is in principle impossible to predict because in this case, code selection constitutes a system of stylistic meaning; speakers may alter or create social contexts through style selection. The aim of the analysis is instead interpretation, a task as challenging as that of prediction, and one that requires careful attention to the details of social context—including, in this case, the structure of domestic space.

1.1.2 The Javanese Style Phenomenon in Suriname

The Javanese language is familiar to sociolinguists as an extreme case of stylistic elaboration, encoding aspects of social relationship in a more or less precise fashion by means of a pervasive set of lexical status-marking alternants (described in chap. 5). The obvious parallel is the European system of pronominal alternation (discussed in chap. 7), but whereas the European pronouns encode a binary stylistic opposition (familiar/polite) in a single, binary lexical paradigm (*tu/vous*; or, more broadly, T/V), the Javanese style system comprises hundreds of lexical paradigms in which two or more alternants are available for a given lexical item. Lexical alternation affects not only the personal pronouns but also such everyday referents as personal actions (come, go, sit, eat, bathe), personal possessions and attributes (home, child, many adjectives), and other terms (number, time of day, locatives, deictics, interrogatives).

Such an elaborate style system has obvious functional relevance for the rigidly stratified social world of the urban Javanese aristocracy known as *priyayi* (concisely analyzed in Errington [1988: chap. 2]). Centuries of foreign colonial rule induced ever greater stylistic elaboration of speech and conduct, perhaps the principal vestige of traditional political authority under the Dutch regime. Far more problematic for sociolinguistics is the relevance of such a style system for rural villagers, whose lives—given the historical absence of widespread feudal landholdings—traditionally revolve around the social relations of an essentially homogeneous community of small- to minute-scale family farms (see Geertz 1968). This question frames the present study, though it is not fully answered.

This study presents observations made among the Javanese immigrant community in Suriname (formerly Dutch Guiana, situated on the Caribbean coast of South America), a community whose origins predominantly are in rural Central Java and whose isolation from "high" Javanese culture is almost complete.[1] Even casual observation confirms that the values of formal politeness—though much attenuated in linguistic expression—do have an important place in Suriname-Javanese life.[2] For first-generation immigrants, stylistic competence is an indispensable social accomplishment; for all rural dwellers, such skills command admiration if not necessarily emulation. For a few of the urbanized second- and third-generation Suriname Javanese, stylistic competence has become a matter of studied affectation. ("Urbanization" in the Suriname context has a different connotation from that in Central Java, where it is associated with the cultural dominance of the aristocracy and the court tradition. Urban life in Suriname is much like urban life elsewhere in the Western Hemisphere, associated with interethnic mingling and the adoption of more "modern" life-styles.) In the 1970s, the Indonesian embassy's promotion of Javanese cultural activities and the presence of a Javanese-language radio station (which broadcasts almost exclusively in formal speech style) helped sustain an awareness of and interest in traditional linguistic skills, though generally below the level of mastery considered requisite in even the most rural districts of Central Java.[3]

More interesting, however, than this occasional use of elaborately formal speech style is the evidence that for *any* social interaction with nonfamily members (and for many interactions within the family) there are certain lexical paradigms whose mastery is essential for all adult and adolescent speakers. It is only in contrast to elite Javanese speech style in Indonesia that the Suriname-Javanese style system can be considered simple or crude; compared to the simple binary code of

European T/V pronouns, even the most minimal Javanese politeness repertoire constitutes a complex structure of lexical alternants.

Universalist models of stylistic repertoire invariably adopt the Brown and Gilman (1960) framework, in which two factors of social context—power and distance—are encoded stylistically as congruent signals (see chap. 7). In other words, differences of power between two speakers are encoded as asymmetric social distance; conversely, social distance may be represented as mutual (symmetric) deference. For Suriname-Javanese speakers, however, the "power semantic" is all but irrelevant, stylistically speaking, in intra-ethnic Javanese-language interaction. Suriname Javanese do, of course, move within a power structure, but one defined by the larger society and peopled largely by non-Javanese—and signaled in terms of Dutch, not Javanese, styles. The only context in which I observed an asymmetric use of formal Javanese style (as distinct from "respect" style) was the interaction of senior and junior bureaucrats within the single Javanese-dominated government agency, the Department of Agriculture. Among Suriname Javanese, asymmetric relations in general belong to the category of "respect," not power, and are based on seniority rather than social or political status. Such relationships are encoded linguistically in what I term "respect politeness," a style that communicates both social closeness and negative politeness. This combination of meanings is an option not anticipated in universalist models of style, but it has fundamental significance for the definition of social relationships.

1.2 ANTHROPOLOGY AND SOCIOLINGUISTICS

The study of social interaction owes much to the innovative analyses of Erving Goffman (especially 1967, 1971, 1976), inspired in turn by the classic works of Emile Durkheim and A. R. Radcliffe-Brown. The key anthropological insight underpinning Goffman's analyses of urbanized ("Western") social forms is the idea of a normative structure that presents a conceptual opposition: positive versus negative interaction ritual; front-region versus back-region norms of social behavior. His work has not been the preserve solely—or even primarily—of anthropology. Sociolinguistics, along with ethology, proxemics, and ethnomethodology, has made fruitful use of Goffman's analytic insights while refining the techniques of data collection and interpretation. His positive and negative ritual have become key concepts in the sociolinguistic study of forms of politeness (see sec. 1.4). Less use has been made of his opposition between front-region and back-region interaction norms, possibly because of the relative social invisibility of the latter and the methodological difficulty of observing the movement of individual speakers across contextual boundaries. In the present study, however, Goffman's distinction between front region and back region has provided the conceptual framework necessary to contextualize the selection of speech style in Suriname Javanese.

Sociolinguistics is far, however, from being a branch of anthropology. It draws important inspiration from other fields of linguistics, as well as from semiotics and (particularly in British sociolinguistics) the philosophy of language. If anthropology has provided a pull toward an expanded view of social context, certain trends in the philosophy of language have provided a distinct push in the same direction (though at a pace that may seem grudging from an anthropological perspective). The philosophical concept of "speech act" has had far-reaching influence, pointing to aspects of speech that have performative (rather than strictly referential) force and impelling closer attention to the immediate context of speech as "situated." The closely related subfields of pragmatics and discourse analysis take an explicitly interactive perspective, focusing on the speaker-hearer dyad rather than the isolated speaker as the relevant unit of analysis and sometimes including audience as well. But pragmatics begins where semantics leaves off; questions of reference, presupposition, and implication thus tend to take precedence over more anthropological concerns such as role, status, ethnicity, and social function. (For British overviews, see Levinson 1983 and Coulhard 1985; Schiffman 1986 provides a pertinent critique.) Significantly, anthropology and linguistics have been most thoroughly integrated in the areas of politeness strategy (Brown and Levinson 1978, 1987; Tannen 1986) and codeswitching (Heller 1988), as will be discussed more fully.

1.2.1 The Anthropological Perspective

American approaches to sociolinguistics have been influenced directly by anthropology, adopting as their broadest definitions Hymes's parallel formulations "ethnography of communication" (1964) and "ethnography of speaking" (1971). A key insight entailed in Hymes's perspective is that the performance of speaking—like grammatical competence—has a structure that can be investigated and analyzed using a combination of ethnographic and linguistic methods. Hymes's (1967) term "communicative competence" enlarges the Chomskian concept of "competence" to include the speaker's necessary responsiveness to elements of social context in framing speech; his conception of "speech event" (Hymes 1974) brings speech style (or genre) into focus as a significant feature defining units of interaction. Anthropological treatments of verbal competence/performance have made important use of the concept of speech event in describing and analyzing highly structured political, social, and juridical discourse (e.g., Rosaldo 1973; Bloch 1975; Irvine 1979).

More broadly, the anthropological perspective has engendered an interpretive approach to sociolinguistic analysis, supplementing the predictive models favored by linguists (Gumperz 1982). In codeswitching, notably, a "dynamic" model has supplanted the "typological or deterministic" models: speakers are viewed as dealing with "multiple frames of reference" and employing codeswitching as a "resource . . . to accomplish interactional goals" (Heller 1988:3). The task of interpretation requires attention to such standard sociolinguistic concerns as social boundaries and political-economic distinctions, but it treats them as having strategic rather than deterministic import (Heller, 1988; Gal 1988).

An anthropological approach to meaning necessarily differs from that of semantic or pragmatic linguistics, which begins with the literal signification of a text. A key feature in the anthropological treatment of codeswitching has been the focus on the *indexical* meaning of distinct codes: "the study of codeswitching . . . becomes a means of understanding how such verbal resources, *through use,* acquire conventional social, discourse, or referential meaning" (Heller 1988; emphasis added). Only a few of the Suriname-Javanese stylistic elements derive their significance from their literal semantic content, even by implication processes. Crucial elements of stylistic meaning are compounded rather from (a) the *contrastive* or paradigmatic salience of a particular feature— e.g., the use of a (close-polite) expressive particle in phrase-final position, where a (respectful) vocative might otherwise occur—and (b) the *resonance* of contextual association, as in the close-polite use of a "crooning" intonation pattern typically associated with the care of children. These two nonsemantic components of meaning interact in every case: the close-polite "crooning" intonation, for example, stands in paradigmatic contrast to the more clipped and even intonation of formal (distant) politeness.

Perhaps the most significant potential contribution of anthropology to the understanding of stylistic variation goes back to the central insight of Goffman—and of Durkheim and Radcliffe-Brown—into the oppositional nature of social distinctions. This understanding is basic to the "compartmental model" presented in chapter 3, and it is implied in several other treatments of sociolinguistic strategy. An early example is Robin Lakoff's (1973) model of politeness strategy, framed as a set of "maxims," two of which —"Don't impose" and "Be friendly"—

have mutually contradictory behavioral implications; the speaker must choose between these politeness categories as competing (and not rankable) options.[4] Lakoff's model provides the framework for Tannen's (1986) incisive analysis of domestic interaction styles. In the anthropological approaches to codeswitching cited above, speakers are viewed as making choices with respect to a relevant social boundary; the speaker's selection and/or combination of codes can serve either to *maintain* or to *level* the boundary. Heller nicely summarizes the social opposition underlying this stylistic choice: "the notion of separate domains ... is, I believe, fundamental to codeswitching, while codeswitching itself, seemingly paradoxically, is the direct contradiction of separation" (Heller 1988:7).

This strategic approach has impelled a significant reworking of the concept of grammatical choice, moving away from the emphasis on prescription and co-occurrence. Scotton (1988) proposes a gradient of "markedness" reflecting the degree to which a particular code choice conforms to the expected usage in a given context and requiring the speaker to decide how closely he or she will adhere to the norm in a particular case: "what the norms do, then, is give all speakers a *grammar of consequences*" (Scotton 1988:155, emphasis added; for a related view, see Parkin 1983). The compartmental model of stylistic variation presented here may be viewed as the diagram of a "grammar of consequences," encoding two mutually opposed standards of acceptability. From this point of view, stylistic rules function more as social rules than as transformational ones: violations of stylistic rules not only occur but are meaningful—they have consequences.

1.2.2 Strategy, Ritual, and Markedness

Discourse analysis aims at extending the notion of grammaticality beyond the limits of the sentence, to regularize as much as possible the entire repertoire of discourse elements. Where a linguistic approach has prevailed, the concept of "grammaticality" has implied a degree of "predictability," whereas the anthropological perspective has tended to promote a view of choice that resists prediction (e.g., Scotton's grammar of consequences). But an anthropological perspective must also take note of a broad range of discourse phenomena that might well be modeled by a predictive grammar. This range of phenomena might be termed "ritualized" interaction, and it includes such marks of mutual recognition as greetings and leave-takings—comprising, in some cases, a great deal of the material of an exchange.

The term "ritual" is here meant quite literally, and speech communities vary widely in the degree to which interaction is normally ritualized. The concept of a gradient of markedness may serve to integrate the ritual and strategic perspectives: for fully ritualized interaction, all departures from the norm are highly marked, whereas in most strategic interaction, the repertoire of options will include some of low-level markedness (see Scotton 1988).

In traditionally "anthropological" nonurban contexts, locality and kinship often provide a clear-cut (not to say insuperable) classification of social events and participants corresponding to clearly prescribed intractional forms. Such a structure presents a sharp contrast to the settings analyzed, for example, in the work of Goffman, which deals primarily with the conventional or normative treatment of strangers, passersby, and casual or business acquaintances—categories of interaction far more salient in the urban than the village setting.[5] A pervasive urban concern seems to be the careful adjudication of degrees of participation, serving to exclude (but perhaps not pointedly) or to include (but not absolutely). Such interaction can be described as "negotiated," in that the relationship emerges and is shaped by the interaction itself; in such a social context the scope for strategic manipulation of politeness forms may be virtually total, so that the most routine of formulas is potentially a marked stylistic element. (Hence the well-worn comic routine in which the formulaic greeting "How are you?" elicits reflexive suspicion: "I wonder what he meant by that?") This rich field of implicature is explored in Brown and Levinson (1978, 1987).

Interaction codes in nonurban cultures may present stylistic discriminations that are at once more blatant and less negotiable than those of Western urban society, mapping enduring, preexisting patterns of social units and relationships with sometimes limited scope for negotiated interaction. An extreme example is the classic opposition between "joking" and "avoidance," analyzed by Radcliffe-Brown ([1940] 1965) in terms of the obligatory interaction styles adopted vis-à-vis specific (generational) categories of affinal kin. The "joking relationship" dramatizes rather than mutes the boundary between categories of social participation, underscoring the classification of the individual's social world according to well-defined categories of kinship and affinity: while the form itself enacts a kind of verbal dueling, the *choice* of form is a matter not of strategy but of prescription. More generally, contrastive norms of interaction may mark social boundaries of any kind, registering not only the movement of individuals between categories of relationship (in-group versus out-group) but also the distinctive interactional roles associated with particular social categories (e.g., men versus women, married versus unmarried, elder versus younger generation).

It may prove meaningful, then, to compare ethnographic cases with respect to the conventionally permitted latitude for negotiation in the application of such contrastive stylistic categories. The Javanese case, I suggest, occupies a kind of middle ground. Social units (in Java as well as in Suriname) are not lineages but rather nuclear-family households and corporate villages, located within a ramifying household-centered network of bilateral kin plus neighbors (and even neighbors' kin). There is ample scope here for negotiated interaction, as speakers attempt to place themselves relative to one another, but such negotiation occurs within a clearly defined structure of distinct interactional categories and contrastive stylistic options.

1.2.3 Interaction Norms and Social Boundaries

Stylistic distinctions (as defined in chap. 10) mark culturally significant boundaries. These boundaries may or may not coincide with the sort of demographic divisions—ethnic, geographic, and socioeconomic—that have been a mainstay of sociolinguistic analysis. At least three other sorts of boundaries are involved here and in other anthropologically oriented studies of language use: Fishman's concept of functional domains; the Radcliffe-Brownian boundaries based on kinship, affinal, and generational relationships; and Goffman's event-oriented boundary between "regions" of participation. I will argue that Goffman's person-oriented distinction between positive and negative "face" may also be interpreted in some cases as an aspect of an individual-centered boundary between close and distant social relationships.

The "compartmental" model of interaction presented in chapter 3 takes systematic account of the structuring impact of social units and social categories. An interaction code is "compartmentalized" to the degree that the norms shaping interaction are substantially different (contrastive) for different categories of interaction (in-group versus out-group; men's versus women's speech; front region versus back region, etc.).[6] An interaction code that functions in a context of salient social boundaries—boundaries that must be recognized, dramatized, transgressed, deprecated, or otherwise dealt with interactionally—may well be subject to the kind of compartmentalization described here for Suriname Javanese. That is, a style appropriate in one social context may be, ipso facto, wholly out of place in another, depending on such variables as status of participants and setting of the interaction.[7] Alternative styles cannot be viewed simply as strategic options when there are conflicting rules of appropriateness governing their application: the speaker must redefine some aspect of either the relationship or the context to switch successfully from one politeness style to another.

1.2.4 Spatial Context and Meaning

A very useful framework in this connection (as in studies of codeswitching) is Fishman's concept of "domains," spheres of activity delimited by social structural (macrolevel) factors and associated with contrastive (microlevel) interactional codes: for example, the domains of family, work, and religion (Fishman 1972). In the case of Suriname Javanese, an indispensable middle term is Goffman's "regions"—an on-the-ground demarcation of interactional boundaries providing a conceptual map of normative interactional distinctions that relate ultimately to the structural domains of kinship and community.

The spatial framework is invoked here principally, however, as a key to the meaning of stylistic options. Specifically, the structure of domestic space is compartmentalized along much the same lines as the structure of speech style: the front region corresponds roughly to the use of formal speech style; the back region implies the use of ordinary style; and the inside region is associated, in certain contexts, with the use of respect style. But this one-to-one correlation is merely suggestive rather than predictive, and creative departures are an inherent part of this communicative code.[8] A sociolinguistic approach typically treats the spatial setting as part of the context of utterance—as one of the situational factors determining speech-style selection. Following the work of Blom and Gumperz (1972), sociolinguists accordingly have distinguished between "situational" codeswitching, which is cued by contextual factors and is therefore in principle predictable, and "metaphorical" codeswitching, in which the speaker deliberately uses a contextually incongruent code for specific communicative effect; such metaphorical usage is, of course, inherently unpredictable. A similar distinction may be useful in the case of the Suriname-Javanese spatial setting but must be framed in somewhat different terms. In many instances, speech style and spatial setting are congruent, as when formally styled interaction takes place in a front-region setting. In other instances, however, speech style is used to *create* the setting, defining as front-region (for example) an interaction taking place in a bus or on a ferry or defining as temporarily back-region a setting that is typically formal, such as the front room. Such creative uses of speech style are not metaphorical in the sense just described; I would term such usage "noncongruent" rather than "incongruent." The use of formal style in an anomalous setting does not in any way call attention to the apparent anomaly but rather erases it: speech style is fully substitutable for other contextual cues. It is as true to say that speech style defines the interactional context as to say that the context determines the style of speech. In effect, speech style serves as a completely flexible means of structuring social context, adapting the framework of spatial categories established in the normative use of household space. From this point of view, domestic spatial organization does not constitute an independent context of utterance in the sociolinguistic sense; the household itself constitutes a communicative code only slightly less fluidly adaptable than speech itself (see chap. 9). In anthropological terms, domestic space can be seen as a meaningful structure of oppositions paralleling the structure of speech-style contrasts. As a flexibly adaptable component of interaction, spatial context bears a relation to speech that is structurally identical to that of speech style itself.

1.3 Cultural Conceptions of Speech

A striking feature of Javanese style is the pronounced cultural emphasis on patterned interaction. Smoothly patterned social interaction is considered essential to maintaining personal equilibrium and, indeed, mental health (to import a Western concept). A correspondingly high value is conventionally placed on "social harmony," in which properly patterned speech plays a crucial role. This cultural emphasis creates a special strategic environment, as well as perhaps a special perspective on the requirements of individual "face." Elements to be factored into a strategic model must include the speaker's personal stake in speaking properly and, conversely, the loss of face to both speaker and hearer entailed in any disruption of proper patterns of speech. The emphasis on cultural harmony serves as a background norm that enhances the force of interactional norms and thus militates against individual speakers' latitude for negotiating interaction in any given case.

Formal speech style (see chap. 2), from this point of view, not only has the negative or defensive function of maintaining interpersonal distance but also serves the positive cultural value of creating a satisfying and harmonious surface to daily life. At stake for Javanese speakers, ultimately, is an entire social order in which the proper (hierarchical) relations governing the whole ideally are mirrored in the properly (hierarchically) ordered relationships of each part. (This classic Southeast Asian conception is set forth in Heine-Geldern [1942] and reinterpreted with specific reference to Java in Anderson [1972]. Its relation to language is best expressed in Keeler [1987], especially pp. 136-40.) Individual strategies of speaking from this point of view must serve not merely an immediate interactional goal but also a larger good;

not only the particular relationship but society itself is given structure by the act of speaking.

1.3.1 Powerful Speech

The Javanese conception of speech as powerful requires that speech be used with great discretion (Keeler 1987:124-40; 1984:321). In a further step, the awareness of powerful speech creates a special strategic environment in which the speaker must control not only his own speech style but that of his interlocutors, because their lapses may impugn his spiritual potency as well as his social status (Keeler 1987:70-73, 85-86). As Keeler makes clear, Javanese do not recognize two separate mechanisms for controlling speech — one's own by direct volition, that of others by indirect pressure. Rather, spiritual potency is the factor that keeps *all* speech — one's own and others' — within the proper channels. (See also Siegel's discussion of the implications of the speech compulsion known as *latah* [1986:28-33].) Remediation of lapses is from this point of view not a possibility, because adequate personal power would have ensured that lapses not occur at all. Individual face may thus require avoiding situations in which one risks being shown as powerless (by others' inappropriate speech) or even being seen as concerned about one's power (Keeler 1987:70-77, 116, and passim).

1.3.2 Greetings

In the case of Suriname Javanese, the interaction of daily life is far removed from the cosmological center — the court cities of Central Java — but it nevertheless has its own defining social reality. The act of speaking structures the household itself and its penumbra of supporting and dependent relationships. The polite formulas of domestic interaction (discussed in chap. 4) themselves have some of the efficacy of ritual, in the sense of creating and sustaining a social order. Taken together with the compartmental structure of the system, which has as its underlying logic the task of placing people appropriately, Javanese politeness is a system less oriented toward redress or remediation than toward the signaled personal recognition we may term, speaking somewhat broadly, "greeting" (see chap. 4).

In a compartmentalized style system, the act and choice of greeting may serve both to map relevant features of social structural classification and to orient speakers, appropriately or advantageously, toward one another. The greeting (or absence of one) provides the crucial context for any further interaction. From this point of view, greeting can have substantial strategic importance as participants attempt to impose a preferred classification on a particular interaction. Greetings also have a certain coercive force, as in adults' interaction with children: the adult greeting brings the child within the orbit of adult interactive expectations. A systematic examination of greetings would usefully relate social structural categories to interactional phenomena.

1.4 CLOSE AND DISTANT POLITENESS

In the Suriname-Javanese style system, the most salient compartmental distinction is between "insiders" and "outsiders," as defined in relation to a particular household and as reflected stylistically in the basic choice between codes of "close politeness" and "distant politeness." I use the latter terms in preference to the currently used terms "positive politeness" and "negative politeness," to reflect the social boundary orientation of the model.

The concept of "positive" and "negative" interaction strategies, originally introduced by Goffman, derives directly from Durkheim's discussion of primitive religion, with its positive rites of prestation and negative rites of avoidance.[9] The broad utility of these terms in describing urban social interaction arises, it may be argued, from the urban necessity of treating each social encounter as strategically problematic, given the absence of structuring frameworks—as literally analogous to the Durkheimian interaction of humans with divinity. The interaction rituals described by Goffman are also forms of negotiation, something that cannot be true of fully prescribed ritual forms, e.g., some forms of greeting.

Goffman locates the opposition between positive and negative interaction ritual in an analytic distinction between the positive and negative aspects of individual face—the individual's desire for approval and ratification, on the one hand, and his or her desire to be let alone, on the other. This insight is at the heart of the model of politeness strategy developed by Brown and Levinson (1978, 1987): a very broad range of politeness phenomena can be analyzed in terms of positive and negative implication, and these alternatives take their place, for Brown and Levinson, in a ranking of politeness strategies that also includes (at the polite extreme) the options of reticence and indirection together with (at the nonpolite extreme) the option of unmediated directness.[10]

1.4.1 Close/Distant and Positive/Negative

The utility of such a ranking of politeness strategies depends crucially on the nature of the social boundaries in the particular case. In the Western urban setting, one might describe the social environment in terms of a continuum of degrees of intimacy, mirroring the continuum of politeness strategies; in the sorts of non-Western environment sketched in section 1.2.2, however, social boundaries impose categorical choices between "in-group" and "out-group" interaction styles (analogous to patterns of codeswitching). In the Javanese case, social distinctions, though not completely clear-cut, have a similar categorical quality: relationships of closeness require ratification through positive politeness, while relationships of distance call for a consistent pattern of negative politeness. (Note again the "greeting"—rather than redressive—function of expressions of positive politeness.) Here a compartmental rather than ranked model is required.

Where politeness forms are oriented to social boundaries, their relation to individual face may be rather remote. Specifically, the form of a positive-polite utterance may be less directly derived from the attention to individual "wants" than the Brown and Levinson model suggests.[11] Such derivation operates in some cases at a metaphorical remove: what is attended to in positive politeness may be not the individual's supposed actual wants but rather some conventionally imputed ("as-if") wants, as in offering food in spite of refusals. Alternatively, actual wants may be given purely ritual recognition, as when an offer is made with a conventional expectation of refusal. Although such gestures *mime* a relationship of want fulfillment, the key referent is not necessarily the individual and his or her wants but rather the social model of care-giving closeness that is thus invoked. These positive-polite forms are not very far removed from the Javanese ritual in which a bride, on the day before her wedding, emerges from her house and sits alone wrapped in batiks, to be doused with dipper after dipper of flowered water ladled in turns by the entire assemblage of senior kin—who by that token identify themselves as such. The ritual mimes the care given a child by the parents in the act of daily bathing, but none of the participants needs to imagine that the additional ladleful of water serves a want-fulfilling function. Here we are clearly in the realm of metaphor—but note that the closeness of the individual relationships, and the support that is thus ritually gestured, may be very real.

If social closeness and distance are clearly defined in a compartmental style system, positive and negative politeness may be correspondingly difficult to distinguish. This paradox reflects the ritualized and obligatory character of boundary-oriented social interaction. As Goffman points out, "greetings can be analyzed as a correction, a remedy, for what otherwise would become an offense. The same is true with an offer . . . and other members of the class of ratificatory rituals" (1971:158).

The formulaic character of much Javanese social interaction, both close and distant, tends to blur the distinction between positive and negative politeness, between gestures of solidarity and gestures that serve to mitigate an imposition. Is the host's offer of beverages—obligatory for formal visits—a gesture of positive politeness? Is the guest's formulaic request for permission to enter (*Kula nuwun*) an instance of negative politeness? Such a view may make sense at some level; for example, the formulaic request for permission to enter serves "as if" to mitigate the imposition of intruding on the household. But the visit itself may be quite obligatory and the "intrusion" nil, as in the case of the foster granddaughter's visit described in section 9.2.2. Here the request for permission is simply an element of the visiting ritual, itself a positive gesture. Conversely, the "positive" gesture of offering beverages is equally expected, and its omission would be felt as a notable oversight. It does not seem useful, on the whole, to distinguish between omitting the request to enter as a "violation" and neglecting to offer a beverage as a "slight," the terms Goffman (1971:63) uses for lapses in negative and positive ritual, respectively. It is more useful to say that the interaction, as a patterned whole, simultaneously serves the positive function of affirming a social relationship and the negative one of avoiding potential awkwardness or upsetting missteps. Guest and host have a shared script, as well as a shared cultural preference for the fact of patterning itself (discussed in sec. 2.4.1), a preference that holds also, to some degree, in close interaction. Interaction strategy, or decision making, is thus contained within the bounds of rather rigidly patterned social expectations; it enters in most importantly, perhaps, at the point of selecting the category of interaction as close or distant.

1.4.2 Forms of Close Politeness

In Suriname Javanese, the distinction between close and distant politeness thus tends to supersede the analytic distinction between positive and negative forms of politeness. In close interaction, for example, both sorts of politeness are encoded as a kind of self-dramatization, using the first-person pronoun confessionally ("I'm hungry!" "I'm full!" "I'm tired!" "I like this!"). (See chap. 7 for the "confessional" first-person.) In distant interaction, self-deprecation rather than self-dramatization is the norm for both positive and negative politeness.

The phenomenon of close politeness has received relatively little scholarly attention, certainly in the case of Javanese speech style, but for Suriname Javanese it represents a centrally important social skill. To fail to communicate closeness is to communicate distance, whether politely or negligently, and to communicate a sense of distance in a context wherein closeness would be appropriate is to commit as great an offense as the converse.

The code of close politeness comprises not only the set phrases that I call "politeness formulas" but also intonation, gestures, and lexical style. It nevertheless tends to escape the attention of observers, perhaps because it appears as a spontaneous or "natural" mode of expression. The apparent spontaneity may nevertheless be part of the stylistic code; the expression of social closeness may be thought of as a kind of "as-if" intimacy in which each gesture contributes to the overall effect of congeniality. Such signals are especially noticeable, for example, in the conduct of those household guests who may be closely related to the host family but who rarely visit owing to factors such as geographic distance. Such visitors may, if they choose, participate as "insiders" rather than "outsiders" by making use of interrogative formulas, expressive particles, and dramatic intonation (see chaps. 3 and 4). Such stylistic devices ought not to be construed as simple spontaneity: their appropriate use may be as rigorously mandated in enacting a close-polite relationship as is the use of formal lexicon in distant-polite contexts.

1.5 Sociolinguistics and Meaning

In keeping with prevailing linguistic concerns, sociolinguistics generally has given closer attention to the formal aspects of style systems than to their meaning for social participants. Social meaning is often handled in shorthand fashion, as if such concepts as ethnic identity, deference, and imposition have unvarying content and uniform cross-cultural significance.[12] Indeed, much the same can be said of the classic study of stylistic alternants, Brown and Gilman's (1960) essay on pronominal choice (see sec. 7.1). In that elegant work, the two "semantics," "power" and "solidarity," are essentially structural labels with only brief treatment of ethnographic content.[13]

Aspects of meaning can nevertheless have far-reaching implications for structural logic, necessitating specific adaptations in a theoretical model. Several examples of such structural implication emerge from an overview of Javanese usage as reported in the literature.

1.5.1 Stylistic Meaning and Personal Face

Social interaction codes that function as important boundary markers may in general have a different sort of significance for participants than do those politeness codes that are oriented essentially toward the interactive dyad, as presented in pragmatic analyses. Performance may be thought of less as a function of personality, less as an expression of "self," than as a token of behavioral conformity. Social behavior, from this point of view, is situationally compartmentalized rather than integrated with the self. Such an understanding eliminates one potential threat to individual face: a successful performance does not require sustaining the illusion of either stylistic consistency or sincerity. Siegel (1986) describes, for Central Java, the striking compartmentalization of classroom interaction, in which students converse freely among themselves in unrestrained Low Javanese but shift readily to formal Indonesian to address their teacher. Keeler (1984:88-89, 166) similarly notes (also of Central Javanese) the abruptness of shifts in conversational tone within a single interaction and observes that "these sudden shifts in and out of a colloquial tone [into very formal speech style] do not embarrass the Javanese and require no dissimulation" (1984:275).[14]

1.5.2 Information as Imposition

There are other crucial respects in which culturally specific meanings seem to have structural implications for interaction analysis. These have to do with an understanding of the nature of social imposition, a central concept in the Brown and Levinson analysis.

Javanese norms of distant politeness seem to offer support for a key premise of the Brown and Levinson model, that the requirements of information communication are potentially in conflict with the requirements of politeness. Counter to the working assumption of the Brown-Levinson model, however, primacy in the Javanese case is accorded to the politeness function of speech; information is treated either as a vehicle of politeness (in close-polite interaction) or as an imposition (in distant-polite interaction). Analytically, a style system that is oriented referentially to interactional boundaries does not need to view politeness forms as irrational or inefficient deviations from a "working assumption by conversationalists of the rational and efficient nature of talk" (Brown and Levinson 1987:4). Rather, the conversational efficiency maxim applies instead in its *negative* form, as a corollary to distant politeness: "Offer new information only when necessary." More than one observer has noted the heavily formulaic character of interaction patterns observable among Javanese. What appears to be an exchange of information is often simply a reiteration of common knowledge: "Almost any topic in Java elicits certain popularly accepted views [which are] expressive of polite amiability, something much prized by the Javanese"; "the Javanese habit of telling each other what they already know . . . is an important part of making everyone feel that they are in comfortable accord" (Keeler 1984:337, 209). The strong Javanese preference for patterned interaction extends to a preference for predictable conversational topics, at least within certain broad outlines. Such interaction is, again, better analyzed as a form of greeting than as an enactment of strategy. Far from motivating interaction style—as the strategic model predicts—the topic of discourse may function instead as another aspect of style, to be selected primarily on grounds of appropriateness. For Suriname Javanese, topic and speech style are very much interrelated in this counterpredictive way, even in the domain of close politeness (see the discussion in chap. 4 of the domestic "agenda" as reflected in interrogative "greetings").

The interactional premise of Javanese politeness seems to be that interaction is directed toward proper placement and recognition of social others—that is, a politeness function. To seek or to provide information is (in distant-polite interaction) always an intrusion on this central function and always requires what might be termed "remedial" bracketing. The syntax of the language (like that of Indonesian as well) makes provision for this in the form of sentence-initial "topic posting" (Keeler, 1984:36-37), which I interpret as a kind of bracketing signal to warn the listener that information is about to be offered or requested. Topic posting can be accomplished with varying degrees of signaled hesitation, giving the bracketing function greater or less emphasis: a conventional device is to bracket the topic itself with a prefatory fumble—"The watchamacallit, that thing, . . ." (*Anu, niku, . . .*).

In close-polite interaction, by contrast, seeking and providing information are mainstays of conversation. Bracketing may appear in close-polite speech style, but it is given dramatic intonational emphasis as if to insist on the importance or uniqueness of the event or situation to be discussed. (See sec. 4.3.2 on the "interrogative dialogue.")

1.5.3 Imposition and Remediation

Interaction in Javanese generally exhibits a pronounced sensitivity to what Goffman has termed "imposition," but again, this sensitivity seems to operate differently here than in the urban Western cultural setting Goffman has analyzed. In the Javanese (and Suriname-Javanese) context, one may distinguish between impositions that are routine and indeed expected—the imposition of offering a greeting (see the next section) or of requesting permission to enter—and those that are remediable but neither routine nor expected. In some traditional circles, at least, the latter category is virtually an empty set: imposition that is not routinely expected ought not to occur, and no acceptable amelioration is provided for such nonroutine imposition.[15] (This is the obverse of the highly patterned quality of interaction.) There are ways of offering apology, but such is the degree of sensitivity to imposition that even rather formal phrases of apology come to be used to ameliorate such routine impositions as taking one's leave or passing in front of someone who is seated. An entire range of interactional strategy simply does not exist for these conservative speakers. So far from asking someone for a "free good" ("Have you got a light?"), in distant interaction, one does not even presume to drink one's tea until the second or third formal invitation to drink (Keeler 1984:122-25).

To say that nonroutine imposition ought not to occur is not to say that it is thought never to occur. On the contrary, errors in speech are considered inevitable but nonetheless serious. A striking feature of any formal interaction, whether a polite visit, a speech, a ritual invocation, or a performance, is the obligatory preface of begging pardon of the listener: "If there may occur any errors of mine, I ask forgiveness." (Keeler [1984:80, 84, 89] gives formulas of varying formality.) Begging forgiveness in fact constitutes a central element of life crisis and family ritual: the bridal couple to their parents at the wedding; junior kin to senior kin at Lebaran (Idul Fitri, the end of the fasting month); wife to husband, to ease a difficult childbirth (H. Geertz 1961:88). Remediation ritual is taken very seriously as a form of speech act, but as such it is enacted formally and generally rather than as specific remediation.

One way of accomplishing event-specific remediation is—perhaps counter to prevailing sociolinguistic logic—by switching from a more formal to a *less formal* (close-polite) style. (I have no examples of the converse—remedial switching from a less formal to a more formal style—though this may also occur. Respect style probably functions in this way as remediation, with or without the addition of formal stylistic elements.) The most striking example I have observed involved individuals who were not Suriname Javanese but rather elite Javanese: two women in their thirties, both originally from Solo (Surakarta, Central Java) but currently living in Jakarta. They were rehearsing for a "cultural morning" that would include a dance performance, and when I first met them I was struck by their consistent use of Madya (intermediate formal lexical style) with each other. In Jakarta, Javanese functions as an in-group code for elite Javanese, who are otherwise equally comfortable in Indonesian (not to mention English and, in many cases, Dutch). For two young women, the in-group register would normally be Ngoko (familiar style, perhaps with honorific address); if they were not close enough for that, Indonesian would be normal. I surmised that the setting—Javanese dance rehearsal—motivated the choice of

Javanese. At a later rehearsal the picture changed dramatically. Evidently the two had been rivals for the place of lead dancer and used Madya to express a distinct stiffness in the relationship; so when one of them offered to take a position in the back the tension disappeared, and for the rest of the rehearsal they maintained a lively interchange of questions, shared complaints, and even some mutual praise, all using Ngoko. The redressive offer itself was formulated in dramatic, close-polite style: "I'd better stand in the back, I'll make mistakes! I already forgot the dance!" This was phrased not in Madya but in a mix of English and Ngoko, directed to no one in particular. (The young woman's embarrassment was real; in the run-through she had made a few very visible errors.) Her rival immediately responded with close-polite reassurance, emphatically disagreeing with the thought, and this ameliorative response was in plain Ngoko.

The sensitivity to imposition in fact enhances its symbolic value in close interaction: a high level of imposition is routine and even obligatory among insiders. The interrogative greetings ("Where are you going?" "What are you cooking?") are the most obvious example of obligatory imposition. What I term the "respect" relationship may be seen as a form of close relationship in which such insider impositions, though obligatory, nevertheless require the amelioration of a distinctive close-polite speech style (described in sec. 2.1.2 and discussed in sec. 2.2).

What might appear, then, to be a potent ameliorative tactic—the use of polite lexicon—is effectively neutralized in the most distant-polite interaction contexts, where the use of polite lexicon in effect functions as an obligatory amelioration for the minimal imposition implied in interaction itself. Indirection and avoidance thus remain the sole tactical options for amelioration of nonroutine impositions in distant-polite interaction. A fairly minor request, for example, calls for elaborate indirection in any but close interaction, and a major request may require the mediation of a third party (who will herself employ indirection).[16]

The most striking example of indirect request I observed was when one of the elderly ladies (Ba Loro; see sec. 9.3.2) who regularly visited my host household in Paramaribo came to the house but did not enter, instead taking up a squatting position just outside the front door. From this the entire household understood that she was (once again) short of money and would gladly accept a "loan." Her request was considered rather a bold imposition just the same, and she was permitted to remain squatting outside for about a half hour while the household went about its business. Incidentally, her speech style vis-à-vis the grandparents retained its thoroughly informal character on the occasions I subsequently observed; it is nevertheless possible that at some point she directly acknowledged their assistance using a more formal speech style.

Perhaps the only kind of ameliorative tactic possible in presenting a major request is, in effect, to redefine the relationship itself to imply a new kind of mutual obligation or interdependence. This is what the petitioner was hoping to accomplish in this case, by presenting herself visibly and more or less publicly as a dependent of what she regarded (for the moment at least) as a patron household. It is quite possible that a similar transformation might be sought in some cases by a stylistic shift to a more deferential lexical style, though I have not observed such a case.[17] Such a gesture is analytically different from amelioration, for it requires the petitioner to offer some sacrifice of social status by taking on, for example, a dependent role (cf. Jay 1969:152-54, 263-64, 285).

An error of my own perhaps illustrates the sharply limited ameliorative power of the polite lexicon. The landlord of my host household in Paramaribo, who lived in the larger house he had built behind the very modest one he now rented to Ba Pèn,[18] was invariably cool in his manner toward me. As the time for his sons' circumcision party approached and the preparations became visibly elaborate—including the construction of a roof over the yard, in case of rain—I took the opportunity to make what I thought was a friendly (but not too friendly) overture. Using polite lexicon and the appropriate vocative kin term, I asked, referring to what was very clearly the task at hand, "Are you building a roof, 'Father?' " (*Damel griya Pak?*) His response was rudely phrased in familiar vocabulary, with no kin term appended: "Something the matter with it?" (*Ora apik?*) Clearly, for whatever reason, I was not part of the social circle from which even routine and duly mitigated imposition was expected.

1.5.4 Inequality and Imposition

A final framing observation about Javanese interactional style relates to the discussion of "directional" interaction in chapter 4. One may speculate that the Javanese sensitivity to imposition reflects the unequal character of most substantive social relationships in Java, including those within the family (see Jay 1969: chaps. 5 and 9; H. Geertz 1961: chaps. 1 and 2). The assumption is that of inequality rather than equality, and so any imposition that is enacted first must be scrutinized as a token of the degree and direction of inequality.[19] Hierarchical relationships are much attenuated in Suriname-Javanese society, but the background assumptions perhaps persist. Inequality implies a special sort of social distance in which every gesture carries reverberations for sensitized participants and observers; in the extreme case, there is no possibility of positive gestures upward, as one's very presence constitutes a kind of imposition of which a lowered gaze and deep bow are the obligatory mitigations.

If formal lexical style has limited usefulness in accomplishing ameliorative tasks, how then does it function in (distant-polite) interpersonal interaction? It is at minimum a way to reiterate the character of a relationship potentially so delicate that the utterance of the merest negative or interrogative may present a potential challenge that requires systematic and simultaneous remediation. Lexical politeness seems to serve a broader function as well, quite apart from its role in shaping individual relationships. In keeping with the cultural emphasis on orderly and patterned social interaction, the shift to polite lexical style satisfies a very basic want, namely, that the social order be properly "Javanese." The opposition between ordinary speech and polite speech, as enacted in the shift between Ngoko and Krama, calls to mind Lévi-Strauss's opposition between the raw and the cooked, the precultural and the cultural. For Javanese the metaphor might be more aptly framed as an opposition between *unclothed* and *properly clothed*—stylized—speech, although the model of speech styles is far more complex than a binary opposition.

1.6 METHOD

The fieldwork on which this study is based took place in the summers of 1976 and 1977, seven months in all. The analysis of the material, as well as the choice of focus, is the product ultimately of a much longer period of interaction with Javanese speakers, going back to a 1962 homestay in Yogyakarta (Central Java) as an American Field Service exchange student. In view of the relatively short period of fieldwork, the observations offered here must be regarded as provisional; nevertheless, several factors suggest that further fieldwork might not materially counter these first and second impressions.

The investigation of stylistic categories presents a topic that calls not only for substantial knowledge of the performers but also, paradoxically, for a fresh perspective on the performance. In many cases the most significant observation regarding a particular interaction was simply the way in which it challenged a non-Javanese set of assumptions: the tolerance for extended silences and nonresponses; the use of exaggerated intonation patterns and the abrupt shift between styles of speech; the salience of kinship terms as vocatives, as well as other forms of direct address. These facets were far easier to capture at the beginning of each fieldwork stay than toward the end.

Nor was this completely new territory for me. I was forced to sort out some of these issues in my initial encounter with Javanese culture in Yogya in 1962. Language training in Javanese during the year prior to fieldwork similarly had entailed learning something about the categories of interaction style as—in true Indonesian fashion—my language teacher in effect adopted me into a circle that included her own family and other Javanese families resident in Washington, D.C.

The subject of Javanese speech style was one that I had wanted to pursue ever since my experience of living in Yogya. Once in the field there was no need to cast about for a research topic: the Suriname setting presented itself almost as a laboratory for studying minimal stylistic refinement in Javanese. The interim period between the two fieldwork trips served to focus first impressions and to distill questions and categories to be pursued during the second visit; the headings on my note cards correspond remarkably closely to the headings of the final draft.

Domestic social interaction is, moreover, a topic that must necessarily occupy any guest's attention at the start of an extended visit. I was fortunate, in my initial introduction into a Suriname-Javanese home five days after my arrival in Suriname, to be regarded less as a foreign anthropologist than simply as a young woman visitor, albeit substantially less adept than the nieces and cousins who might visit the household from time to time. Linguistically, I was identified, for practical purposes, as an Indonesian speaker, because that was the language of convenience when translation was needed (as it frequently was in the early weeks: the Javanese dialect spoken in Suriname drops initial consonants, among other idiosyncrasies it shares with regional dialects in Java). I was soon being corrected freely, not only in speech style but also in dress and other points of conduct, as well as in the performance of routine household chores. As my status became more clearly that of a household insider, I found that I could no longer be present at the more formal men's visits and ceremonies, as my outsider status had initially permitted. What was thereby lost in the documentation of formal Javanese speech style was compensated for by the opportunity to appreciate the importance of the inside social realm for both men and women in the Suriname setting.

I had the privilege of extended periods of residence in two very different households, as well as brief stays in three others (and visits to neighboring and related households). The first household I lived in was a relatively prosperous one belonging to the assistant headman of a large village not too far from Paramaribo, the capital. The second (distantly related to the first) was a very modest rented home in a Javanese neighborhood of Paramaribo. Most of the households I visited were in these two areas. The bulk of the linguistic observations reported here are from the Paramaribo setting; where nonurban styles are reported, they are noted as such.

The means of data collection was primarily on-the-spot note taking, which, given my interest in language, was readily accepted by my hosts. Notes were transcribed and contextualized as soon as possible, usually nightly—that is, annotated as to setting, participants, and other factors. Tape recording presented several difficulties. Soon after my arrival in the initial household, my host received a visit from one of the two Javanese cabinet ministers in the government at that time. This august visitor pointedly refused to shake my hand and was afterward quoted as alleging a CIA connection on my part. For reasons of prudence as well as etiquette, I resolved to make tape recordings only after obtaining the permission of the participants. This ground rule made it rather difficult to record greetings, which are commonly uttered before the entrance of the new arrival and which by definition take place before another topic (such as tape recording) can be negotiated. Other taping difficulties were technical: noises from trucks, motorcycles, neighbors' radios, roosters, dogs, goats, and children rendered normal discourse inaudible for portions of every tape. On-the-spot note taking was in any case essential for correlating spatial interaction (entrances and exits, as well as shifts in seating and other gestures) with the flow of talk and nontalk.[20]

This "low-tech" approach to data collection is the traditional anthropological method of participant observation. Linguists reasonably may be dismayed at the consequent lack of precision regarding frequencies of occurrence, but perhaps at the same time they will recognize the value of participant observation for investigation of the meanings associated with stylistic choices. Among the most revealing data regarding meaning were speakers' reactions to lapses, which were usually errors of my own; participation in the style system was in general an essential aspect of observation.[21]

The Suriname-Javanese style system is presented here as a distinct sociolinguistic case rather than as a variant or subset of Javanese as used in Indonesia. Reference must be made, however—especially in chapters 5 and 8—to the background context of Javanese usage and social structure. The Suriname-Javanese community is a development of this century, and at the time of fieldwork it was still informed by the cultural code of a large community of first-generation arrivals from the prewar period. My own perspective on the Suriname-Javanese material has been enlarged (though not substantially altered) by the experience of three years' residence (1986-89) in Jakarta, the Indonesian capital, which though not itself an area where Javanese predominates, nevertheless has strongly influential elements of Javanese culture. In this period I benefited greatly from the view of Javanese scholars and other Javanists, as well as from discussions with anthropologists working in other areas of Indonesia. Many of the points made here regarding Suriname Javanese apply equally in much of Java, and it is my belief that the three-way model described here for Suriname Javanese underlies usage in Java as well.

1.7 Setting: The Javanese Community in Suriname

The historical connection between Java and Suriname, which are located on opposite sides of the globe, arises from their shared colonial relationship with the Netherlands. Java, as the politically central and most populous island of the former Dutch East Indies (now the Republic of Indonesia), constituted the core of the early Dutch colonial possessions by 1620. Suriname (formerly Dutch Guiana), acquired a half century later, was an important addition to the expanding colonial agriculture plantation system.

Unlike Java, Suriname (in common with the Caribbean area generally) presented a picture of chronic labor shortage from the point of view of an inherently exploitative production system. Responding to the abolition of the slave trade and the subsequent emancipation of existing slaves, and to the eventual cutoff of labor importation from British India, the Netherlands in 1890 began importing contract laborers from overpopulated Java to the labor-absorptive agricultural economy of Suriname.[22] Labor importation from Java continued for almost five decades, until 1939, and by 1960 the Javanese community in Suriname numbered over 40,000 — one-fifth of a population that was otherwise composed primarily of "Creoles" (descendants of African slaves) and "Hindustanis" (descendants of contract laborers from British India). The population also included much smaller numbers of ethnic Chinese, indigenous tribal groups, and, most interesting perhaps, communities of Maroons, or Bush Negroes, who are the descendants of escaped slaves, still living in remote rain-forest areas (see Price 1979). By the time of the 1971 census, the Javanese community numbered amost 60,000 — a sizable absolute increase since 1960 but a smaller relative share at less than 16 percent. By 1976 the demographic picture had changed, reflecting the very substantial emigration of Surinamers (predominantly Hindustanis) to the Netherlands, which took place in the two years preceding Suriname's independence in 1975. Observers estimated that, though their numbers had also decreased, the proportion of ethnic Javanese had increased by perhaps 2 percent (historical sources are Lockard 1971; Malefijt 1963; Derveld 1982; Mintz and Price 1976; census data from the *Encyclopedia Britannica*).

The Suriname-Javanese community, especially in the rural districts, presents to the observer the picture of yet another regional variant within the spectrum of Javanese culture rather than a totally new social and cultural form. As late as 1975, the Javanese remained the least integrated of the various ethnic groups, continuing in predominantly agricultural occupations and resisting the trend to urban migration. The Dutch plantation system had maintained a strict homogeneity of immigrant labor groups in the form of distinct Javanese and Hindustani plantations. On leaving the plantations, the Javanese settled in largely homogeneous communities and neighborhoods, and in a few cases established Javenese-style village administration.

The culturally conservative, homeward-looking ethnic identification of the Javanese community is clearly reflected in religious affiliation. The distinction between Indian and Indonesian Moslems is rigidly maintained in the form of separate mosques, with distinctive religious communities and forms of ritual. The more conservative Javanese mosques not only use Javanese as the primary language of worship but actually orient their prayers toward the west, as Indonesian Moslems turn westward to face Mecca. These traditional "west-facing" mosques in effect refuse to legitimate the relocation of the Suriname Javanese from the Eastern to the Western Hemisphere. Cultural and religious reform, for Suriname Javanese, has thus been identified with reorienting prayer and mosque itself toward the east—hence, the "east-facing" mosques, with their generally younger and more activist congregations—as well as with adopting Arabic as the primary language of worship. Certain prayers are indeed chanted in Arabic even in the west-facing mosques, though the invocations and sermons are in formal Javanese; conversely, the use of Arabic appeared to me to be limited in the east-facing mosques by the participants' competence in the language. Nevertheless, the attitudes toward the use of Javanese in prayer seem to differ sharply between the two groups, the former regarding it as an essential and revered tradition, the latter as a necessary concession to circumstance. Efforts toward education in reading Arabic were evident in the reformist community.

Suriname's population is concentrated markedly along the Caribbean coast. Sandwiched between the other two Guianas—British (now Guyana) on the west and French (still French Guiana) on the east—Dutch Guiana shared a coastal highway linking all three with their dominant neighbor, Venezuela, on the west. Thirty to forty miles inland from the coast begins the mountainous jungle that extends through most of the Guianas and much of northern Brazil. The Surinamers predominantly still live clustered along this coastal highway, most heavily concentrated in Paramaribo, the capital, and Nieuw-Nickerie, the western border town; settlements also extend southward along the rivers to the interior, most markedly along the Suriname River. (The exceptions to this demographic pattern are the indigenous tribes and the Maroon villages already mentioned.)

With relatively frequent bus and ferry service, travel from one end of Suriname to the other was at the time of fieldwork a quite simple matter, and there was no such thing as an isolated Suriname-Javanese community. Readily available transportation presumably helped replicate the Javanese pattern of small-scale rural and semiurban marketing (described in Dewey 1960). It may also have aided in maintaining rural identification, as young people were able to remain in their villages without necessarily forgoing altogether the attractions of town life.

By 1977 the situation of the Javanese community was undergoing significant changes. At that time Suriname had been an independent republic for only two years, having retained the status of a partially autonomous territory of the Netherlands until 1975. Independence brought to the fore the ethnic and class divisions that are culturally so apparent. For some of the Suriname elite (who were and are drawn predominantly from the Creole community), independence was regarded as a kind of demotion from their established rank as, so to speak, honorary Europeans. For the Hindustani community, which made up the bulk of the technical, professional, service, and entrepreneurial personnel, the prospect of independence created graver misgivings, including a widespread fear of black dictatorship. (Fears of erupting racial conflict proved unfounded, but in 1980 democratic rule was indeed terminated in a military coup. By 1986 vigorous armed resistance, led by the Maroon tribes, had closed down aluminum mining and other operations. Republican government was restored in 1987.)

The colonial power itself engineered Surinamese independence. The Netherlands found itself in the position of having to pay a generous subsidy (in the form of a $1.5 billion, ten-year development program) for the conversion of Surinamers' Dutch passports and the cessation of open Surinamese immigration into the Netherlands. In the two years between the announcement of independence and its consummation, however, what had been a regular flow of immigration became a flood:

high estimates put the total Surinamese emigration for the two years at one-third of the total Suriname population.

Compounding the demoralizing effect of this flood of out-migration, the fleeing thousands of Surinamers included the bulk of the (largely Hindustani) professional and managerial personnel. But the obverse of this demographic vote of no confidence was the dramatic expansion of opportunities for those remaining behind—especially the Javanese. Derveld (1982:17) reports that the Javanese made up less than 5 percent of the emigrating population; for many Javanese, opportunity beckoned not in the Netherlands but at home. The influx of Dutch development funds, as well as the continuing presence of foreign commercial enterprise (chiefly Alcoa's bauxite-mining and smelting subsidiary, Suralco), provided an abundance of slots on the socioeconomic ladder that waited to be filled. At the top of the ladder, the massive emigration had left positions of authority and responsibility vacant in every field; at the bottom of the ladder, the government was quickly becoming the employer of last resort, even hiring as street sweepers those who couldn't qualify for the burgeoning agency staffs and development project teams. Add to the picture the introduction of full-scale electoral politics and it can be readily understood that the public mood, rather than reflecting the pre-independence panic, was one of expansive optimism and a certain rhetorical self-congratulation.

For the Javanese, these events made a dramatic difference. In electoral politics, the Javanese held the swing vote between the Creole and Hindustani blocs, neither of which could achieve a parliamentary majority without Javanese support. In the socioeconomic shuffle, Javanese moved into occupations and positions they previously had not held: shopkeepers, taxi drivers, bank tellers, government office staff. Motorcycles and stereos had become commonplace household features when I visited in 1977, even in homes without plumbing—or, in one case, flooring. I had the impression of substantial numbers of Javanese youths, male and female, who only recently had come to Paramaribo seeking employment. My initial village of residence, not too far from the capital, had the character almost of a suburb, with little agricultural production apart from household gardens and villagers commuting daily as much as an hour for employment in Paramaribo or in the aluminum operation inland. With the introduction of fully mechanized rice agriculture, the Javanese agricultural tradition seemed to be on the verge of disappearing altogether.

Nevertheless, the Javanese retained their traditional place in the market stalls and the roadside *warung* (food stands), raising vegetables on ditchside strips of land, keeping chickens and livestock, and fishing by night on the river piers of the city. Javanese women continued to work in their homes as seamstresses and small-scale caterers and on bicycles as door-to-door vendors, in addition to their traditional food-selling occupations in the market.

The process of urbanization has direct consequences for language use. Although Suriname villages are clearly defined along ethnic lines, urban neighborhoods are less so. Urban dewellers, moreover, live their lives in daily contact with shopkeepers, bus drivers, co-workers, and others who do not speak Javanese. The young people migrating to the city are generally competent in Dutch as well as in Sranang (Suriname creole), owing to the strong tradition of compulsory primary schooling even in rural areas, and in all the urban families I visited there was a systematic effort being made to raise the younger children using Dutch rather than Javanese.

This trend away from Javanese had not yet left much of a mark on the rural communities, even the almost suburban village I lived in. In 1977 one still heard Javanese almost exclusively in the rural areas. Schoolchildren were literate in Dutch, at an elementary level, but apart from "playing school" they used only Javanese outside the classroom. (An interesting exception was the invariable use of Dutch in counting; children appeared to be unfamiliar with the Javanese numbers beyond ten.) The older generation, outside the city, are still generally unacquainted with Dutch but have a working knowledge of Sranang, the language of the market as well as the first language of the Creole community. In intra-ethnic interaction, however, the rural Javanese use only their own language, except occasionally for market price transactions.

Not only language use but also ethnic traditions of clothing, cooking, and eating styles, and even gestural communication serve as valued aspects of ethnic identity for Suriname Javanese. In the urban households I visited, the traditional custom of removing one's shoes at the door was scrupulously maintained, even when the shoes were not slip-on sandals but buckled, high-heeled platform shoes. And in most of these households, the use of domestic space followed roughly the traditional pattern of front/back functional division described for rural Java (see chap. 8).

1.8 MEANING AND CONTEXT

This study of Suriname-Javanese speech style does not aim at producing a generative model of verbal behavior for any of the individuals observed. No scholar (or, for that matter, speaker) of the Javanese language would venture to predict with complete confidence the precise social style a speaker will use in a given context, but this is neither a defect of the analytic apparatus nor merely an unfortunate consequence of the world's complexity. For Javanese speakers, speech style cannot be predictable because it is *meaningful* rather than strictly constrained. Similarly, no linguist or philosopher takes as his or her task the prediction of the semantic content of an utterance, though he or she might work at its interpretation. In the case of Javanese, conversely, where a prominent function of speech is what I term its "greeting" function (see secs. 1.3.2 and 1.5.2), the content of an utterance is in some cases much easier to predict than its precise stylistic presentation, which may in fact be the point of the utterance. For example, the customary greeting between other-than-close acquaintances is "Where are you going?" using some degree of formal lexical style; but the degree of lexical formality and syntactic completeness, especially the use or omission of the formal second-person pronoun or kinship term, conveys a great deal, not only about the relationship of the interactants and the situation of the interaction but also about the speaker's current attitude toward the interaction.

The inclusion here of such paralinguistic data as spatial organization and ritual practice also reflects the central concern of anthropology with the problem of interpretation or meaning. For purposes of cross-cultural comparison and generalization, sociolinguists are forced to adopt a transcultural terminology, using such terms as "social distance" and "positive politeness" as if their meanings were transposed readily from one ethnographic case to another. The argument implicit in this study is that the problem of meaning is not extraneous to the problem of structure; on the contrary, the paradigm of structural alternatives cannot be untangled without a rather thorough sense of the paradigm of social relationships and their culturally specific meanings. Three chapters, therefore (chaps. 4, 8, and 9), have been devoted to the description and analysis of the context of domestic social and spatial relations as the indispensable referential context for categories of social interaction.

The argument presented here is thus twofold. First, I argue that the stylistic distinctions in Suriname Javanese represent a complex structure of meaning in which a choice must be made, at any given moment, between the mutually exclusive social values that we may label, for simplicity, "closeness" and "distance." (The argument is taken a step further in chap. 10 by presenting this complex structure as a kaleidoscopic map.) The second part of the argument holds that the specific cultural content of these opposing social values can be detailed, in this case, only with reference to the setting in which they are enacted: that is, the domestic context, with its culturally dictated "agenda" of daily activity and its culturally defined spatial divisions that give shape to the style system.

If there is indeed a grammar of stylistic competence, it entails not only a process of selection among opposed meanings but also an extensive knowledge of the proper "arrangement"—here understood literally as well as metaphorically—of the various participants in the social drama. This structure of opposed meanings and meaningful arrangement is described, however tentatively, for Suriname-Javanese domestic interaction. Whatever formal analysis is offered is nonpredictive and nongenerative, a map rather than a flowchart. The focus is on the meaning of specific gestures—verbal and nonverbal—in their given contexts, determined through the traditional anthropological means of observation, imitation, and participant error.

NOTES

1. Nevertheless, certain feudal forms, virtually obsolete in Indonesia, could be heard in Suriname, for instance, *ndara,* "lord" (accompanied with a nearly prostrate bow) uttered by an elderly woman to an Indonesian embassy official.

2. The terms "formal" and "formality" are too useful to be avoided in this study; see section 2.1 for discussion and definition.

3. The Suriname setting provided an invaluable opportunity for learning *Ngoko* (familiar lexical style) as the primary style of communication with my hosts. This I regard as a rare privilege for a foreign student of Javanese language.

4. "Close politeness" and "distant politeness," as used in this study, may be read as elaborations of these two maxims (see sec. 1.4). Smith-Hefner (1981) makes use of Lakoff's framework in explicating the contrast between Javanese politeness styles and those of the Tenggerese, a mountain-dwelling Javanese-language community regarded by Javanese as sociolinguistically marginal, similar to the Suriname Javanese.

5. Goffman (1971:162) emphasizes that the interactional phenomena he describes are culture-bound and not necessarily universal.

6. My compartmental model differs from the classic model of diglossia in that values as well as usage are compartmentalized into distinct domains or contexts. Thus, crosscutting the classic valuative dichotomy of "high" and "low" speech codes is an alternative value paradigm, most broadly identified as "out-group" versus "in-group."

7. In the Javanese case, topic selection must be treated as an aspect of style selection rather than as an independent variable determining style selection (see sec. 1.5.2). The exception is any formulaic utterance that has a ceremonial function, such as the spoken invitation to *slametan* ritual; this calls for formal

speech style even within an informal interaction, not because it represents an imposition, but because it is itself part of the ritual (see Keeler 1984:275 ff.).

8. The correlation of spatial region with speech style is normative rather than statistical. The argument that the spatial model makes sense of speech-style repertoire does not rest on any assumption regarding frequencies of occurrence.

9. Goffman (1967:72) is as usual elegantly direct: positive interaction ritual comprises "things that must be said and done to a recipient," and negative ritual comprises "things that must not be said and done." Violations of the latter category give rise to a broad array of what Goffman terms "remedial interchange"; see particularly Goffman (1971:62-65) and Brown and Levinson (1987: chap. 5).

10. Brown and Levinson (1987:69) use other glosses that require some contextual amplification. Presented as a tree of choices, from most polite to least polite, are the following five strategies with respect to doing a "face-threatening act" or FTA (with my glosses): don't do the FTA (reticence); do the FTA off record (indirection); do on record with negative politeness (formality or deference); do on record with positive politeness; do the FTA baldly, without redressive action (unmediated directness).

11. The extreme case is the purely "indexical" meaning of a particular code or language in cases of codeswitching (e.g., Scotton 1988), in which code selection can communicate an "in-group" relationship.

12. Brown and Levinson (1987) take note of this problem, specifically with reference to evaluating the weightiness of an imposition.

13. Rosaldo (1982) makes this argument with reference to speech act theory.

14. The three examples of such shifts provided by Keeler (1984) are motivated differently, as follows: (1) broaching the substantive topic of a visit is signaled by a shift from partial formality to more fully formal style; (2) interaction among three speakers of whom two are intimates will accommodate startlingly abrupt shifts between intimate and formal style, as speakers redirect their attention from one dyad to the other; (3) a ceremonial formula of invitation to a *slametan* must be in fully formal style, even though the participants have been exchanging informal speech up to that point. (This latter circumstance is the only instance of switching between style categories within a single dyadic interaction.)

15. Remediation in close-polite contexts is treated more pragmatically, though with far less variety than is presented, for example, in Brown and Levinson (1987). Standard remediating formulas are "Don't be angry" (*Ojo nesu*) and "Excuse me" (*Amit*; or, more elaborately, *Amit sewu*). Explanation may be offered, often by using the confessional first person ("I'm tired!" or "I can't [do it]!") or by briefly invoking circumstantial hindrances: "It was raining hard!" or "Don't you know it's already late?!"

16. Nor does formal lexicon serve to ameliorate an imposition in close interaction, where such formality simply has no place and indeed can convey insult. The sole exception is the ritual of begging pardon from close senior kin, which (as previously noted) occurs annually at Lebaran as well as on life-

crisis occasions. An elevation of formal speech style may perhaps serve ameliorative functions in moderately distant-polite interaction, but I have no example of such an effect.

17. Jay (1969:140 ff.) draws attention to the "exchange" value of linguistic and other gestures; in the matter of food gifts, for example, "relatively poor hearthholds choose to give unilaterally to those well-to-do hearthholds from whom they have had or hope to receive preferential gifts of cash, wage work, or sharecropping concessions" (248).

18. I use "Ba" as a short form of *Mbah*, "grandparent"—the obligatory title accorded to all senior-generation Suriname Javanese. (In Java, this usage has an old-fashioned or condescending sound.) All names are fictitious.

19. This observation may appear to conflict with the earlier description of the village as an essentially homogeneous social entity. Perhaps the simplest way to capture this complex social reality is to invoke Freud's conception of the "narcissism of slight differences." From a structural point of view, the sensitivity to gestural inequality is perfectly compatible with an overall socio-economic homogeneity; interaction ritual is a component of social structure, not an image of it.

20. The tape recordings proved invaluable for eliciting reactions from (among others) my Javanese teacher, who identified the speakers' dialect with that of the mountain areas of Central Java. Suparlan (personal communication) identifies the Suriname Javanese as originating primarily in the Magelang, Banyumas, and other Outer Mataram areas of Java.

21. I do not mean to suggest that there is an inevitable tension between participant observation and the more technical methods of data collection. In some circumstances, however, combining the two approaches requires very considerable social dexterity, since one's perceived identity as a marginal "insider" to the household may be constantly undermined by the technological trappings of one's observer status.

22. Suparlan (1976) provides some dramatic personal accounts of labor importation and plantation experiences.

CHAPTER 2

The Style System of Suriname Javanese

2.1 Categories of Polite Speech

In the very substantial and fascinating literature on Javanese language (including works in Javanese, Indonesian, Dutch, French, and English), primary attention has focused on the lexical aspects of speech style.[1] The focus of the present study is quite different. The interactional style system of Suriname Javanese revolves around social distinctions and linguistic devices that must be analyzed independently of the lexical style system. To put it another way, patterns of lexical alternation in Suriname Javanese constitute only one element—and by no means the dominant linguistic element—in a richly communicative structure of stylistic choice.[2]

The conventional focus on lexical alternation goes along with an oversimple model of the structuring categories of Javanese stylistic choice. The basic lexical alternants are structured as sets or paradigms, clearly ranked from "low" to "high": the lowest vocabulary form is labeled *ngoko*, the "familiar" form; there may be an intermediate form, labeled *madya*, "middle"; and the fully polite variant is labeled *krama*— a term with no adequate translation. Where an honorific is used for respectful personal reference, the form is termed (somewhat misleadingly) *krama inggil*, literally, "high krama." The implicit model thus forms a ladder of increasing politeness:

1. ngoko
2. madya
3. krama
4. krama inggil

Even Javanese speakers who don't know all the terms are aware of the ladder model, which they may give in an abbreviated form, often omitting level 2 and sometimes level 3 as well.

Not surprisingly, these terms are also commonly used by Javanese to refer to overall style of speech: one is said to speak Ngoko or Krama, for example, as if they were distinct languages.³ The conventional view of Javanese speech style, then, is informed by a single standard of politeness as a bipolar continuum from less polite to more polite—the ladder of language "levels." (A more detailed account is given in chap. 5.)

The overall style system of Suriname Javanese (and possibly that of non-elite Javanese speech as well) presents a compartmental structure of stylistic choices and associated social contexts. In place of the conventional bipolar continuum of more polite and less polite speech, we must begin with a three-way model, in which the shift to formally polite speech style is only one of the three basic stylistic choices or strategies. Informal (or "ordinary") speech style has its own definite stylistic character, described in chapter 3; it is associated with positive (close-polite) cultural values quite distinct from the distant-polite cultural values enacted in formal speech. The third category of speech style is a form of politeness I term "respect," which is socially and linguistically distinct from formal speech style.⁴ Respect style, as we will see in this chapter, is an expression not of social distance but of a positive (and asymmetric) relationship of marked closeness, represented stylistically in nonlexical features that have received little systematic attention in the literature of Javanese speech style.

The term "formal" has been much criticized as imprecise (by Irvine 1979, among others) but continues to be useful in practice (e.g., J. Errington 1985:13). I use the term formal to refer to a style of performance that adheres relatively closely to a set of prescribed interactional forms (gestural as well as verbal) that are clearly contrastive with the patterns of interaction recognized as spontaneous in a given culture. These prescribed forms themselves are also termed "formal." (The stylization of close politeness, on the other hand, consists of forms appearing as either an exaggerated or a modulated version of spontaneous interaction patterns; the most obvious example is the stylized "joking" relationship referred to in chap. 1.) A formal interaction, for a particular individual, is one that requires him or her to adhere to the prescribed formal interaction style; a formal occasion or setting is one that requires formal interaction styles of the participants in general.⁵

In the case of Javanese, spontaneous interaction is viewed as naturally rather loud, dramatic, and intrusive (summed up in the word *ramé*). Whereas the gestures of formal style convey a consistent reassurance of quiet restraint and nonintrusiveness, the gestures of *ordinary style* give the drama and intrusiveness of everyday life a predictable, nonthreatening, and even formulaic shape. In *respect style*, the intrusive formulas of close politeness are accepted and even expected, but in a form that is further modified to provide stylistic amelioration directed specifically to the addressee. This sort of specifically ameliorated intrusiveness is perceived as deferential, and the archetypal case is the treatment of grandparents within the domestic setting (see sec. 2.2.2). Respect style nevertheless carries no further implication of obedience, substantive inequality, or even self-effacement; it can, in fact, be offered mutually or even "downward," as toward a child who is too young to show proper respect.[6] The specifically ameliorative devices of respect style consist of the use of the kinship term as vocative along with characteristic crooning intonation. These ameliorative elements can also be combined with formal interaction style to create a style of "formal respect."

2.1.1 Formal and Respectful Styles of Politeness

Formal speech style (abbreviated F) appears to take as its model the clipped enunciation and monotone intonation of ceremonial speech, particularly the formal invocation at a *slametan*, the core ritual meal described by C. Geertz (1960:11-14). (Similarly clipped enunciation characterizes public political speeches as well, but with an occasional dramatic emphasis varying the monotone intonation.) Syntactically, formal style tends toward completeness of utterance, without the element of ellipsis that characterizes informal speech. Extremely formal style, as in public invocations or speeches, exhibits the opposite of ellipsis—a programmatic redundancy (see Keeler 1984:13 and *passim*).

Some use of polite lexical form invariably is associated with the use of formal intonation and syntax, though in Suriname this factor varies widely with the linguistic competence of the speaker. (The lexical style system of Javanese is described in chap. 5 and that of Suriname Javanese in chap. 6.) The range of commonly used polite lexicon is far smaller in Suriname than in urban Java, but certain polite variants are obligatory as markers of even minimally formal conversational style (negatives, interrogatives, deictics, plus certain standard phrases).

In addition to the use of some polite (madya and/or krama) lexicon, the avoidance of ellipsis in formal speech may entail using certain items of familiar (ngoko) vocabulary that, because of their rarity in informal conversation, have a stilted sound. For example, the conjunction *utawa* ("or") has a distinctly formal sound in Suriname Javanese, because the usual way of presenting alternatives in informal conversation is simply to list them without using a conjunction. When a conjunction is used in informal speech, it is likely to be *opo* (literally, "what") rather than the formal-sounding *utawa* ("or").

Respectful speech style (R), like formal style, usually lacks the dramatic emphasis of informal conversation. Instead of the formal style's monotone intonation, however, it tends toward an intonation pattern usually described as "crooning." This intonation pattern is characterized by the elongation of phrase-final syllables, typically with an overall downward intonation and a slight upward lilt at the end. The example most often used by native speakers in educating a foreigner is the polite form "please," used as an invitation:

    3   1-1-2
1. Monggo-o-o.

This chapter contains several examples of intonation patterns as I observed and noted them, according to a system that requires some explication. I have used a line of numbers above the line of text, ranging from 1 to 5 (low to high) and representing around an octave in tonal range. A hyphen between two numbers represents a smooth glide.[7]

If there is a lexical hallmark of respectful style, it is not the use of a particular level of vocabulary but rather the obligatory use of an appropriate kinship term in a vocative function. (There is no grammatical inflection of cases in Javanese.) The appropriate kinship term— more often than not, a term of "as-if" rather than factual kinship— is always appended to a respectful utterance (as a coda) and often is used also, as internal "punctuation," at the end of a phrase. Because it is usually a much older person who is addressed in respectful style, the most commonly heard kinship term is *mbah*, "grandparent," but other kinship terms are used in this way also: *pak*, "father";[8] *oom*, "uncle"; *tante*, "aunt"; *wa* or *siwa*, "senior aunt," "senior uncle"; perhaps less commonly heard are *yu*, "elder sister," *bik* or *bibik*, "junior aunt," and *dhik*, "younger brother or sister."

Unlike formal speech style, respectful speech employs ellipsis in more or less the same degree as informal style. This tends to enhance the effect of the crooning intonation pattern and the kinship-term vocative, so that respectful speech seems to be made up of brief but sometimes drawn-out phrases, exhibiting a consistent intonation pattern:

    3ˉ   1 - 2
2. _____, mba-ah.

The next section presents respectful intonation and phrase structure in greater detail. The point to be made clear at the outset is that these respect features constitute as definite a stylistic norm as does the use of polite vocabulary in formal speech style. On more than one occasion

I was explicitly corrected for omitting to use the kinship-term vocative in addressing someone substantially senior. Such corrections always took the form of repeating the phrase, with the appropriate kinship term appended, in an exaggerated crooning intonation. The crooning intonation and the kinship-term coda were presented as if inseparable elements of a single formula: to omit the coda destroyed the intonation, and to shortchange the intonation perhaps vitiated the respect conveyed in the kinship term.

In one instance, the person who offered such a correction was a woman visitor, correcting my style of addressing the "grandmother" in whose house I was staying. Her own style of addressing the "grandmother" was indeed consistently respectful (though without using any polite lexical forms)—never omitting the kinship term *mbah* ("grandparent") and invariably using some degree of crooning intonation. In correcting my utterance she used a crooning intonation much more exaggerated than her own customary style, repeating my own words and adding the forgotten kinship term:

    2   2-3'   1---------2
3. Dayoh okeh, mbaaah!
"(There were) many guests, grandmother."

The exaggerated crooning pattern seemed to have a double significance in this context. Not only was it an explicit form of instruction, giving me (as the pupil) a clear model of respectful style to imitate, but at the same time it duplicated the tone of voice that is commonly used in addressing someone else's child (as discussed later). The exaggerated croon was thus a way of acknowledging that the speaker was treating me as if I were a child being indulgently corrected—a mark of quasifamilial involvement that softened the implied criticism.

2.1.2 Respectful Intonation and Phrase Structure

The common denominator of respectful intonation (based on analysis of notations that were made at the time of observation) is the intonation sequence 3-1-2 at the close of a phrase or utterance. Variations on this basic pattern are numerous, as is illustrated in the following material. There is usually some material preceding this crooning pattern, so that the intonation of the utterance as a whole would take the form 2-3-1-2, with the stress falling on the highest-pitched syllable: 2-3' 1-2. Some typical examples of this form are as follows:

   2-3'   1-2
1. Ora, mbaah.
  "No, grandfather."
   2-3'   1-2
2. Muleh, mbah.
  "(I'm) going home, grandmother."
    2   3'   1-2
3. Teng 'stadt,' mbah.
  "(I'm going) to town, grandfather."

I have represented the word for "grandmother/grandfather" in two different ways: the standard spelling (*mbah*) and a prolonged version (*mbaah* or even *mbaaah*). This is a way of suggesting the possible variations within the same basic intonation pattern; the final lilt can be rendered as a very smooth croon (the prolonged version) or in a more abrupt, shortened form. My intention in providing these three examples is to represent the realistic interaction of sense and style. Example 1, "No, grandfather," is a potentially offensive utterance simply because it is a negative; examples 2 and 3, by contrast, are inherently polite because they are the "announcement" of an intention (specifically, a leave-taking or *pamitan*, as discussed in chap. 4). For this reason, an abrupt intonation pattern would have a less respectful sound in the case of example 1 than in the case of 2 or 3. Taken as a whole, therefore, example 1, with its slightly prolonged final syllable, is probably no more polite than the more abruptly rendered utterances 2 and 3.

Though perfectly respectful, these three utterances are not at all formal. Only in example 3 is there any use of polite lexicon, and that is in abbreviated form: *teng* is the short form of the krama variant *dhateng,* meaning in this context "to." The first two examples are marked in fact by the use of strikingly informal vocabulary: the words *ora* and *muleh* both have widely used and well-known polite (krama) variants in Suriname Javanese, *mboten* and *wangsul,* respectively. In both cases, the ordinary lexical variant may be described as a kind of marker of informal style (just as its polite counterpart would be a marker of formal style). This combination of informal vocabulary with perfectly respectful phrasing and intonation is by no means unusual; indeed, it is the hallmark of informal socializing, particularly where there are generation differences between speakers.

A final note on vocabulary: the use of *stadt,* "city," illustrates the tendency to borrow from Dutch lexicon, as do certain of the kinship terms already cited (*oom, tante*). Both Dutch, as the official language of Suriname, and Sranang, as the lingua franca, serve as sources for loan words. Such borrowings tend to be fairly standardized rather than idiosyncratic; in all three of these examples, for instance, no other word is commonly used in place of the Dutch borrowing.

Variations within the basic crooning pattern are not necessarily as subtle as the difference I have represented in examples 1, 2, and 3 as a contrast between *mbah* and *mbaah*. The final syllable can, in the most respectful style, be rendered as an extremely elongated glide: 3' 1--2. At the other extreme, the intonation pattern can be rendered with no glide at all, almost in the clipped intonation of formal speech style: 3' 2. For example, the simple statement "That is the one, grandmother" will sound quite different in these two distinct renderings:

    2 3'   1--2
4. Iku, mbaah.
"That (is the one), grandmother."
    1-3'   2
5. Iku, mbah.
"That (is the one), grandmother."

For extreme respect, the entire crooning phrase can be rendered as a glide, as is done in formulas such as the standard polite (krama) invitation:

    3'-2-1-1-2
6. Monggo-o-o.
"Please (come in, etc.)."

(Note that the nasal consonants of *monggo* lend themselves to this kind of glide far more readily than most other consonants. The same is true of the initial nasal of *mbah*, which makes it so well suited to serve as the final syllable of the crooning pattern.)

A crooning pattern in an interrogative utterance is marked by a slightly higher pitched ending, typically taking the form 3 2-3. This pattern, too, can be rendered in more abrupt form (3 1-3) or more respectful form (3 1-2-3). Three examples with the same semantic content are the following, quite standard, utterances:

    3'   2-3
7. Ndi mbah?
"Where (are you going), grandmother?"
    3'-3   1-2
8. Pundi mbah?
"Where (are you going), grandmother?"
    2   2-3'   1-2-3
9. Teng pundi mbaah?
"Where (are you going), grandmother?"

These three examples exhibit progressively more formal lexical style.

In 8 and 9, *pundi* is the krama variant for *endi* (shortened also to *ndi*), "where?" In 9, *teng* is the short form of *dhateng*, "to"—also a krama form, and one that makes the utterance syntactically more complete and thus more formal. This kind of lexical variation is not essential to the rendition of varying intonation: any of the three intonation patterns conceivably could be used in any of the lexical styles. The lexical progression is nevertheless realistic; the intonation pattern in example 8 would sound rudely abrupt if used with the ordinary vocabulary of example 7.

There is thus some interaction between formal and respectful styles, in the sense that they complement rather than duplicate each other. In overall style, examples 7 and 8 are equally polite, the first simply respectful and the second more or less simply formal. Example 9 is clearly more polite than the others, combining fully respectful intonation with a more fully formal lexical style.

A final variant of respectful intonation may be termed *partial respect*. In this intonation pattern, the overall downward intonation is maintained but without the final upward lilt. Instead of the pattern 3 1-2, partial respect shows the pattern 3-2 or 3 1.

     3'- 2
10. Ndi mbah?
"Where (are you going), grandfather?"
     3'   1
11. Ten mbah.
"No, grandmother."

Again, example 11 is less respectful in intonation but more formal in lexical style than example 10. *Ten* is a shortened form of *mboten*, the krama variant of *ora*, "no." If example 10 may be characterized as "partial respect," example 11 probably should be labeled "minimal respect plus minimal formality."

The examples given so far have been polite announcements and formulas, whose brevity is easily adapted to the crooning intonation pattern. Longer utterances are handled in respectful style by being broken up into short phrases, each of which may be rendered in crooning intonation. Each such phrase may be punctuated with the kinship term as vocative. I term this form of syntax "punctuate phrase structure" and contrast it with the "discursive" syntax of formal speech style (sec. 3.2).

The following example was part of a lively conversation between members of the household in Paramaribo. The elder (foster) daughter, Sita, was addressing her "grandfather":

      2   2-3   2   2 3   3   2   3   2 -3

12. Mbah! Abené aku 'verjari,' mbah, montoré Min dianu,

  2 3' 3'   1

dicoplok mbah!

"Grandfather! When I had my birthday party, grandfather, Min's car was, you know, was vandalized grandfather!"

In this example the element of respect is somewhat submerged in the sense of drama of the reported event. The utterance was rapidly delivered in a rising rather than downward intonation. It is the triple use of the kinship term *mbah*, together with the final drop of the voice, which marks the utterance as essentially respectful, at least in the context of a close personal relationship. (It is quite unlikely that this speaker would have used so lively a style in addressing a much older person unless closely related.)

In another example, an utterance is broken up into brief phrases not by using a kinship term but by inserting the affirmative or interrogative particle *ya*, "yes." This was an utterance directed to me by a nine-year-old girl, who was clearly uncertain what, if any, kinship term could be appropriately addressed to me:[9]

      2-3   2   2 3' 1-2   2   3'

13. Aku arep dolan, ya, nèng isor.

"I'm going (out) to play, okay, downstairs?"

In this case, the entire utterance is a polite one, since it is a form of leavetaking (a *pamitan*). The interrogative particle *ya* is given fully respectful intonation, just as if it were a kinship-term vocative; the final phrase, however, is given strictly interrogative intonation, without any crooning element. A more completely respectful intonation (which would have been excessively polite in our relationship) would have been achieved by using a second interrogative particle at the end of the sentence:

     2   3   2-3

. . . neng isor, yaa?

2.2 Social Contexts of Respectful Style

Respectful speech style, with or without some element of formal lexicon, is a pervasive feature of everyday social interaction. *Simple respectful style* (without formal vocabulary) is usual in addressing any member of the "grandparent" generation who is closely related to the speaker or who lives in the same household. Both children and adults use respectful intonation in this context. In general, children use some degree of respectful style in addressing all adults, for example, by routinely adding the appropriate kinship term at the end of an utterance.[10] Omitting the kinship term certainly occurs, but it is apt to be regarded as a sign of the sulks, particularly if the utterance is brief.

Respectful style (without formal lexicon) is used also between same-generation adults on occasion. For example, adult sisters may use some degree of respect if there is a significant difference in age and if they are not in everyday contact. The younger sister will make a point of using the kinship term yu^{11} ("elder sister"), and the elder may (if she chooses) reciprocate with respectful intonation and the use of the personal nickname as a vocative.

Respectful style with formal lexicon is used chiefly by adults addressing members of the "grandparent" generation, particularly "grandparents" who are not members of the same household. Here, however, there is great individual variation, and the nature of the setting will also influence the degree of formality employed. One woman of about forty (a second-generation Surinamer living in the capital city) consistently used formal lexicon in addressing her own parents, who lived nearby and who kept the shop next to her own market stall (*warung*). Another woman, somewhat older and a first-generation immigrant, used no formal vocabulary at all when visiting the "grandparents" with whom I was residing, even though the "grandfather" in particular was usually addressed with some degree of formality by adult visitors, because he was a founding member of the local mosque and something of a cultural expert in the Javanese tradition. My impression was that the use of formal respect has roughly the same status as the writing of thank-you notes has for middle-class Americans: the rules of appropriateness are fairly clear, but there exists a wide latitude for individual adherence. Among urban-dwelling young adults, in fact, the use of formal lexicon seems to be the exception rather than the norm. One twenty-year-old woman, visiting the house I lived in, explained apologetically to the "grandmother" that she didn't know any formal language, a circumstance that she evidently found somewhat embarrassing but that was taken in stride by the grandmother.

Unlike the mastery of formal lexicon, the use of respectful style is by no means an esoteric or refined accomplishment. Even those urban children whose command of Javanese is quite limited are able to use respectful intonation in the brief, everyday phrases they do know. This may be an important factor in the preference for using Javanese to address one's elders, even though both parties generally may be more comfortable in Sranang or even in Dutch: only in Javanese can the respectful crooning intonation pattern be applied.

In the family I lived with in Paramaribo, the seven-year-old foster daughter, Lan, spoke Sranang when playing with other children and often when talking with her (much older) foster sister. To her elderly foster parents, however, she normally used Javanese. Although she was not (by Javanese standards) either well-versed in etiquette or restrained in deportment, she nevertheless rarely omitted the kin-term vocative "grandparent" in addressing her foster parents. Her intonation followed a pattern of modified respect, somewhat abrupt but maintaining the outline of the 3-1-2 crooning pattern, as in this example from my notes:

    1   3' 2 2-1   2
1. Dèk sopo iku mbah?
"Whose is that, grandfather?"

Note that it is quite possible to use the kin-term vocative without using respectful intonation, either maintaining level intonation (1-2-2-2), which gives a distant feeling, or using the dramatic intonation of ordinary style without the final upward lilt of respect (e.g., 1-3-2-1), which conveys a definite sense of familiarity.

Intonation, then, must be regarded as a politeness feature independent of lexical style. Not only does intonation vary between distinct social settings and relationships, but it is if anything more subject to variation within an interaction than is lexical style. A speaker who customarily uses formal respect style in a particular relationship is more likely to omit the respectful elements than the formal elements in reacting, for example, to a momentary irritation.

In one case (which I was unable to note verbatim), the forty-year-old woman mentioned previously sharply reproved her elderly mother (and, by implication, her father as well) for some omission. Her intonation was indistinguishable from the normal scoldings directed at children, and her voice was raised well above normal speaking range. Her vocabulary, however, was nevertheless formal; as far as I could determine, her lexical level did not deviate from her normal polite usage with her parents. Though her anger eclipsed the sense of closeness conveyed in respect style, it left intact the sense of formal deference owed to seniority.

A final observation about the social context of respect style has to do with its *directional* character (see sec 4.5 for a fuller discussion of this term). In most cases I observed, respect style was used by the junior party and not reciprocated by the senior; at most, the senior party might use the nickname of the addressee as a kind of vocative ending of an utterance, with the final drop in intonation that I have identified as minimal respect:

     2   2 3'   1
2. Min! Réné, Min!
"Min! Come here, Min!"

But there is also an occasional downward-directed use of fully respectful "crooning" intonation—by an adult addressing a young child (typically, someone else's).[12] This pattern is likely to be used as an expression of indulgent concern for a friend's or kinsman's child, or as a way of softening an explicit instruction. In place of a kinship-term ending, a term of endearment will be used as a vocative—*woq* in addressing a girl, *liq* for a boy. For example,

     2 3'   1-2-3
3. Ombé wo-o-oq!
"Have a drink, dear!"
     2   2 3' 1 2--3
4. Ojo lali to, li-iq!
"Don't forget now, honey!"

This kind of respectful usage also tends to be unidirectional, because most often it is directed to a child who is not yet able to reciprocate with respectful crooning intonation, though this is not always the case. Generally, only adults make use of this full or exaggerated respect intonation; the style used by children (at least up to teenage) is apt to be more perfunctory. Full crooning style, therefore, is rarely reciprocated fully: it is used by an adult either to a "grandparent" or to a child, and is reciprocated at most by partial respect.

Like the use of polite lexicon, the use of respectful intonation patterns shows individual differences in use as well as differences based on setting, relationship, and other features of social context. But since respectful style is a stylistic device much more widely commanded than the polite lexicon, it perhaps tends to be attuned more closely to the features of social context and less determined by individual competence.

2.2.1 Respect as a Conscious Stylistic Device

The use of respect intonation is probably as conscious a mark of politeness as the use of formal vocabulary, or very nearly so. I overheard a striking example of respect politeness, in downward-directed use, while waiting at a corner bus stop in the Javanese neighborhood in Paramaribo. A middle-aged woman was instructing a couple of neighborhood boys (about ten years old) to run an errand for her. She phrased her lengthy instructions entirely in Sranang—in which city children are most comfortable—but appended as a polite finish two perfectly redundant phrases in Javanese, using a definite crooning intonation:

    3   1-2   3   1-2-3
5. Jikuk liiq. Golèq liiq.
"Take (it), dear. Fetch (it), dear."

The substantive and stylistic content of the message was apportioned neatly between Sranang and Javanese, respectively. The Sranang request was entirely matter-of-fact in style, even rather abrupt; the Javanese phrases were, by contrast, distinctly coaxing, but so unspecific as to be virtually contentless.

An awareness of *word order* as a stylistic element was illustrated by the self-correction of an elderly visitor (a first-generation immigrant) who was giving me examples of lexical politeness. As "Krama Inggil" she offered first

6. *Pun dhahar, sampéyan?
"Already eaten, have you?"

using formal vocabulary but with the word order characteristic of respectful or ordinary speech style. Recognizing the anomaly, she immediately revised the example to the more distant-polite version:

7. Sampéyan pun dhahar?
"Have you already eaten?"

using the word order of formal speech style along with the formal lexicon.[13]

In another instance, the use of crooning intonation became the explicit target of childish mockery. In my Paramaribo household, the "grandmother" treated me as a favored grandchild; in speaking to me she made full use of the kinds of politeness formulas described in chapter 4, and these were usually delivered in a fairly marked crooning intonation. Frequently, when there was no subject at hand for particular remark, she would simply croon my name. (This is a not uncommon form of interaction between young children and their elder relatives.) On one occasion, Lan, the six-year-old foster daughter, began to imitate this crooned refrain, with remarkably accurate intonation:

    1-4   4-1
8. Clare, Clare.

The grandmother took this bit of mockery in good humor and gave her own imitation of herself:

    1-4   3-1   1-3   3-1
9. Clare, Clare, mangan Clare.
"Clare, Clare, come and eat, Clare."

Lan's comment: "Grandmother talks like singing!"

The "grandfather" had overheard this exchange without comment, but a bit later he had his own little joke when he called Lan to eat supper using the grandmother's crooning style (which, however, was rarely used with Lan herself):

       3   1   1-3   3-1
10. Mangan ta, Lan, Lan
    "Come and eat, Lan, Lan."

The conscious awareness of intonation is demonstrated also by the fact that in recounting a previous conversation a speaker will reproduce, as a matter of course, the intonation of the quoted utterances. Not only exaggerated crooning but also partial crooning intonation is reproduced in quotations, as if inseparable from the substance of the utterance. (In American usage, in contrast, such a device would be used only to make a particular point about the sound of the quoted conversation.) It was my impression that the omission of some degree of crooning intonation, in quotations where it would seem appropriate, would be taken to indicate that the speaker being quoted had omitted proper intonation.

My notes contain two clear examples of such intonation quotation. In one case, a youngish woman quoted her own use of an exaggerated crooning intonation to address an older woman. (Her current interlocutor was a woman approximately her own age.)

      1-3'   1-2
11. Inggeh waa.
    "Yes, (senior) aunt."

The crooning intonation is here coupled with the formal variant of "yes" (*inggeh*), producing a style of formal respect. This may well have been the only formal lexical item (or one of very few) used in the quoted conversation, because this item is one of the first to shift into formal style.

The second case was an elderly woman quoting a third person addressing her, using a modified crooning intonation:

     1 3   2   3'   2
12. Aku ora pasa mbah.
    "I don't observe the fast, grandmother."

All the vocabulary in this example is in familiar style, even though two of the words used ("I" and "not") are typically among the first vocabulary items to shift to formal style. The overall style was thus moderately respectful and without formal elements.

In neither of these two cases did the speaker appear to be making a statement about the attitude expressed in speech style. It seemed rather that the intonation pattern was an integral part of the utterance (just as the level of vocabulary is) and so had to be specified in direct quotation. (In general, the use of direct quotation in conversation is markedly more frequent in Javanese than in American usage. Reciting earlier conversation seems to be a standard form of socializing, even when there may be no particular point to be made and nothing remarkable about the conversation being quoted.)

Intonation in Javanese, then, is an integral part of stylistic "level," and for Suriname-Javanese speakers it constitutes a politeness style in its own right—the style I have termed "respect." Lexical alternation plays no part in determining respect style, though polite lexicon can be combined with this basic respect style to create a further range of "formal-respect" styles. The use of formal vocabulary alone *without* any element of respect style (i.e., without kin-term vocative or respect intonation) constitutes a fundamentally different sort of politeness— one that conveys a dignified social distance rather than deference.

2.2.2 Respect Style as "Close Politeness"

Respect style in Suriname Javanese may best be seen as a special variant of social closeness. For Javanese, the closest possible relationships (other than the mother-child relationship) are those associated with respect: archetypically, the grandparent-grandchild relationship, described by Jay as a relationship of "easy indulgence" and "relaxed, comfortable assurance" in a context of stylistic respect (1969:159-60). Kin relationships in general are thought of as asymmetrical to some degree, shaped by considerations of seniority even between near siblings (H. Geertz 1961:20-22); Geertz makes it clear, however, that the substance of kinship seniority is precisely the payment of stylistic respect, including (in Java) the use of polite lexicon or other "minor suggestions of respect" (ibid.).

Kinship thus provides a highly valued model—perhaps the only model—of a comfortably (asymmetrically) patterned close social relationship.[14] To refer to the "payment" of respect, in domestic contexts, misleadingly suggests an element of self-abnegation or of accepting a diminished status. My sense of the relationship is almost the opposite: by enacting respect one in effect establishes a claim to the listener's indulgence and concern, "as if" the listener were one's own grandparent. Jay invokes an exchange model in describing relationships of seniority among kin: "Between kinsmen of different generations the normative conceptions of kinship require that a person use well-defined patterns of respect and deference to his senior and provide him with services on demand. The senior kinsman is expected to return expressions of indulgence and care and gifts or loans of goods and money" (Jay 1969:159). Such patterns of exchange are ritualized in the gifts of cooked food sent to senior kin on ceremonial occasions: "An individual offers services to a senior kinsman, including prepared food . . . and in return he receives goods from the senior, including gifts or loans of produce (that is, unprepared food). The offer is made with gestures of deference and the return with gestures of indulgence and solicitude" (Jay 1969:176).

The stylistic expression of respect or deference is not strictly a matter of accepting inferior status; it is also an assertion of certain claims, as of a dependent. Siegel observes of the use of Krama Inggil (in relationships of distant respect) that the expression of deference "lacks all sense of subservience": "To indicate deference . . . is to free oneself from having to *experience* a feeling of inferiority. In this sense the conventional nature of Krama is used for self-protection" (Siegel 1986:27, emphasis added). Siegel notes a corresponding absence of status competition in the form of trying to use the lowest possible speech style with one's interlocutor: "Rather, it seems to be the other way around"; "Javanese find an advantage less in the form of address they receive than in the role of deference-giver they accept" (Siegel 1986:26, 315). The patterning itself has inherent value for all the participants, which is merely enhanced (at least in the Suriname context) by the substantive implication of a closely interdependent relationship. Kin-term reiteration and crooning intonation are used to express not only deference "upward" but also the reciprocal attitude of indulgent concern "downward." The respect relationship might best be summarized as one of "close deference."

2.3 A Three-Way Model of Politeness

In place of a bipolar continuum (formal/informal; more polite/less polite)—the ladder model implicitly assumed in descriptions of Javanese language "levels"—a model of the style system must include respect style as a separate category capable of combination with either ordinary or formal speech style. The basic model thus presents three distinct stylistic options, as in the roughly triangular schema of figure 2.1—shaped rather like a baseball diamond to allow for the stylistic admixture described below as Formal-Respect.

Although there is no implied politeness ranking between formal style and respect style, each of these styles comprises a range of more polite

Figure 2.1 The basic three-way model.

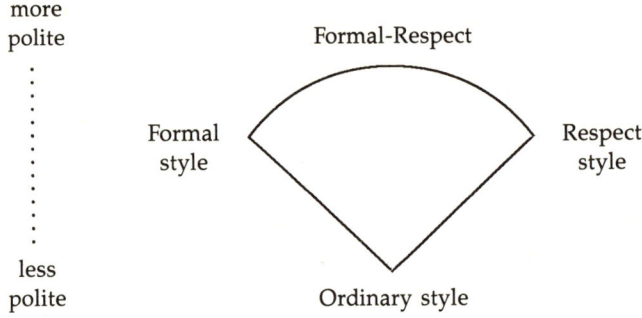

and less polite variations. Figure 2.2 shows the stylistic elements of formal and respectful politeness as diacritic features: whereas a fully respectful style (for example) will exhibit both of the diacritic features of respect, a style of partial respect or minimal respect uses just one of these features, the kin-term vocative. That is to say, the diacritic features *within* each of the basic politeness styles are indeed "ranked" in an implication series.

As figure 2.2 shows, ordinary style entails none of the four diacritic features. Partial respect (r) entails feature (1) only—the kin-term vocative; full respect (R) entails both (1) and (2)—the kin-term vocative plus crooning intonation. Partial formal style (f) entails only feature (3)—some polite lexicon; whereas fully formal style (F) entails both (3) and (4)—polite lexicon plus syntactic completeness and monotone intonation.

With these diacritic features in mind, we can elaborate the basic

Figure 2.2 Diacritic features of basic polite styles.

Speech Style	Respect Features		Formal Features	
	(1) vocative kin term	(2) crooning intonation	(3) formal lexicon	(4) syntactic completeness/ monotone intonation
ordinary	−	−	−	−
r	+	−	−	−
R	+	+	−	−
f	−	−	+	−
F	−	−	+	+

model of figure 2.1 to include partial and full politeness styles of each type, as shown in figure 2.3.

The use of binary notation in figure 2.2 represents a considerable simplification. Every politeness feature entails a "more-or-less" rather than a "yes-or-no" choice; even the use of the kin-term vocative can be exaggerated, through repetition after every phrase of an utterance. Instead of a distinct line between minimal and full styles of formality or respect, there is a possible continuum in each case. This binary and componential analysis is intended to show only the characteristics of a truly minimal politeness style as distinct from a maximally polite utterance in each case.

Figure 2.3 The expanded model.

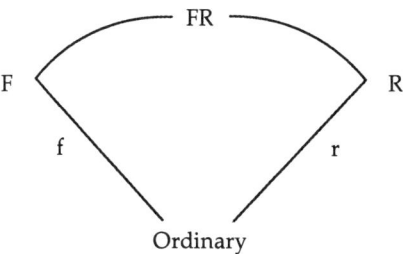

Neither figure 2.2 nor figure 2.3 gives any indication of the range of possible combinations of formal and respectful style. In fact, in Suriname one hears only rarely the combination of maximal formality with maximal respect (the style indicated by FR in figure 2.2). Far more likely is a partial admixture, combining some element of respect within an overall formal style (Fr) or some element of formality within an overall respectful style (fR). Indeed, a simple summation of the two styles is difficult to imagine, since their respective features tend to interact negatively. Crooning intonation is associated with the punctuate phrase structure of respectful speech style—a phrase structure that interferes with the syntactical completeness required in fully formal speech style. Conversely, the overall monotone of the fully formal style entails some modification of the crooning intonation pattern that would otherwise make such an utterance also fully respectful. The following section gives some examples of combined politeness styles.

2.3.1 Combined Formal-Respectful Styles

Formal and respectful styles occur frequently in combined forms. A polite utterance may be characterized as predominantly formal or as predominantly respectful according to the particular mix of lexical and intonational features, briefly outlined as follows. (Note that either style may also be modified in the direction of "ordinary" style, as discussed later.)

Within an overall *respectful* speech style, an element of formality may be introduced by using polite lexical forms (to a greater or lesser extent). Unless the syntactical structure of the utterance is expanded, such an utterance would retain a predominantly respectful rather than formal character, which can be represented by the notation fR (formal-Respectful). For example, the brief but respectful (R) announcement

     2 3'   1-2
13. Muleh, mbah.
    "(I'm) going home, grandmother."

can be rendered in slightly more formal style (fR) as

     2 3'   1-2
14. Wangsul, mbah.
    "(I'm) going back, grandmother."

—with no expansion of syntax and no change in intonation pattern.[15] This can be compared with a still more formal version of the same utterance, in which expanded syntax goes along with a modulated intonation pattern:

   2 2   2 3'   1-2
15. Kula wangsul, mbah.
    "I'm going back, grandmother."

Example 15 exhibits the same crooning pattern as examples 13 and 14, but the expanded syntax adds an initial, monotone word/phrase and thus creates an immediately formal impression. Subtle modifications of the final crooning intonation may also enhance the formal monotone effect: the entire utterance may be pitched lower, and the intervals (1-2-3) may be diminished. In this form the utterance can be characterized as Formal-Respectful (FR).

The examples just cited belong intrinsically to the category of respectful rather than formal politeness: this is one of the commonest politeness formulas, and it functions as a request for permission to depart (*pamitan*). As such, it affirms both the "connectedness" and the "directional" quality of the relationship. (For discussion of these terms see chap. 4.) But discursive utterances, too, can be given a tone of respectful politeness. This is most simply effected by the use of a vocative-function kinship term to end the phrase, with or without an adjustment of intonation in the direction of crooning.

In an utterance of otherwise formal style, the simple addition of the kinship term produces the stylistic category rF (respectful-Formal). This style may be heard in conversation between relative strangers who are of clearly disparate ages. The insertion of the kinship term, almost as a kind of punctuation, serves as a gesture of status recognition on the part of the junior party but doesn't imply a personal relationship or substantive commitment of any kind. The monotone of formal intonation is preserved, as in the following hypothetical example:

        2   2   2 2'   2   2   1
16. Sampun teng mrika, mboten ènten mbah.
"(I) already went there, he wasn't there, grandfather."

The same utterance can be rendered in a more crooning intonation, thus becoming fully respectful as well as, in Surinamese usage, fully formal (FR):[16]

        2   2   2 3-3   2   3   1-2
17. Sampun teng mrikaa, mboten ènten mbah.

Along these lines, the component features of formal and respectful style can be combined in various ways to yield an array of combined formal-respectful styles, as presented in figure 2.4. Each of the two basic styles is shown as having two stylistic components, or diacritic features: respectful style entails the use of the kin-term vocative and possibly some degree of crooning intonation; formal style entails some

Figure 2.4 Diacritic features of combined politeness styles.

Style	Respectful		Formal	
	kin-term vocative	crooning	lexicon	complete syntax/ monotone
ordinary	−	−	−	−
r	+	−	−	−
R	+	+	−	−
fR	+	+	+	−
FR	+	+	+	+
RFF*	+	+	++	++
rF	+	−	+	+
F	−	−	+	+
f	−	−	+	−
rf	+	−	+	−

*RFF is reserved (in Suriname usage) for stereotypic utterances that have formal ceremonial function and that are interpersonal rather than publicly directed; for example, the speech used in presenting a ritual gift of food (*punjungan*) to a senior kinsman is RFF.

use of polite lexicon or a tendency toward complete syntax and monotone intonation. The ten resulting speech styles shown in figure 2.4 are in fact an abstraction from the markedly fluid reality of stylistic modification.

2.3.2 Stylistic Transformations

As in the case of the lexical "levels" as described in the literature (chapter 5), the styles listed in figure 2.4 may be seen to some extent as transformations of one another. That is, in many cases a single utterance can be rendered in any of the enumerated styles without affecting semantic content.[17] In certain cases, however, this is not so. There is no "ordinary" or "moderately respectful" (r) form of the stereotypic invocation at a *slametan* (in formal style), just as there is in practice no formal variant (F) for certain everyday, familiar greetings.

Figure 2.5 provides, for illustrative purposes, stylistic variants of a single utterance that might be delivered appropriately in any of these styles. Obviously, such an illustration must be constructed rather than taken from direct observation, and the construction will necessarily be somewhat arbitrary: intonation and syntactical expansion are subject to minute gradation. The interaction of style elements itself is a source of considerable variation, so that for the "mixed" styles there is no single appropriate form of the utterance. Each of these style categories should be seen as representing a range of possibilities, the choice of which depends on individual speech-style usage and situational factors. Accordingly, the versions given in figure 2.5 differ slightly from those just given in the preceding section.

These stylistic categories and notations may give an unwarranted impression of systematic clarity — as, indeed, the descriptions of lexical "levels" tend to do. The system is one of contextual *contrasts* rather than clear *categories,* and the context of an utterance decisively affects the interpretation of its style. For example, the utterance labeled rF (respectful-Formal) is neither syntactically complete nor very elevated in lexical style. In the Suriname dialect, however, a casual conversation is not likely to be more formal than this. There are, however, occasions when this same utterance would be only minimally polite, as, for example, in a conversation between previously unacquainted guests at a *jagongan* (in Suriname, *pejagongan*). (A *pejagongan*—from *jagong,* "to sit"—is a formal but unstructured gathering, often on the morning of a *slametan,* when friends and distant kin pay their respects to the host household to mark some important event.) On this sort of occasion, one might hear the syntactically more complete and therefore more formal (rFF) variant:

18. Kula sampun dhateng mrika, menika mboten wonten mbah.

(The notation rFF indicates the especially formal character of this style, in Suriname usage.)

Figure 2.5 Examples of style transformations.

Style	"I was already there, he wasn't there."
ordinary	$\begin{cases} \text{2 } \text{ 2 } \text{ 2 3' } \text{ 2 } \text{ 2-3'} \\ \text{(Aku) wis rana, ora ènèng.*} \\ \text{3 } \text{ 2 } \text{ 2 3' } \text{ 2 } \text{ 4'3} \\ \text{(Aku) wis rana, ora ènèng.} \end{cases}$
r	1 1 2 2' 1 2-3' 2 Wis rana mbah, ora ènèng mbah.
R	2 2 3' 1-2 2 2 3' 1-2 Wis rana mbah, ora ènèng mbah.
fR	2 2 3' 1-2 2 3' 3 2 Pun mrika mbah, mboten ènten mbah.
FR	$\begin{cases} \text{2 2 } \text{ 2 } \text{ 2 3' } \text{ 1-2 } \text{ 2 } \text{ 3' 3 } \text{ 2} \\ \text{Sampun teng mrika mbah, mboten ènten mbah.} \\ \text{2 3 } \text{ 2 } \text{ 2 } \text{ 2 3 } \text{ 2 } \text{ 2 } \text{ 2 3' } \text{ 1} \\ \text{Kula pun teng mrika mbah, mboten ènten mbah.} \end{cases}$
rF	2 2 2 2' 2 2'2 1 Sampun teng mrika mboten ènten mbah.
rf	2 2 3' 1 2 2 3' 2-3 Pun mrika, mboten ènten mbah.
F	2 2 2 2 2' 1 2 2 3' Kula sampun teng mrika, mboten ènten.
f	2 3 2 2 3' 2 2 3' Kula pun mrika, mboten ènten.

*Glossary:

	ordinary	polite
"I"	aku	kula
"already"	wis	pun (sampun)
"go there"	(m)rana	mrika (teng mrika)
"not there"	ora ènèng	mboten ènten

2.4 Discussion: Boundaries and Stylization

The social context of rural Javanese and Suriname-Javanese speech-style usage calls for a model that begins not with individual speakers and their choices but with the arrangement of social units and their membership. Social boundaries in the Javanese village largely have to do with kinship relations; these are not defined rigidly, however, as by lineage affiliation, but rather expansively, as a bilateral network. (See

H. Geertz 1961:15, 24-26; Jay 1969:156ff.) The basic units of the network are not so much individuals as households; for example, when a married woman participates in the ritual (*slametan*) preparations of another household, it is usually as a representative of her own household. If her own kin are hosting, then her husband will normally also make an appearance during those preparations. One of the functions of stylistic usage is to place participants relative to one another within this constellation of interrelated households.

In general, an individual participates on a given occasion as either an insider or an outsider to a particular household. If the former, his or her speech style will be adapted to express close politeness and the putative absence of social boundaries. If the latter, speech style will observe norms of distant politeness and thereby affirm the existence of a boundary. (The interaction need not take place within the household setting, though the particular setting may influence the degree of stylistic formality.)

Respect style, by contrast, is not household oriented but is directed specifically toward a particular individual, either as a member of the respected elder generation or, more specifically, as occupying a senior (usually kinship) position vis-à-vis the speaker. In the Suriname-Javanese context, the use of respect style nevertheless is anchored firmly in the structure of social units—in the patterned intergenerational relations that structure both the individual household and the ritual relations between households.

2.4.1 Stylization as a Cultural Value

All three styles, ordinary, formal, and respect, must be understood in relation to a distinctive cultural preference for stylized interaction—that is, interaction that is patterned according to more or less rigidly prescribed conventions and that is therefore to some degree predictable for all participants. This is a theme in much of the literature about Javanese culture. As Geertz has observed, "etiquette provides the *alus priyayi* [refined gentleman] with a set of rigidly formal ways of doing things which conceals his real feelings from others. In addition, it so regularizes behavior, his own and that of others, as to make it unlikely to provide unpleasant surprises" (C. Geertz 1960:241-42). Keeler details the way conversation is patterned, both at times of stress and in general:

> The Javanese mark rites of passage with conventional phrases. Situations which might give rise to mental upset require concerted effort to stave off the expression—and as much as possible the experience—of strong and troubling emotions.... The constant

repetition of conventionalized remarks is one part of this effort to keep everyone's emotional balance. (Keeler 1984:292)

Java is . . . full of small talk, and polite conversation draws on a large store of stereotypical remarks. To use them is not thought stultifying, as some Westerners find, but rather gracious, comfortable, indicative of the desire to make every encounter smooth and effortless for all concerned. (Keeler 1984:xvii)

Accordingly, "one has arrived, in Javanese, when one has come to enjoy making the obvious comment at the proper time in the appropriate tone" (Keeler 1984:358).

Siegel summarizes the art of highly formal conversation: "To be *alus* [refined] in speech is to speak appropriately, that is, to use the language appropriate to one's listener and to please, or at least not to upset, him or her. . . . If one is speaking High Javanese, it means phrasing one's sentences so that they are long and, if possible, full of archaisms. Given the right opportunity and a skilled speaker, the result can be a pleasing vacuity, one that stills whatever tumultuous feelings one's listener might have while one says as little as possible" (Siegel 1986:17). To note this lack of content in formal utterances may sound (from a Western perspective) condescending, given the primacy normally accorded to substance over style. The Javanese view of interaction begins from a different point, one that assumes the existence of difficult feelings or issues and that attempts to achieve not an impossible resolution, as by open discussion, but rather a quite possible and indeed "normal" state in which all feelings are submerged beneath a harmoniously patterned surface.[18] There is a spiritual and psychological corollary to this emphasis on smoothly patterned interaction, which Geertz has defined in the context of life-crisis ritual: "This state of weakened emotional investment in one's immediate environment, or self-induced distance and disciplined aloofness from all events in the transient world of men . . . is among the most valued of Javanese feeling patterns: *iklas*" (C. Geertz 1960:53). Formally polite speech thus has a value that transcends situational etiquette. Its practice is one of the ways in which individuals can produce a sense of tranquillity in both speaker and listener. For some speakers, formal conversation is literally an art form, pursued for its own sake rather than as a socially imposed necessity or a means to social ends. Refined speech for them is—or ought to be—the stuff of life.

This point is worth emphasizing, because it conflicts with certain key assumptions about social interaction that have informed the literature of interaction studies. What is to be explained, ostensibly, is the use of politeness forms, perhaps in terms of interaction strategy; what is assumed as background is the individual's normal tendency to express his or her wants, needs, and reactions. For the Javanese, however, it may be safe to say that it is rather the tendency toward self-expression that requires an explanation, or at least an accounting, in terms of the individual's lack of "normal" self-control or lack of concern for spiritual consequences.

This preference for conventional patterning is not restricted to the use of formal speech style, though that is its fullest expression. What I have termed ordinary speech style may also be highly patterned, but according to a different standard of performance. In ordinary conversation style, what is valued is a sense of liveliness and drama, so that even rather unremarkable occurrences are given an air of excitement. Possibly this nonrefined (that is, not *alus*) form of sylization is directed toward a similar aim, to encompass social events in a kind of "clothing" to minimize the unpredictable. In this case the clothing is not so much a way of disguising feelings as a way of "costuming" them. As Siegel observes, "in part it is the nature of Javanese that its speakers can practice the emotional detachment (*iklas*) they so much value by speaking of things in order to avoid being possessed by them. Thus Javanese dislike being surprised, and consequently they frequently exclaim, 'lho,' indicating that they are surprised, in order to avoid feeling it" (Siegel 1986:27). In the same way, the use of respect style has a definite value, to speaker as well as hearer, simply because it enacts a well-defined interactional pattern. Stylization of interaction is in itself, then, a positive aesthetic and spiritual value, in all three basic forms of speech style.

This is not to say that there is no place in interaction for "spontaneous" or unself-conscious speech. The ordinary speech style I refer to here (described further in chaps. 3 and 4) is a category quite separate from the unadorned and unself-conscious speech heard between close family members (e.g., between husband and wife, or from elder sibling to younger sibling), which might best be termed familial and which is further described in chapter 4. This is the form of Ngoko that Siegel describes as "quick, abbreviated, abrupt, and usually harsh": "Low Javanese often sounds as if the speakers are quarreling. To speak Low Javanese means that one need not attend to the position of one's hearer, to his social standing. Stripped of the tones that designate consideration for others, Javanese sounds quite harsh" (Siegel 1986:18-19).[19]

This "nonlanguage" (as distinguished from "language," *basa*) is likened to thinking aloud, without the necessity of giving order to one's thoughts or, for that matter, of supplanting them altogether (Siegel

1986:25). In the Javanese view, this sort of familial speech stands as an unstylized background to the almost pervasive patterning of social interaction—a pattern in which, I will argue in chapter 3, the close-polite stylization of ordinary speech has a prominent place.

2.4.2 Stylistic Distance

The emphasis on stylization in Javanese interaction recalls Bernstein's ([1958] 1974) distinction between "mediate" and "immediate" forms of linguistic expression. (In Bernstein's use, however, these two modes appear not as elements of individual politeness repertoire but as distinct social dialects.) Bernstein distinguishes between "public language" and "formal language" as, respectively, immediate and mediate forms of expression: "Where the symbolism is descriptive, tangible, concrete, visual and of a low order of generality, where the emphasis is on the emotive rather than the logical implications, it will be called a *public* language. . . . A particular form of indirect or mediate expression where the subtle arrangement of words and connections between sentences conveys feeling . . . will be termed *formal*" (Bernstein [1958] 1974:28). Disregarding the corollary distinctions Bernstein perceives between verbal and nonverbal means of expression and between higher and lower orders of symbolism, we can adopt this conception of a "stylized code" as *one in which the speaker maintains a certain distance between himself and the utterance*—that is, one in which prescribed forms mediate the quality of expression and in which personal qualification serves to label the utterance, more or less explicitly, as serving a particular purpose within a specific social context.

No less than the prescribed forms of polite lexicon, the prescribed forms of crooning intonation and respectful vocative serve such a distancing or labeling purpose. The speaker is careful not to drop his personal reactions or concerns too abruptly into the social interaction, but rather provides the hearer with some (stylized) assurance that the utterance can be handled within the terms of the existing relationship; he categorizes the interaction. Such expression is indirect rather than direct, mediate rather than immediate, and may indeed be rich in implied qualifications. Though it is easy to confuse this sort of stylistic distance with the concept of social distance, what is maintained here is not necessarily or even primarily an interpersonal boundary, but rather a more general sense of orderliness.[20]

The value placed on smoothly patterned interaction creates a bond, however transitory, between the participants, quite apart from any more substantive relationship. Siegel notes the "air of complicity" in the performance of a conversation in High Javanese, "as if the speakers were sharing something no one else knew about" (1986:28). In Siegel's view, this shared secret is the avoidance of Ngoko. An alternative way of viewing the performance is as an act of collaboration, in which the participants must rely on one another for the accomplishment of an essential social ritual. To undertake a formal conversation is fundamentally an act of trust in the ability and willingness of a coparticipant to sustain the necessary pattern; an individual will "avoid interaction with people ... whose [stylistic] judgment in interaction cannot be trusted" (Keeler 1984:338).

The three-way model I have proposed is an observer's, not a participants', model of Javanese speech style. Nevertheless, there exist terms for referring to stylistic performance in all three of these speech-style categories. Most obvious and most frequently heard is the phrase used to approve a performance of formal speech style, *inter basa* ("capable of or skilled in [polite] language"). Parallel formulations also exist for the other two styles: *inter omong*, "skilled in talking," and—heard on one occasion, regarding my own speech style—*inter "mbah"* ("capable of using *mbah*"). The latter formulation is not normally heard, perhaps because the accomplishment is considered so trivial: the kin-term vocative is required of children almost as soon as they begin to speak. It is an invisible accomplishment precisely because it is a centrally important one for "becoming Javanese," as the acquisition of proper manners is routinely described.

Of the three categories, the liveliness of ordinary style appears to be taken for granted, or perhaps mistaken for spontaneity, by native speakers as well as by observers. There are, however, stylistic elements of "skill in talking," as the following chapter describes in detail.

All three of these basic speech styles are associated with definite social values: formal speech style with the value "refinement" (*alus*); ordinary speech style with the value "liveliness" (*ramé*); and respect style with the Javanese value translated as "respect" (*urmat*). The relationship among the three basic interactional values—refinement, liveliness, and respect—is not adequately represented in the three-way model of stylistic choice; it requires a compartmental model, as presented in the next chapter.

NOTES

1. A few notable exceptions include Uhlenbeck (1950 and 1978) on syntax, phonology, and morphology and G. Poedjosoedarmo (1977) on intonation; Keeler (1984) details some of the syntactic elements of speech style. (See chaps.

5 and 6 for descriptions of lexical alternation in Javanese and Suriname Javanese, respectively.)

2. Lexical variation in Suriname Javanese plays a far less prominent role in social interaction generally than appears to be the case for most Indonesian Javanese dialects. It is nevertheless by no means absent in Suriname usage, as chapter 6 demonstrates in detail.

3. Following J. Errington (1985), I reserve the capitalized form of these terms (Ngoko, Madya, Krama) to refer to overall style of utterance. Where individual lexical variants are discussed I use the lowercase forms.

4. The term "respect" in this context is not intended as a translation of the Javanese concept *urmat*, but has the specifically linguistic reference described in section 2.1.2.

5. I have tried to avoid using the term "formal" in the broader sense of pertaining to form (e.g., of an utterance), except where reference to another work seems to require it.

6. The respect relationship is inherently "directional" (see sec. 4.2) because its key stylistic feature is the use of the appropriate kinship term as a vocative coda. The Javanese kin-term system is hierarchically structured, consistently distinguishing between junior and senior categories of kin even within the same generation, so any utterance that specifies kin relationship will express an asymmetrical relationship. The use of respect style "downward," therefore, conveys an indulgent or condescending note that it does not convey "upward." Note that, though directional in its message, the respect style can nevertheless be reciprocated—as in the Western example of the deferential "after you."

7. This system represents an ad hoc adaptation of the graphic intonation line used by John Wolff for Bahasa Indonesia in his classes and his text (1986); numbers proved a quicker and more reliable way of taking on-the-spot notes. I should mention that I achieved some facility in noting intonation patterns during my two years of working with Wolff, both as a student and specifically in editing intonation lines for the grammatical text. Moreover, informants found it perfectly natural for me to repeat their utterances, reproducing the intonation pattern—a practice that made it much easier to transcribe and that also elicited corrections. Nevertheless, I make no claim to complete accuracy and would not attempt to use the material for close tonal analysis. The illustrations are intended simply to support my argument (a) that intonation carries stylistic meaning and (b) that it is consciously attended to. (For Javanese pronunciation see Keeler [1984: xxv-xxxvi].)

8. The term "mother" is not used in metaphorical extension; a term for "aunt" would be used instead.

9. This speaker, whose father was non-Javanese, used Javanese only outside the home (with neighborhood children, for example). This utterance was my first indication that she was in fact aware of the syntactical rules of respectful politeness. Her speech style in general was quite abrupt, even with her Javanese grandmother and other adult Javanese villagers.

10. The kinship term is the appropriate form of address (and in most cases

the only title) used among Javanese speakers in Suriname. As in Java, it is used to address a foreigner only as a special mark of courtesy.

11. Short for *mbaqyu* (avoided in Suriname, where it has an insulting implication).

12. Goffman takes note of the downward use of respectful styles as a general phenomenon: "There are deference obligations that superordinates owe their subordinates; high priests all over the world seem obliged to respond to offerings with some equivalent of 'Bless you, my son' " (Goffman 1967:59). More broadly, the use of diminutives in address may represent a general case of downward-directed deference or respect.

13. In elite usage in Java, the honorific verb (*dhahar*) would call for the honorific second-person pronoun (*panjenengan*). This is an example of the tendency noted by C. Geertz for non-elite speakers to use the formal variant as an honorific form, even for items that have an honorific variant.

14. A premise of Western interaction going back at least to Aristotle holds that equality is the soundest basis for friendship; for Javanese, however, relationships of near equality, even among kinsmen, are considered somewhat anomalous and inherently problematic (see Jay 1969:159-62, 201-6).

15. In standard Javanese, the polite variant of *muleh* ("go home") is not actually *wangsul* (literally, "go back") but *mantuk*. In Suriname usage, the former is more often heard in this sense.

16. In fact, the utterance would be fully formal only if it were more complete. The pronouns ("I" and "he") are still elided, and the word *dhateng* is still in shortened form. A fuller version would be unusual in Suriname Javanese, especially in a respectful utterance; it might occur between two elderly gentlemen on a formal occasion, but without the respect features. See the additional examples of the next section.

17. But note Suharno's argument that all Javanese speech-style selection takes place at a semantic level (1974).

18. See, for example, H. Geertz's interesting discussion of attitudes toward marriage and divorce: "To the Javanese, 'pretense'—*étok-étok*—is without any disvaluing connotations and is actually positively valued as a good way to deal with troublesome situations" (1961:134). Elsewhere she remarks the "deep-rooted Javanese conviction that it is best to avoid or to play down divisive or conflicting tendencies between individuals in the hope that by verbally ignoring them social relationships will flow more smoothly" (1961:18).

19. This description, accurate for what I term "familial" speech, is too broadly labeled as referring to Ngoko generally. The "tones" that communicate consideration must be viewed as distinct from the question of polite lexical alternation.

20. The concept of stylistic distance provides a useful perspective on the respect relationship. In the western European languages analyzed in Brown and Gilman (1960), deference is registered stylistically as the nonreciprocal expression of social distance; that is, the superior may use a "close" style

whereas the subordinate must observe a correct social distance. The Javanese respect relationship is mutually close, but there may be an asymmetry in the two participants' respective obligation to maintain stylistic (not social) distance.

PART TWO

The Repertoire

CHAPTER 3

Expressive Features of Ordinary Style

3.1 Introduction: Formal/Informal Contrasts

Like the use of respect style, skill in ordinary speech style is a somewhat invisible accomplishment for Javanese, especially when compared to the explicit attention paid to the mastery of formal lexical style. It is, after all, formal style that embodies the dominant cultural value, "refinement" (*alus*), a consistent negation of the spontaneous, dramatic, and self-expressive elements in social interaction. Refinement, conventionally framed in opposition to the negative value *kasar* ("coarse, rough, crude"), constitutes a cornerstone of Javanese personal philosophy and aesthetics (see, e.g., C. Geertz 1960; Peacock 1968).

Accordingly, any discussion of speech style with elite Javanese speakers inevitably suggests that the stylistic elements of ordinary speech are more or less strongly disvalued and moreover that they are associated with speakers of non-elite social classes. Non-elite speech is perceived as exaggerated in its dynamics and crudely elliptical in its syntax: it is shrill, abrupt, and loud. In terms of lexicon, the range of choice is seen as limited and generally crude, lacking the most dignified variants and permitting the coarsest forms of expression. It is against this background that the stylistic hallmarks of formal speech—polite lexicon, expanded or redundant syntax, modulated intonation—derive contrastive significance.

Such an account of ordinary speech is fairly accurate, as this chapter illustrates (except, significantly, the notion of an impoverished lexicon: see sec. 3.4.1). What is inaccurate is the notion that unrefined speech style is the exclusive province of unrefined speakers. Notwithstanding the pervasive "high" versus "low" imagery, the style system is, in fact, a structure of compartmentalized stylistic values such that every speaker demonstrates the need for all three basic styles (ordinary, formal, and respect). The stylistic features that are disvalued on the refinement axis are positively valued in their own context of use—perhaps by elite no less than non-elite speakers. The exaggerated dynamics and intonation of ordinary speech, although crude according to the standards of the elite speech community, lend drama and expressivenesss to everyday conversation, qualities that are valued aspects of social life. The ability to recount an anecdote in lively and exaggerated fashion is something of a verbal art form for non-elite speakers. (The best-loved characters in traditional Javanese theater are the unrefined "clowns," whose antics contrast sharply with the heroes' dignified restraint.) The stylization devices of ordinary speech (for that is what they are) express connectedness instead of social distance and convey dramatic emphasis instead of refined restraint.

3.2 Intonation and Ellipsis

The prosodics of ordinary conversation exhibit sharp contrasts of pitch, tempo, and vowel quality. Overall dynamic quality is often loud but with contrastive variation. As discussed in the next section, intonation and syntax are related: the punctuate character of ordinary syntax lends itself to dramatic contrasts in pitch. These patterns are readily distinguishable from the "discursive" intonation and syntax of formal speech style, which is characterized by smoothly connected strings of syntactically complete (and often redundant) phrases.

A few examples will serve to illustrate the use of contrastive intonation patterns. The numbers 1 to 7 span nearly an octave, low to high.[1]

    2-1' 1 5-4
1a. Lho! Wis teka?!
    "Well! Look who's here!" (Literally, "Already come?")

This is an example of an informal politeness formula (see chap. 4)—a rhetorical question serving as a greeting, especially between kin or quasi-kin. The formula itself is a gesture of sociability and is inherently stylized. Without the dramatic intonation, however, such an interrogative can easily sound abruptly offensive. Spoken without dramatic contrast or the emphatic particle *"lho,"* this example would sound perfunctory indeed—underlining, almost, the speaker's disinterest in the arrival of the hearer:

    2   3 1
1b. Wis teka?
    "Already come?"

Examples 2 and 3 are similarly given here in two different intonational patterns: the first instance as actually uttered in close-polite interaction, the second (without the dramatic intonation) as a straightforward "task-oriented" statement or question. The dramatic intonation is a more elaborate gesture of sociable involvement.

      5-6'   2-1 3' 4'
2a. Ora! Udan kok!
    "Of course not, it's raining!"

The particle "*kok*" in this example implies a definite retort, contradicting or even ridiculing some statement or assumption of the hearer. Given the dramatic intonation of the entire utterance, "*kok*" suggests a playful rejoinder, in response to the question, "Didn't you go there?"; a more pragmatic intonation would change the significance of the particle from playfulness to annoyance:

      2-3'   1 2'   2
2b. Ora! Udan kok.
    "Can't you see it's raining?"

The third example is, again, an interrogative greeting between close acquaintances, as described in chapter 4:

      5   6'5-6
3a. Tuku nandi??
    "Where did you buy that??"

This exaggerated interrogative intonation is less a request for information than an expression of interest in the object indicated and, by implication, an expression of admiration for the hearer's possessions and activities. The same utterance could be given a less dramatic intonation, making it a straightforward request for information:

      2 1   3' 2
3b. Tuku nandi?
    "Where did you buy it?"

The recurrent use of exclamatory particles (*lho, kok*) and interrogatives illustrated in these three examples creates a sense of dramatic interest around the prosaic details of daily life.[2] Dramatic intonation is an inseparable element in this sociable effect, and its absence would suggest an impersonal or even angry quality.

These dramatic intonation patterns co-occur with a characteristic punctuate syntax structure. Ordinary style exhibits a marked degree of ellipsis, omitting all nonessential or understood elements of the utterance. The resulting semantic kernel is punctuated with phrase-final exclamatory particles and adverbial phrases, producing a syntax that contrasts sharply with the smoothly connected, syntactically complete clauses of formal, "discursive" speech style. This punctuate syntax lends itself to the dramatic intonation patterns illustrated in the previous section. (Such syntax is characteristic also of respectful utterances; in respect style, however, a reiterated kinship-term vocative takes the place of the exclamatory particles, and the elided elements—subject, locative, predicate noun—are supplied in sequential phrases, all given some degree of crooning intonation.)

Apart from its relation to intonation pattern, ellipsis seems to serve a further stylistic function in ordinary conversation. Just as formal conversation requires the speaker to expand each utterance to the point of redundancy, so, conversely, it is characteristic of ordinary conversation to leave something unsaid. Elliptical syntax is valued, perhaps, as a sign of the participants' mutual familiarity—an affirmation of an insider relationship. Close acquaintances will rarely need to specify place names or identifying labels (to the anthropologist's chagrin) but will rather use an indexical (*kana*, "over there"; *mrana*, "to that place") accompanied by a gesture of the head. Similarly, names of individuals are frequently replaced with indexical terms (*iku, kaé*, "that one"; *wongé*, "the person"; *kana*, "[the one] over there"). Any object in the immediate vicinity may be indicated by a slight lifting of the chin and a glance in the object's direction—for instance, in example 3a. An object or person not present may be indicated by use of a filler word (*anu, anuné*, "so-and-so," "the whatchamacallit"). From this point of view, elliptical syntax is simply an extension of the strong indexical component of ordinary conversational style.

Both the indexical and the elliptical tendencies of ordinary style are even more strongly present in the unstylized interaction I have termed "familial." Between household members, particularly in senior-junior (as opposed to junior-senior) interaction, not only the understood syntactic elements but also the embellishing particles and phrases may be omitted. A particular task is likely to be indicated with a single word (e.g., *Kéné!* "Here!"), or by wordlessly handing over the relevant object or implement (such as a broom). In place of the stylized ordinary negative *Ora!*[1-5] a close friend may say simply *Rak!* ("Nope!").

3.3 Interrogative Patterns

Politeness in ordinary style, then, is precisely opposite to formal politeness—dramatic rather than smoothly modulated, elliptical rather than redundant. No doubt the process of stylization works both ways: formal style avoids the forms of ordinary speech, whereas informal style systematically negates the norms of formal (i.e., distant-polite) speech. Phonological contrast provides an example of the former process, as discussed in section 3.4; interrogative patterns of conversation may be a case of the latter.

3.3.1 The Interrogative Dialogue

Elliptical speech provides the basis for a type of extended exchange I refer to as the "interrogative dialogue." Elements that have been omitted as understood frequently are not understood at all, nor are they necessarily supposed to be. Spelling out the elided elements becomes the object of a lively conversation. Such a dialogue is a stylistic device: the first speaker makes no attempt to gauge the actual state of knowledge of the hearer, nor does the second speaker's response accurately represent his or her knowledge. An imaginary dialogue will have to serve as illustration; this example is based on actual conversations, which were not, however, recorded on the spot.[3]

    A: Kerja kana saiki.
       "Working over there now."
    B: Sopo??
       "Who??"
    A: Anu—kana!
       "You know—from over there!" (gesture of head)
    B: Sopo—Nom, kana?!
       "Who—Nom, over there?!"
    A: Iyo ta!
       "Yes, of course!"
    B: Lho! Kerja nandi?
       "Why! Where's she working?!" (etc.)

Such a dialogue may take place even if speaker B is already aware of the information, simply as a way of introducing the subject for further discussion or comment. (B may also omit the interrogative responses and proceed directly to commenting on the news, especially if A and B are well acquainted.) The interrogative device is perhaps a way of politely crediting A with providing new information; more subtly, it may be a way of accepting the slightly superior status of one reported to. Alternatively, B may choose to indicate lack of interest in A's news by refraining from any interrogative response, offering merely an affirmative *Iyo*, "Yes." Or B can communicate disinterest and ignorance simultaneously by offering a single, undramatic interrogative *Sopo?* "Who?" and thereupon dropping the subject. The rudest rebuff, perhaps, would be to begin the interrogation not with "Who?" but with "Where?"—a clear statement of lack of interest, given that the news focuses on the identity of the third party. (The place of work is probably understood—e.g., the market—or, if not, takes second place to the discovery of who is being discussed.) In this case, A would perhaps merely repeat the indexical *Kana*, "Over there"—a bit huffily, as if to say "Never mind!"—and let the subject drop.[4]

The interrogative dialogue serves as a fairly standard conversational device between individuals who are not very closely acquainted, especially in the absence of clear seniority; it is a routine preliminary to an anecdotal monologue by the initial speaker that will disclose the full particulars, the source of the information, and reports of other people's comments on the subject. Where there is a clear difference of seniority, however, the junior speaker would provide a more complete account in the first place:

> A: Anu, Nom kana, kerja kana saiki!
> "You know, Nom over there, she works over there now."

If it is the senior speaker reporting the news, she or he may take for granted the interest of the junior and proceed with an anecdotal monologue, possibly punctuated with expressions of interest by the other speaker.

The politest intonation pattern, in the context of the interrogative dialogue, is the most dramatic: a high-pitched murmur on the part of speaker A, which is more or less the equivalent of our stage whisper (Anu$\overset{2\text{-}1}{-}$kana$^{6\text{-}7'}$), and a rapidly delivered, high-pitched response by B, suggestive of a breathless astonishment overcoming the rules of polite formal discourse (Sopo$^{6\text{-}5}$??). A delayed or more formally polite intonation pattern would express a more moderate degree of interest, suggesting that B's response is more perfunctory than genuinely interested. Least polite would be an intonation pattern that maintains the abrupt interrogative style but in a more matter-of-fact, low-pitched tone (Sopo$^{2\text{-}3'}$?)—as if eliciting the information from a messenger or from one's child.

3.3.2 Formal/Informal Contrasts

The exchange of information is a central part of everyday interaction for villagers, and no item of information is too trivial to be of at least passing interest. This unremarkable observation provided the basis of a major shift in my role as a participant: my work, much like that of the local fish seller, took me from one house to another, and without violating anyone's privacy I found I could enter into conversation simply by announcing, as if giving real news, *Wis masak kono,* "They've finished cooking."

The interrogative patterns of ordinary style pay tribute to this centrally important process of exchanging information. The interrogative dialogue serves as a dramatic overture to the discussion of recent events. Chapter 4 describes another stereotypic form of interrogation among close acquaintances, the interrogative greeting. These two forms together suggest a preference in ordinary style for interrogative formulations, which communicate a sense of interest and involvement. As mentioned previously, such stereotypic forms are given stylized intonation, perhaps as a way of distinguishing them from the task-oriented interrogatives used in daily household interaction. Such pragmatic exchanges have a strongly directional and asymmetric quality that requires stylization to be acceptable in either close-polite or distant-polite interaction (see sec. 4.2).

In formal style, by contrast, the stylization of interrogatives is accomplished not by dramatizing the relationship or the degree of interest of the participants but by modulating the tone of inquiry. Formal lexicon and monotone intonation serve to remove the utterance from the category of stereotypic interrogatives: the air of dramatic mystery (of speaker A) and breathless astonishment (of speaker B) disappears beneath the surface of modulated restraint.

Perhaps in part because it is so characteristic of casual social interaction, the interrogative dialogue is far less commonly associated with formal social interaction. The characteristic pattern of formal conversation is not interrogative but discursive; each of the speakers in turn (if they are approximately equal in seniority) engages in a virtual monologue, punctuated by affirmative responses (*Inggeh,* "Yes") on the part of the other speaker.

It is relevant in this context to note that interrogative words in general are among the first items in an utterance to shift to formal lexical style. Both the dialogue structure and the interrogative element are minimized in formally polite interaction. This seems to be carried out in intonation as well: an interrogative utterance in formal style is delivered in a modulated intonation that may be virtually indistinguishable from the intonation of discursive utterances.

In the most formal polite styles, the use of interrogatives is kept to a minimum. For example, a question is replaced by an affirmative statement that indirectly calls for confirmation or correction by the hearer. I suggest that the modulation and avoidance of interrogatives in formal style are related to the peculiar salience, in formal interaction, of any indication of status asymmetry: formal stylization allows interrogatives to be exchanged between equals in such a way as to avoid the suggestion of either commanding information (as from a child) or of deferential inquiry (as to a grandparent).[5] As chapter 4 illustrates, domestic interaction gives a marked asymmetry to all task-oriented exchanges, including interrogation, and by that token imparts a strong resonance to any lingering overtones of informal usage in a formal stylistic context.

The formal-style requirement of deemphasizing the use of interrogatives lends, in return, an added stylistic significance to their routine use in ordinary conversational style. The dramatized exchange of interrogatives implies that the participants are so closely acquainted as to be unconcerned with questions of status; any asymmetry in the relationship can be comfortably absorbed into the "intimate hierarchy" of kinship seniority, to use Jay's term (1969:249). A further implication is that the topic of conversation is sufficiently absorbing to compel the speaker to forget the requirements of decorum (though, as noted previously, the dramatic intonation is itself a studied stylistic effect).

3.4 Phonological Patterns

Nothing more clearly characterizes ordinary speech style than the use of vividly apt, often onomatopoetic words and particles. The rich lexicon of descriptively detailed terminology is a feature of Javanese language at least as striking as the repertoire of formal and honorific variants, as Keeler (1984:xxiii) has remarked.[6] These two aspects of Javanese lexicon are to some extent mutually exclusive in their application: the sensory and onomatopoetic repertoire that, deftly manipulated, epitomizes the art of conversational narrative in ordinary style must be systematically avoided in the more elevated forms of formal discourse.

Of the abundance of descriptive and onomatopoetic vocabulary included in Horne's Javanese-English dictionary (1974), I have arbitrarily chosen the following series[7] to serve as an example of the minute particularity of sensory descriptive terminology in Javanese:

pendhelis: showing as small, round, smooth surfaces
pendhelus: showing as round, glossy surfaces
pendhilis: lumpy, bumpy (with small bumps)
pendhulus: the sight of many smooth, round objects, e.g., bald heads in a crowd
pendhisil: forming many small bulges, e.g., soybeans floating in a pan of water

Note that a contrast in vowel quality—here, between front and back vowels—is used to suggest the visual discrimination of scale and surface texture. The use of liquid and sibilant consonants is also typical of such descriptive vocabulary series.

The phonological contrast between ordinary and formal speech styles involves more, however, than simply the avoidance of onomatopoeia in formal speech style. As analyzed in the literature, the phonological shape of formal speech is determined by (a) a systematic transformation of ngoko sounds into distinctive krama variants and (b) the avoidance of certain sensory descriptive particles and their associated adjectival or adverbial (onomatopoetic) vocabulary.[8]

The most detailed analysis of the phonological contrast between krama and ngoko variants is that of Poedjosoedarmo (1968:64-66). He identifies nine subgroups of krama forms that are derived by regular phonological transformation of the corresponding ngoko forms. Generalizing from his analysis, two broad tendencies can be discerned.

Of Poedjosoedarmo's nine krama subgroups, six involve a transformation from an *open-syllable ending* in the ngoko (ordinary) variant to a *closed-syllable ending* in the krama (polite) variant. For example, *ganti* in ordinary style becomes *gantos* in polite style. Such regular phonological transformations of final syllables help to shape the overall sound of krama utterances by punctuating utterances with consonantal and nasal endings.

Poedjosoedarmo's three remaining krama subgroups exhibit the patterned transformation of vowels. In one group, final *-o* in ngoko becomes *-i* in krama (for example, *tuno → tuni*). In general, the krama forms show a tendency to eliminate both *-u* and *-u-;* with less consistency, the krama forms tend to eliminate *-o*. The overall preference in krama forms thus seems to be toward frontalization of vowels, eliminating two of the three back vowels (*u, o,* and *aw*). (See Poedjosoedarmo [1968] and Keeler [1984] for the Javanese phoneme system.)

Apart from the phonological transformations involved in the ngoko-krama lexical shift, polite speech also entails the avoidance, to a greater or lesser extent, of certain expressive particles as well as of a broad range of onomatopoetic vocabulary. The commonest expressive particles in Suriname-Javanese usage are probably *lho* (or *lha*) and *kok,* both exclamations of surprise—the former usually introducing an utterance, the latter finishing one. Syntactically, the use of expressive particles contrasts with the discursive style of formal utterances; phonologically, the final *-o* of *lho* and the glottals of *kok* stand in contrast to the favored patterns of krama variants.

In addition to the expressive particles, there are two common descriptive particles that are similarly avoided in formal utterances, according to Uhlenbeck (1950:13). These are the particles *mak* and *pating*, which are always accompanied by a sensory descriptive word. The entire array of this sensory descriptive vocabulary is dropped from formal speech style, with a consequent loss of its characteristic sound patterns. A few examples taken from Horne (1974) will illustrate the phonological patterns, including syllable reduplication, syllable-final glottals, and consonant clusters:

mak blung: a sudden submerging
mak plek: coming into and remaining in contact
mak pleng: a blow
pating brengkok: (people) shouting
pating cekakak: (people) roar with laughter
pating kedangkrang: to dangle (of fringe, e.g.)
pating sliri: keep whizzing past

The switch to Krama is not simply a matter of using alternative lexical forms to say the same thing; rather, formal speech is seen as incompatible with the expressive vocabulary that so enriches Javanese. In turn, the stylistic impact of ordinary speech is enhanced by the clearly contrastive counterpoint of formal speech. The coexistence of two distinct styles of conversation places each in relief against the other, with compounded resonances of stylistic meaning accruing to both.

3.5 STYLIZATION AND STYLISTIC VALUES

The alternative styles of any repertoire, as just illustrated, are constructed of mutually contrastive features. The use of feature A in context A—ellipsis, for example, in contexts of close politeness—is associated in paradigmatic contrast with feature B in context B—complete syntax, used in contexts of distant politeness. Along with the compartmentalization of speech styles, it is necessary to speak of a compartmentalization of stylistic values. In non-elite Javanese speech (at least in Suriname), refinement is not the sole criterion for gauging verbal performance, and other stylistic values have conflicting implications for performance.

In Javanese value terminology, the positive value associated with distant politeness (i.e., formal style) is the dominant cultural value, *alus*, usually translated as "refined" and conventionally set in opposition to the negative value "coarse" (*kasar*). But there exists also an alternative paradigm that presents a contradictory cultural value, "liveliness" (*ramé*).⁹ Though *ramé* has no specific conventional antithesis, on several occasions I heard the term *"alus"* used in this sense with evident negative implication.

In my own experience, I noticed that as my language skills improved the word *"alus"* ("refined") was less frequently used to describe my performance. Instead, if someone wished to compliment my command of polite style he or she would use the term *"basa,"* "polite language": *Lho, inter basa barang!* "Why, (you) even know polite language!" I realized that the use of the term *"alus"* to describe my speech style in the early weeks, though generaly kindly intended, was also a comment about its stilted and bookish quality; it served to warn a new acquaintance that my speech would sound uncomfortably formal.

This is not meant to suggest that refinement is a value entirely alien to the community I observed. The term *"alus"* could be used with entirely favorable connotations in many contexts: of a dance performance, of formal speech as heard on the radio, of classical *gamelan* music (recorded in Java). The use of the term in an apologetic or deprecating sense in my case had to do with the inappropriateness of my speaking style in dealing with presumed friends within the context of everyday hospitality. My closest friend much later confirmed to me that I had seemed initially very timid and stiff (a description she rendered in Dutch); her own way of paying me a compliment, especially regarding social and linguistic performance, was to repeat, *Clare ngguyuaké 'boi'!*"¹⁰ "Clare is really funny!"

As an alternative value of Javanese social life, *ramé* is as strongly positive (in its own context) as refinement but almost diametrically opposed in its performance implications. A *ramé* occasion is lively, noisy, crowded with people, and busy. It is perhaps as great a solecism to be excessively refined in a *ramé* context as it is to be offensively loud in an *alus* context. If polite and ordinary styles are mutually contrastive—in value as well as in form—it can be appreciated that an important part of speech performance is that of *signaling* the particular category of speech intended. This signaling function is the essence of stylization, defining and maintaining the compartmentalization of styles.

Both the respectful and formal polite speech styles show a marked tendency to eliminate the abruptness and dramatic emphasis of "unstylized" or intimate speech; these polite modulations serve to affirm a sense of distance. Ordinary speech style, in contrast, instead of eliminating the qualities of abruptness and dramatic emphasis, gives them a stylized elaboration, in effect stage-managing the dynamics of intimate speech to achieve the drama and liveliness characteristic of ordinary conversation. If the message communicated by formal stylization is the affirmation of social distance between the participants, the message of ordinary speech is the establishment of an "as-if" closeness—a metaphorical degree of intimacy that mimes but does not duplicate the intimacy that exists between true insiders.

Compartmentalization of styles thus becomes a way of resolving the ambiguities inherent in social distance. The problem of gauging social distance is well summarized by Goffman (1967:72-73) in discussing his two main types of "deference." He distinguishes between "avoidance rituals," which establish interpersonal distance, and "presentational rituals," which affirm to the recipient "that others are, or seek to be, involved with him and with his personal private concerns." With regard to these two types of ritual Goffman observes: "To ask after an individual's health, his family's well-being, or the state of his affairs, is to present him with a sign of sympathetic concern; but in a certain way to make this presentation is to invade the individual's personal reserve, as will be made clear if an actor of wrong status asks him these questions, or if a recent event has made such a question painful to answer" (Goffman 1967:72-73).

The stylization of "as-if" closeness is itself a kind of distance marker, as suggested by the use of the term "stylistic distance" in chapter 2. The stylized intonation of an interrogative greeting (described in chap. 4) disavows any claim to an accurate answer. (As Clifford Geertz has noted, the response to such a question is usually quite vague or even misleading.) What allows such stylized interaction to represent closeness is precisely the existence of a distinct form of alternative stylization—formal politeness—whose message is emphatically the avoidance of intrusion and the maintenance of social distance.

3.5.1 The Compartmental Model

In a compartmental style system, the stylistic options carry valuative weight. The contrastive poles are identified as embodying positive and negative stylistic values; the style paradigm thus becomes an opposition. For example, in the Javanese tradition the dominant aesthetic value of refinement stands in valuative opposition to coarseness.

In shifting between stylistic options in a compartmental style system, the performer must switch from one valuative orientation to an inverse one, in which the negatively valued pole takes on a positive reading. In the Javanese case, in the inverse paradigm the dominant value, refinement, is disvalued as stiffness, whereas its antithesis is not coarseness but a positive value, liveliness (*ramé*).

Each of these weighted paradigms has its own context of appropriateness in which it is the dominant paradigm, even though one of the two paradigms may be dominant in the culture as a whole. What is remarkable in the Javanese case is that the individual speaker does not identify exclusively with a single style paradigm but tends rather to move between paradigms, at least to some degree. (Since style is in essence contrastive, compartmentalization cannot go so far as to insulate the stylistic paradigms from one another; in that case, the distinction of context would amount to a distinction between "style communities" on the order of speech communities, as in the case of regional stylistic differences.) The general model of a compartmental style structure is given as figure 3.1. For each paradigm, the positively valued (or weighted) polarity is given in upper case.

It is important to note that contexts A and B are *both* positively valued. The expectation of shifting between valuative perspectives has profound importance in qualifying the participant's sense of opposition. That is, the presence of B as a background value must color the participant's experience of A, even within context A.[11] For Suriname Javanese, and possibly for rural Javanese generally, the structure of the speech-style system can be understood as a compartmental structure, as presented in figure 3.2. In this case, both contexts are positively valued, but the first (as shown by underlining) may be seen as culturally dominant—not because it is necessarily more salient in individual experience but because the values associated with the dominant context are given more elaborate cultural articulation. In the dominant cultural paradigm, the positive value *ALUS* is represented in speech style by the two conventionally polite styles, FORMAL and RESPECT style. In the alternative paradigm, the positive value *RAMÉ* is represented in

Figure 3.1 Compartmental style structure (general model).

CONTEXT A	CONTEXT B
VALUE A/value b	value a/VALUE B
STYLE A/style b	style a/STYLE B

Figure 3.2 Compartmental structure of Suriname-Javanese style system.

<u>DISTANT</u>	CLOSE
ALUS/Kasar	alus/RAMÉ
FORMAL/RESPECT/ordinary	formal/RESPECT/ORDINARY

speech by the two "connectedness" styles, ORDINARY and RESPECT style.

This complex structure of contrastive oppositions is an elaboration of the polarity *ALUS/kasar* = POLITE/ordinary = FORMAL/familiar, which implicitly underlies the conventional ladder model of Javanese lexical style (Ngoko-Madya-Krama). The polar opposition is modified in two ways. First, in certain contexts the polarity of the dominant paradigm is inverted, recasting the terms of opposition in the alternative form: *alus/RAMÉ* = formal/ORDINARY. Second, the addition of a mediating third style, respect, provides a stylistic category that is positively valued in both the dominant and the alternative paradigms. Respect style cannot be said to epitomize either of the stylistic values (refinement and liveliness); rather, it does not conflict with either.

This compartmental structure may help to account for the extraordinary stability of the Javanese style system. Errington (1985:130) notes that the specific forms even of madya vocabulary are relatively unchanged over the past hundred years, in spite of momentous changes in the social, political, educational, and even linguistic environment (though the rules of usage have changed substantially). One might easily imagine otherwise: possibly a trend toward "madyafication," that is, the collapse of distinctions tending toward a noncommittal middle style, with loss of ngoko and krama forms; a trend toward "kramafication," the steady inflation of speech styles toward a general polite pattern of use, with loss of ngoko and madya forms; or, alternatively, a trend toward sharper distinctions of social dialect, so that "high" and "low" come to be associated primarily (rather than secondarily) with the speech of distinct social classes. Such processes may well be at work, but not yet to a degree that has substantially altered the system of style discrimination as a whole. A major development reported by Errington (1985:163-64) for the contemporary Surakarta elite in fact shows sharper stylistic compartmentalization, so that madya begins to be reserved for "out-group" address, with forms of krama and ngoko alternating in "in-group" usage.

Siegel (1986) explains this remarkable durability of the Javanese speech-style system in terms of a philosophical understanding of language, self, and translation inspired by Derrida: he rightly notes the great pleasure associated with the use of Krama, deriving in part simply from the fact that it is not the speakers' first language (1986: "Introduction" and chap. 1). But to speak of Ngoko as "nonlanguage," as he seems to do (1986:7), or as a language of nonself-consciousness (1986:22-25), is to understate its value as a performed style in its own right. Siegel comments on the remarkable compartmentalization of speech styles exemplified in one instance of "triangular conversation," in which "two speakers use Ngoko reciprocally and the third addresses them in Krama and is replied to in kind . . . soothing tones of deference [to the third party] followed harsh tones with no embarrassment at all" (1986:25). He views such interaction as illustrative of the tendency of the "Ngoko speaker" to "disappear from view": "it is as though he is not there when he speaks Ngoko" (1986:25). This seems to be adopting a too thoroughly Krama perspective, which is not necessarily that of the participants; in a compartmental style system, it is perfectly possible to hold firmly in mind two sorts of social reality, entailing two contrastive codes of interaction and, possibly, two coexisting conceptions of the self as a social person.[12]

3.5.2 Ordinary Speech Style as "Critiqued" Closeness

The compartmental style structure suggests an added dimension to the concept of interaction as performance. Speakers have a choice of "genre" to be performed on any given occasion (with a particular other, for a particular audience, in a particular setting). To some extent, the speaker creates the context of utterance by selecting among relevant features of relationship, audience, and setting, signaling accordingly the intended category of performance.

It is also important to recognize the different implications for performance of distinct categories of style. The genres of Suriname Javanese can be arrayed according to the requisite degree of adherence to form—that is, their susceptibility to stylistic critique. What I have termed formal style, as the term suggests, imposes the most rigorous critical standard. The ordinary style of close politeness has its own standards of performance but is less susceptible to explicit critique, at least of a negative sort. Respect style imposes an absolute requirement in the kin-term vocative, but beyond that offers considerable latitude for more or less attentive performance.

All three styles take their shape against a background of what we might term "uncritiqued" speech[13] (the style termed "familial" in sec. 2.4). This is the terse, minimally verbal, and abruptly intoned speech that is permissible and indeed normal in the closest kin relationships: elder sibling to younger sibling, spouse to spouse, young child to any family member. The liberty of such unshaped speech is perhaps the hallmark of an intimate relationship.

To fully appreciate the impact of speech stylization in Javanese, one must recognize just how minimal these unstylized utterances tend to be. I have already noted the strongly indexical element of task-oriented utterances, as well as the latitude for ellipsis and for gesture in place of words. Familial speech is strikingly characterized also by a number of one-word formulations that underline its tendency toward laconicity, including the following:

Nyoh!	"Here, take it"
Emoh!	"I don't want it"
(pronounced /maw/)	
Arep?	"Do you want it?" or "Do you want to?"
(pronounced /arp/, the *r* as a flap)	
Emboh.	"I don't know."
(pronounced /mboh/)	
Ojo!	"Don't do that!"
Wis!	"That's enough; that's finished."
Min!	"Let it be. Don't bother."
Ngapa?	"What are you doing?"

Two other such one-word phrases are also used very widely in close-polite interaction: *Ayo*, "Let's go" or "Get going!"; and *Aduh*, an all-purpose exclamation of pain, surprise, or mild disapproval. Intonation patterns of familial speech are similarly minimal, lacking both the dramatic contrasts of close politeness and the smooth elongation of formal politeness.

This background of uncritiqued or familial speech brings into sharper focus the performed or stylized (critiqued) quality of ordinary speech style. This performed quality is an aspect of the stylistic distance that mediates an utterance, serving the "negative politeness" function of protecting the hearer from potential aesthetic "shock" (to adapt Siegel's term to a different context). In ordinary speech style, however, the accomplishment is to let stylization communicate closeness rather than social distance. If intimacy is an assumed, unshaped, and unattended closeness, what ordinary speech style accomplishes is a gestured or mimed—a *performed*—closeness. Social distance is maintained precisely by the speaker's "pointing to" the closeness of the relationship.

The stylized closeness of ordinary speech has a broad range of applicability in the social landscape of rural Java no less than in Suriname. Kinship in Java is structured as a multiply ramifying, bilateral network of kinsmen, foster-kin, and step-kin. (H. Geertz [1963] provides abundant evidence of this structure; see also Jay [1969: chaps. 6 and 7].) The individual's circle of kinship is bounded more by circumstance than by genealogy, and categories of kinsmen are discriminated only by the broadest distinctions of sex, generation, and laterality: "grandparent," "aunt," "uncle," "elder sibling," and "younger sibling" are virtually the only kinship terms required in social interaction. The resulting very sizable kindred constitutes a community of potential or actual insiders to any household.

Enhancing this pattern of kinship extension is the cultural preference for expressing social relations in terms of kinship. The obligatory titles of polite address—extending even to terms of address and reference for Indonesian officialdom—are the kin terms "father" and "mother" (in gradations of formality: *Pak* or *Bapak*; *Mbok* or *Bu*). Neighborship, too, is enacted ideally in quasi-kinship terms: Jay (1969:198) reports the difficulty of getting informants to distinguish explicitly between neighbors who are kin and those who are not. Social distance may well be the operative mode of such relationships, but interactional expectations tend equally toward an "as-if" closeness. (Siegel [1986:50] reports that neighbors, "with some exceptions," exchange Ngoko; Keeler [1984:289], however, reports the use of Ngoko only between "closest friends.")

Stylized closeness provides a means for dealing with this loosely defined realm of secondary and "honorary" kin. In the next chapter, I examine the range of formulas and patterns of performed closeness that make up the repertoire of domestic politeness.

NOTES

1. My original notes contain an interesting discrepancy brought to my attention by P. Brown. Implicitly assuming an 8-tone scale, I used numbers 7 and 8 to register tones pitched about an octave higher than the base tone (1). In fact the tonal steps are a bit steeper than this, and as a result the number 5 never appears in my notes. I have regularized the intonation markings by using a 7-tone scale; the numbers 6, 7, and 8 in my notes appear here as 5, 6, and 7. (The seven-tone scale spans a bit less than an octave.)

2. Keeler (1984:263) observes of quoted speech in Java that "people ... will often quote an interlocutor as speaking in some highly stylized manner: extraordinarily polite, or wildly insolent, or shrilly curious. The past in Java turns into *kethoprak* (folk drama) almost instantly."

3. The setting of many lively conversations, including those represented here, was the roadside food stand owned and tended by Bu Nardi (sec. 9.4). She had never learned to read and was clearly made uncomfortable by my note taking. We got along best when I could busy myself with some clearly useful job, like packaging peanuts for the food stand. It was less that she needed the help—she was extraordinarily capable—than that this placed me clearly as a junior household member.

4. One or two of the women I had opportunity to observe were masters of this sort of putdown, perhaps not liking to be the second to hear a piece of news.

5. Goody (1978) discusses the status implications of question formation.

6. One of Keeler's (1984:xxiii) examples nicely illustrates also the high degree of consciousness of interactional phenomena: *ngegongi*, "to punctuate someone else's long-winded remarks with 'yes, uh-huh,' like the strokes on the gong."

7. My orthography follows that adopted by Keeler (1984), so I have substituted *dh* for Horne's dotted *d*. (These terms do not necessarily appear serially in the dictionary, nor do they exhaust this particular series.)

8. The phonological shape of Krama utterances is strongly affected also by morphological variation. The morphological ending *-ipun* (allomorphically, *-nipun*) is the krama replacement for the ngoko-madya ending *-é* (*-né*) (a possessive suffix as well as nominalizer); the passive prefix *dipun-* in krama replaces ngoko-madya *di-*. Javanese syntax makes lavish use of constructions requiring these possessive, nominalizing, and passive-forming morphemes, so that the sound of Krama (but not Madya) is heavily shaped by the recurrence of the smoothly intoned syllable *"pun"* (often rendered, in phrase-final position, *"puun"*).

9. The value *ramé* can itself be understood, accordingly, as either a positive value ("lively, bustling, fun") or a negative ("overcrowded, chaotic, disconcerting") (Keeler, 1984:338).

10. *Boi* is a Sranang loan word.

11. I am indebted to Clifford Geertz for this approach to softening the concept of "opposition."

12. Keeler (1984:166) notes in this context that "speech is primarily a one-to-one encounter for Javanese, so that what happens between one pair of speakers hardly affects what happens between another such pair"—even though one speaker participates simultaneously in both pairs.

13. The term "uncritiqued" is defined in the discussion of stylistics and criticism in chapter 10.

CHAPTER 4

Domestic Politeness

4.1 INTRODUCTION

The interactional skills most called on for Suriname Javanese are probably neither the skills of formal speech style nor the ability to discourse entertainingly in ordinary style but rather mastery of the brief but obligatory signs of mutual recognition and occasional respect that make up the repertoire of domestic politeness. There are two major categories in this area: "politeness formulas," which mark the transition of participants into and out of the domestic compass, and "task-oriented" stylization, which acceptably patterns the verbal exchanges involved in accomplishing the sizeable range of domestic tasks.

4.1.1 The "Uncritiqued" Background Style

Perhaps every stylistic repertoire takes its place against a background of what might be regarded as unstylized usage (or, better, "uncritiqued" usage; see chap. 10), associated, for example, with interaction among intimates or with undirected (or self-directed) speech. For Suriname Javanese, the normal usage in intrafamilial interaction—what I term "familial" speech—contrasts sharply with the stylization even of close politeness and respect politeness. Utterances tend to be minimal, almost as if the activities of speaking, moving, and interpreting constitute a burden to be avoided as far as possible.

For Suriname Javanese, two salient and interrelated characteristics of unstylized familial interaction are its marked *directionality* (asymmetry) and its practical, *task-oriented* focus.[1] These two features strongly shape the stylization of polite interaction, which stands as a sort of studied contrast to unstylized interaction. In close-polite interaction these elements are given a modulated form: the directional element is stylized as some degree of respect (upward or downward), and the task-oriented focus is echoed in a repertoire of interrogative greetings that politely mimic the task-oriented interrogatives characteristic of unstylized domestic interaction. In distant-polite interaction, stylized forms are constrastive rather than resonant: formal speech style is normally symmetrically distant as opposed to directional, blandly conversational as opposed to task-oriented.[2]

The material in this chapter is based on participant observation and note taking. Neither task-oriented interaction nor the "domestic greeting" is well suited to documentation via tape recording, unless it is employed on a continuous or voice-activated basis: both sorts of interaction generally occur unpredictably and are of extremely brief duration. Moreover, neither type of interaction presents itself as a socially acceptable topic of scholarly attention—as does, for example, the category of formal discourse for Suriname-Javanese. Judgments regarding participants' attitudes, as well as regarding the social efficacy and cultural "normalcy" of utterances (and silences), are my own.

Some of the conclusions presented here come under the heading of what Hymes (in a 1977 lecture) has termed "positive patterning"—the accumulation of observations that presents a general pattern. The category of domestic greeting is such a case, emerging only in the course of weeks and months of observed comings and goings. A few of the conclusions exemplify what Hymes calls "negative patterning," in which a single test case can establish a significant contrast. For example, the conclusion that silence has a more accepted place in Javanese than American interaction rests on the reaction of a single American—myself—to the unanticipated occurrences of silence. Other such instances are the occasions when I either deliberatedly or inadvertently tested a cultural rule by violating it and was (sometimes explicitly) set right.

4.1.2 Visiting

At least three categories of household visiting can be distinguished for Suriname Javanese: ritualized, social, and pragmatic. Specific examples of each occur in this and following chapters. A brief general outline may be useful here.

Certain occasions require a ritualized visit, in which the visitor delivers a formally phrased (often quite brief) performance. For example, an invitation to a *slametan* (a household ceremony) is always delivered in person, possibly by a child of the host household, in the form of a brief ceremonial utterance usually accompanied by a written invitation. On the occasion of a death in the neighborhood, women visit the bereaved house at daybreak not only to offer a formulaic condolence but also to bring a customary contribution of raw rice, an egg, and fruit to help feed the mourners and helpers after the burial. Another sort of ritualized visit is required a bit later on the day of the burial, as neighbors (both men and women, sometimes from considerable distances) come to "sit" (*jagong*) in attendance at the bereaved household, even though the family members may be too busy with ritual preparations to receive even brief condolences. Interaction among the visitors on these occasions is somewhat subdued but is not necessarily formal in style.

Ritual preparations, especially the heroic amounts of cooking customary for any celebration, require what might be termed a working visit. The backyard of the house becomes the setting of a well-organized joint effort, in which helpers (mostly women and a few male kin) engage in more or less informal conversation as they go about their assigned tasks. There is a general expectation of reciprocity: women of the neighborhood gather to assist with the cooking at whichever house is preparing a *slametan* (ritual meal), so that on the next occasion the roles of host and helper will change around. Where there is such a disparity of status that there is no likelihood of role reversal, the helper is compensated by an outright monetary payment. *Slametan* assistance can be repaid by other sorts of help as well. A respected widow may help with *slametan* preparations and in return expect help with house repairs or other chores, because she will not herself be hosting a *slametan*. Within the circle of kinsmen and quasi-kinsmen, indirect rather than direct reciprocity is the norm. The assistance given by junior kinsmen (including ritual preparations) is compensated by ritual and other expert assistance and sometimes by gifts of food, clothing, or money.

In addition to these highly structured occasions of visiting, there is a range of less structured visits. Any visit to another town, for whatever purpose, calls for at least a brief stop (*mampir*) at a relation's home. If overnight accommodation is needed, it is provided without question and with no advance arrangement, and the guest will help provide the meal and help with household chores as if in his or her own home. The overnight visit with kin may in fact be the purpose of the trip, but still no advance arrangement is required.

Even nonritual visits have a certain customary structure. A guest normally announces his or her arrival at the threshold, and if not immediately greeted will find the appropriate spot—a chair on the porch or at a minimum a shaded patch of ground in the front of the house—to wait. Someone is virtually always at home, if only a child, and the guest will be brought in to be seated and eventually served a drink—traditionally tea, but now preferably a prestige bottled soda, and often a water-and-colored-syrup drink called *"setroop"* (served cold if refrigeration or ice is available). Because telephones are nonexistent in rural areas and are a luxury in the city, there is no expectation that the householder will be at home at the moment of the guest's arrival, and even if at home it is understood that he or she may have chores to accomplish. To sit and wait, even after being served the drink, is an expected part of any visit. A visitor who chooses to define himself—more often, herself—as an insider to the host household need not sit and wait, however. After being ushered into the house, she may walk into the kitchen to find a drink and a snack or even a meal, or may busy herself with a chore of some sort such as sweeping, or may make use of the bathing place without asking permission. In general, overnight visitors seem to present themselves as quasi-insiders, the role I was assigned in my dealings with several (kin-related) households. Unlike the uncritiqued interaction of true insiders, such as household members, the participation of quasi-insiders is stylized as a form of close politeness. The two broad categories of such stylized domestic interaction are (a) the negative-polite forms of task-oriented utterance (see sec. 4.3) and (b) the positive-polite forms of domestic greeting (see sec. 4.4).

Frequent visitors to the house may act much as true insiders, for example, entering directly by the kitchen door without preliminaries of any kind, perhaps using the domestic greeting: "[Have you] already cooked?" "*Wis masak?*" I have even seen an entire visit conducted, without greetings of any kind, through the side window of a house, as the woman visitor leaned in to talk with the female head of the household. The normal structure of visiting may thus be suspended, serving as an index of closeness of the relationship. (In at least one case it seemed to me that the degree of closeness assumed by the visitor was greater than the householder would have willingly granted.)

A final category of visit is strictly pragmatic (to use the term in its nontechnical sense of having a practical purpose): for example, offering items for sale or delivering items already ordered; obtaining a service of some routine kind; or passing information regarding neighborhood events (for example, a mosque-building meeting). Again, in the absence of telephones all business must be transacted face-to-face, and the degree of formality reflects, first, the preexisting relationship between the participants and, second, the nature of the task at hand: a mosque-building meeting would be more formally announced than an offer of fruit for sale.

Informal social visiting is given structure by a culturally shared agenda of activities considered necessary and appropriate for each time of day. The normal daily routine includes two "slots" that are especially appropriate for visits, the midmorning period after the early household chores are accomplished (*siang*) and the late afternoon period, after the midafternoon nap and bath (*soré*). As will be seen in part 3, culturally shared assumptions regarding the use of household space also give shape to informal social interaction.

4.2 Directionality

In spite of the emphasis on equal and reciprocal relationships between households within the Javanese village, the working assumption in many interpersonal relations — particularly among kinspeople — is that of inequality (Jay 1969:281-88, 124-26). Among Suriname Javanese I observed a number of ways in which this assumption of inequality was expressed in interaction. I refer to this phenomenon as directionality. (The term "inequality" has a conventional association with differential property or status rights, irrelevant in the present context. Asymmetry — the commonly used interactional term — seems to exclude the possibility [discussed in sec. 4.4] of a symmetric exchange of inherently directional formulas.)

Prominent in this respect is the category of task-oriented interaction, in which I include commands, questions, and responses. Within the household context, such interaction has a stronger directional character than it would in a middle-class American household. Again, the use of space and the use of language are congruently patterned. These two aspects of directionality can be summed up in two related questions: "Who moves?" and "Who speaks?"

4.2.1 Who Moves?

Among the Javanese families I observed, a parent is less likely to fetch a child than to stay put and call for the child to come. If the child is obviously out of earshot, a second child will usually be sent to fetch the first. Children are summoned to perform a range of tasks, sometimes very minor ones, and rarely offer overt protest beyond a grimace or a shrug.

In the family I stayed with longest, in Paramaribo, the relationships between the two foster sisters offered the most dramatic evidence of directionality. The elder, whom I call Sita, was already twenty-one years old and acted in some respects as a mother to the younger sister, Lan, who was only seven: school registration and payments were taken care of by Sita, for example, Along with this unusual degree of responsibility, Sita assumed a perhaps unusual degree of authority over her younger sister — though I am in no position to provide similar particulars of other families' relationships. In this case, it was striking enough that Lan was expected to be available to perform virtually any personal service for her elder sister. For example, Sita would invariably summon Lan from her games when something had to be thrown away, and for such personal tasks as removing lice or tweezing hairs, Lan performed exactly as a well-trained personal servant (though in my presence, at least, she would permit herself a conspiratorial grimace of defiance).

This relationship may have been an exaggerated version of what Jay terms the "errand-boy" function of small children in a family (1969:264). Certainly, small children were routinely expected to fetch and carry in all the households I observed, and older children would perform such tasks as giving messages between households, picking up purchases from the neighborhood store, and, once they were able to ride a bicycle or motorbike, fetching heavy sacks of rice or fruit.

What is striking in these task-oriented family interactions is not the actual assistance rendered (which was usually unremarkable) but rather the style of task-oriented requests. Typically, the senior made no gesture of meeting the child halfway. For example, an American (middle-class) parent calling to a child would almost certainly move at least slightly toward the child: if the child is outside, the American parent will go to the door or window to call; if the child is in the next room, the parent will turn toward the communicating door while calling or at least lift his or her head in that direction. What I observed among the Suriname Javanese amounts to a studied immobility on the part of senior participants, who often would address a child without turning at all, whether the child was playing outside or sitting in the same room. Similarly, in handing an object to a child, the senior might barely lift a hand in circumstances wherein an American would automatically stretch out an arm or even get up to hand it over. This apparently studied immobility is characteristic only of intrafamilial (or intrahousehold) relations. With other people's children, the Javanese style is apt to be more solicitous (using downward respect style, for example) than the American.

The directionality of kinship relations extends to the use of property. In general, I found it impossible to give a gift (except of candy) specifically to a child without having it preempted by a senior household member. (This pattern is no doubt related to the custom of giving small gifts of money to children as a way of repaying their parents for a favor—with no expectation that the child will actually keep the money.)

In one case, I gave a child (not Lan) the gift of a plastic bubble-blowing kit, which turned out to be a source of great amusement to the adults of the household: the kit was used up in a single afternoon,

Domestic Politeness

and if the children had a turn, it was a brief one. Sita and Lan enacted a similar episode in a perhaps exaggerated form. I had given the younger sister the impressive gift of a set of colored markers and a drawing pad. Not only did the elder sister make lavish use of them before the younger had a turn, but she insisted on being punctiliously waited on in the process of consuming the materials. Lan was required to stand at Sita's elbow, handing her the particular color requested after having first uncapped it. When the game was over, the colors and paper were carefully locked away in the elder sister's closet. (Lan was too awestruck this time to express even covert resentment.)

This incident also provides a clear illustration of the phenomenon of studied immobility. Part of Lan's job was to place each marker in its turn in Sita's hand. What made the job difficult was Sita's unwillingness to even glance toward her hand; like an operating surgeon, she kept her eyes on her work and simply poised her hand to receive the desired implement. And like a well-trained assistant, the younger sister made the necessary adjustments to position the implement properly and was sharply reprimanded for slowness or sloppiness. In this possibly extreme example, the junior was expected to adjust her movements to meet the kinesthetic expectations of the senior.

4.2.2 Who Speaks?

Language style follows a similar principle. Instead of studied immobility one might call this phenomenon studied taciturnity: two words are not used where one will do, and in practice almost any command (given the flexibility of syntax in conversational Javanese) can be reduced to a single word.

The use of silence, sometimes accompanied by a gesture, is generally more common in Suriname-Javanese interaction than in middle-class American settings. Schegloff and Sacks (1973) suggest as one of two basic rules of American English the rule "no silence." Such a rule does not seem to exist for Javanese interaction generally.[3] A formal visit may be characterized by extended silences, during which neither host nor guest feels compelled to make conversation. On special occasions, the household receives a broad range of visitors whose social obligation is literally to sit (*jagong*), usually in the front yard or porch area; beyond offering routine greetings, such visitors might say nothing at all, either to the host or to one another.

In domestic interaction, a senior may respond to a question from a junior with silence, indicating a negative response. (For American speakers, silence is conventionally interpreted to mean that the question was not heard and so invites reiteration—an easily tested hypothesis.) In

Javanese, silence means that the question has been heard and should not be pursued further. Almost any other response, such as asking the speaker to repeat the question, asking for other information, or responding "yes," is best interpreted as a "maybe." In domestic interaction, a positive response takes the form of a command, whether nonverbal (such as handing over the object requested or pointing to it) or verbal ("Go on!" "Take it!").

Similarly, a senior may ask a child a question by simply calling the child's name and geturing with the head or may give a command wordlessly by handing something over (for example, to be put away or to be thrown out). Such gestures are not softened by smiles but are allowed to speak matter-of-factly for themselves.

Such taciturnity has a decidedly directional quality. Silence is downward-directed interaction in task-oriented situations. (The silences of formal visits are not directional in Suriname Javanese.) The complementary upward-directed style is that of respect, and this involves the obligatory use of kinship-term vocatives even if nothing else is said. A child will properly respond to a request with "Yes, mother" (*Ya mak*) or even just "Mother" (*Mak*). Alternatively, a child being called should respond *Kula* ("I," formal variant), often shortened to *La*.

Suriname-Javanese households vary widely in the degree to which the rules of respect are observed in intrafamilial (or even extrafamilial) interaction. In two of the households I visited frequently, children also made use of the gestures of nonrespect, giving silent answers to questions or making requests with gestures instead of words. Nonrespect in these relatively mild forms seems to be generally tolerated as childish sulkiness. More extreme forms, however, seemed to occasion some embarrassment in front of an outside observer (myself).

Sita's style with her foster parents (whom she addressed as "grandparents"), particularly her style toward her "grandmother," exhibited a sometimes striking degree of nonrespect. The grandparents had long since retired, and Sita was chief breadwinner, still unmarried at twenty-one. She deferred to the grandparents in important issues and did not regard herself as an entirely free agent in her social activities, but in day-to-day interaction her style alternated between the filial and the peremptory. Extreme nonrespect occurred only with the grandmother, and I had the feeling that with her grandfather Sita would not have dared to do more than perhaps leave a question unanswered. With her grandmother, however, she would tease unmercifully, especially when she was asked for money, repeating "grandmother" in a mockingly exaggerated croon while holding a few guilders just out of reach. (She never to my knowledge actually withheld requested funds.) I interpret such teasing as normally more appropriate among siblings, probably idiosyncratic as a form of child-parent (or grandchild-grandparent) interaction.

Nevertheless, Sita was in fact better versed in the rules of respectful conduct (including formally polite lexicon) than most of the urban-dwelling Javanese of her age whom I encountered. Her verbal competence was remarked on more than once in my presence. With outsiders—senior neighbors, for example—she was a model of respectful deportment, and in most of the intrafamilial interaction I observed, with both grandparents, she showed a quiet restraint and an unfailing use of kin terms, sometimes with crooning intonation.

The contrast between respect and nonrespect was particularly striking because of the apparent absence of any middle ground of neutral or nondirectional interaction. In this household, as well as in other households I observed, the choice seemed to lie between a taciturn abruptness and a studied decorum, with nothing in-between.

The lack of a middle ground may explain such interaction as the following (as recorded in my notes): "As the evening gets dark the house is besieged by flying insects, and the front door must be closed. The grandfather, the foster daughter, and I are sitting in the front room, and it becomes clear to me that he is waiting for one of us to close the door. Out of curiosity, I stay put to see what happens. Instead of asking either of us to close the door, the grandfather gets up and quietly closes it himself." Reflecting on this episode, I realized that asking us to close the door would necessarily have had the character of a direct command. The grandfather may have felt it inappropriate to issue commands to me, as a guest, and with his foster daughter he perhaps feared noncompliance, which would have been embarrassing.

The problem here is not really a matter of language. In fact, the language does provide, in the form of a third-person passive verb, a moderately polite form of command. Instead of using the passive imperative verb form,

1a. Lawangé tutupen.
 "Close the door." (literally, the door be-it-closed)

the third-person passive verb may be substituted,

1b. Lawangé ditutup.
 "(Let) the door be closed." (literally, the door be-it-closed-by-him).

This latter construction was polite enough to be used by the grandmother in addressing instructions to me.[4]

It is not the linguistic form but rather the social context that makes a command something more than a request. In the example just described, the instruction to "please close the door" would seem to an American quite a casual and even trivial remark. In English such a request can as easily be directed nonspecifically—"Would somebody close the door?" "Let's have the door closed"—as to a particular person. In Javanese, except on clearly ceremonial occasions, utterances are always addressed to a particular addressee (sometimes to the speaker himself). If the grandfather had used the more polite passive verb form, the request would have been clearly intended for me rather than the foster daughter—in itself an uncomfortable choice. It is impossible to know what would have occurred in my absence, but judging from similar situations I surmise that the grandparents tended to avoid giving orders to their bread-winning foster daughter. To have given orders on any particular occasion might well have indicated some larger source of irritation in the background.

It is precisely the directionality of intrafamilial interaction that gives such a seemingly trivial request the weight of a command. The emphasis on junior-senior respect gives any noncompliance, even a casual "I'm busy now," the character of nonrespect. Possibly, even an indirectly phrased request ("The mosquitoes are coming in") would have entailed an issue of obedience and respect. The grandfather's silence was itself a request for service—presented in the only face-saving way available to him.

Not only requests or commands but also questions seem to have an inherently directional quality to them in Suriname-Javanese domestic interaction. In the absence of a neutral middle ground, one either *commands* some information (from a junior) or one *petitions* it (from a senior). This may help explain the use Sita's "grandparents" occasionally made of me as a kind of go-between. On one occcasion, for example, just after Sita had gone out for the evening, the grandparents approached me to ask when she would be home. They had no fear of incurring a direct refusal (or silence) on my part, as they perhaps did from Sita. Indeed, the question may have already been posed and ignored. In my presence, at least, the grandparents seemed to exercise some care not to invite disrespect by asking unwelcome questions of Sita directly.

4.3 Task-oriented Politeness

The basic assumption of directionality in domestic task-oriented interaction may account for the extreme care taken in task-oriented interaction outside the domestic circle of insiders. This category of interaction includes requests, instructions and corrections, questions, and responses to all of these. Such interaction has been noted as central to politeness behavior in general (Ervin-Tripp 1972; Ferguson 1977; Goody 1978; Brown and Levinson 1978).

A thorough examination of task-oriented politeness would require a separate study. All the stylistic devices discussed in chapter 3 are relevant here but in subtly varied ways. The pronounced directional (unequal) character of task-oriented interaction seems to call for compensatory stylistic adjustment. For this reason, task-oriented politeness ideally should be analyzed from three distinct points of view; upward, downward, and equal interaction are each differently stylized, and each is capable of minute gradations in directionality and politeness.[5] Distinct categories of task-oriented interaction must also be individually examined: requests for assistance, responses, and elaborations each entail their own stylistic devices.

Some of these stylistic devices are familiar from the general discussion of distant- and close-politeness styles: syntactical elements (completeness/ellipsis, punctuate phrase structure), lexical elements (formal lexicon, particles, vocatives), and intonation patterns. A few stylistic devices are peculiar to task-oriented politeness: verb form (imperative or passive) and specialized formulas for upward and downward request (see sec. 4.3.3). Also used, though not discussed here, are indirect ways of presenting requests (much like the forms of indirection discussed in Brown and Levinson [1978]).

4.3.1 Spatial and Stylistic Demarcation

Although task-oriented interaction may be completely unstylized between members of the same household, on formal social occasions even intrafamilial interaction will be modified. On such occasions, interaction is demarcated so that task-oriented speech and gestures do not obtrude on the formal social proceedings.

The most obvious demarcating device is the kind of "regional" segregation of activity examined by Goffman. The back area of the house and yard is understood to be the locus of behind-the-scenes preparation involving task-oriented exchanges. (Such exchanges are themselves likely to be muted in the ways described in the next sections.) Front-region participants, although perfectly aware of such back-region activity, are well able to ignore its existence.

Interaction may also be demarcated within the front region itself. On fully formal occasions, task-oriented interaction is kept to a minimum within the front region. If a brief order or instruction is given in the front region, the tendency is toward extreme ellipsis. The instruction may be conveyed completely nonverbally, using gestures of the head and eyes.

In less formal front-room interaction, the intrusion of task-oriented interaction is hedged rather than minimized. A mother may, for example, give a completely audible command to a child; the use of unstylized Ngoko sets the interaction apart from the more stylized interaction taking place in the same region. The effect is as if the unstylized utterance is so obviously directed outside the front-region activity that the front-region participants automatically screen it out of social awareness. Such verbal demarcation shows a clear distinction between verbal respect for the addressee (absent in this case) and an implied respect for the social setting.

Except when demarcated in this way, task-oriented interaction does not enter into formal front-region social activity. The tradition of formal visiting specifically excludes any task-oriented content, to the extent that the substantive concerns that may have prompted a particular visit are broached only after sometimes lengthy preliminaries, and then with as much indirection and prolixity as the participants can manage. (For a description of a traditional marriage negotiation, see H. Geertz [1961:62-63].)

Nevertheless, there are many occasions when task-oriented interaction occurs between people who are not members of the same household, such as market transactions, ritual preparations, construction and maintenance projects, contractual agreements, and contracted services. This category of interaction constitutes a second broad arena of formal (or distant) stylization.

Task-oriented interaction also occurs between people who are temporarily sharing household space in the course of the frequent visiting, especially between kin, that characterizes Javanese and Suriname-Javanese culture. In this case, too, task-oriented interaction is stylized —but using forms of close rather than distant politeness.

4.3.2 Polite Lexicon

Distant politeness in task-oriented interaction is marked essentially by the use of polite lexicon. The most frequently occurring krama and madya items are words with task-oriented application: interrogatives, negatives, and deictics. Such distant-polite stylization clearly removes a task-oriented interaction from the familiar context of domestic activity and— with no alteration of syntax—eliminates the abrupt or peremptory directional quality. For example, the common elliptical imperative

2a. Kana!
"Over there!"

is transposed into the lexically polite

2b. **Mrika.**
"Over there."

(In this section, as in chap. 6, boldface type is used to represent the shift to polite lexical style; see sec. 6.3.) In either case, the unadorned deictic may be used, for example, to enlist someone's assistance with carrying something to the spot indicated or to call attention to a third party waiting to be helped (at a social gathering or in a shop).

However, the simple transposition into polite lexicon is not sufficient for interaction where some degree of respect is appropriate, as between members of different generations. In this case, the respectful kin-term vocative is obligatory in either lexical style. Within the family (especially if the speaker is a child), familiar lexicon may be used:

3a. Kana mbah!
"Over there, grandparent!"

To nonfamily members, polite lexicon is usual:

3b. **Mrika** mbah!
"Over there, grandparent!"

But even the combination of polite lexicon and respectful vocative is not sufficient to render polite an inherently inappropriate request. A senior person's aid is enlisted only if it is clearly necessary (whereas a child can be summoned for any trifling errand). The use of the exclamation point in example 3a reflects the tone of urgency that appropriately accompanies an upward-directed request for assistance in contexts of close politeness.

Deictics occur in contexts other than elliptical requests or imperatives. In narrative utterances, too, deictics function as lexical style markers; that is, in an otherwise ngoko utterance, the deictics may be given in krama or madya. This use of polite-variant deictics probably reflects their prominent use in task-oriented interaction. For example, the familiar form *kono*, "there," so clearly and inescapably echoes the functional imperative *Kono!* (normally used to a child) that its use is therefore (I suggest) avoided in all distant or semidistant interaction in favor of the polite lexical variant. (The same is probably true of the other familiar and frequently used indexical forms: *nang kéné*, "over here," *iki, iku, kaé*, "this one, that one, that [other] one.") (See the related theoretical discussion in Errington [1988:244-46].)

The use of polite lexicon alone—without respect style—conveys at the same time the sense of equality *and* that of social distance. Both elements serve to remove task-oriented utterance from the familial or domestic context, in which task-oriented interaction is both unstylized and strongly directional.

In spite of the well-known and widely occurring association of social distance with social inequality, for Suriname Javanese the two are not invariably connected, even metaphorically. Rather, *the expression of inequality, upward or downward, is strongly associated with domestic (close) interaction.* This is why the use of deferential stylization in the form of respect style can convey an element of closeness in an otherwise distantly polite relationship, softening the tone of a noncommittal equality by implying some degree of personal commitment. This softened tone can be achieved with the use of any appropriate kinship term, whether or not there is any kin relationship (or even any previous acquaintance) between the participants.[6]

4.3.3 Close-Polite Devices

Close politeness in task-oriented interaction is much like close politeness in other contexts. The intonation is apt to be dramatic or urgent; Brown and Levinson (1978) note that the expression of urgency is one possible strategy of positive politeness.

There are, however, specific devices especially characteristic of task-oriented stylization in close-polite interaction. The uses of certain particles, ellipsis, imperative and passive verb forms, and interrogatives are discussed in turn.

Particles. Several particles are used to soften task-oriented utterances in close-polite interaction. Two are particularly frequent in Suriname-Javanese usage. The word *ya*, "yes, okay," is used at the end of a request or an instruction, in effect standing in for a vocative and at the same time asking for concurrence:

4a. Tasé kono, mbok jupuk ya.[7]
""The bag there, please pick (it) up, okay."

The use of *ya* without a (kin-term or nickname) vocative has a slightly distancing effect. A closer version might be:

4b. Min! Tasé kono, mbok jupuk ya Min.
"Min! The bag there, please pick (it) up, okay Min?"

Possibly more frequent than *ya* is the particle *waé*, meaning "only, just." Appended to a request it has the effect of deprecating the assistance or object requested, much like the English phrase "Could you just. . . ." *Waé* is similarly used in giving an instruction or a task-oriented response: *Ngéné waé,* "Just (do it) this way"; *Kono waé,* "(It's) just over there." The effect is more communicative and less abrupt than a simple indexical but less polite than the same utterance with *ya*. (Both particles may be used in a single utterance, as in *Ngéné waé, ya,* "Just this way, okay?")

Both particles have polite lexical variants that are also very frequently heard. The polite variant of *ya* is *nggeh* (short for *inggeh,* "yes"), appended to any kind of task-oriented or discursive utterance. Because "yes" is possibly the first item to shift into polite lexical variant, the polite *nggeh* may occur in the context of overall familiar (ngoko) lexical style. It also occurs as an isolated particle, punctuating a narrative utterance by another speaker. In task-oriented utterance its use is the same as that of the ngoko variant *ya*.

The polite lexical variant of *waé* is *mawon,* also very frequently heard. *Mawon* seems to expand an utterance and make it less abrupt, with or without syntactic completeness. In an utterance that is syntactically incomplete (and especially one that omits *nggeh*), *mawon* may serve as a lexical marker of formal polite style and thus establish a minimal polite (but unceremonious) distance. In task-oriented utterances, *mawon* co-occurs with the polite variants of indexical items. In this case, *mawon* (without other politeness devices) diminishes the abrupt quality of the utterance without implying any element of either connectedness or respect.

Ellipsis. In task-oriented interaction there are two conflicting possible interpretations of ellipsis. One derives from the directional interaction already described: silence and extreme ellipsis are associated with downward-directed interaction in task-oriented contexts. The other interpretation follows from the description of close politeness: ellipsis is a mark of connectedness and positive social involvement.

Without having systematically investigated this topic, I hazard the suggestion that ellipsis is used to convey connectedness in task-oriented contexts but that its use is somewhat modified. Specifically, a task-oriented utterance (particularly a request or an instruction) will not consist of an isolated indexical, except in intrafamilial or other unstylized interaction. For example, a young woman addressing a close friend would use ellipsis in asking her to pick up a nearby handbag, but she would probably soften the request by attaching a nickname vocative, and she would in any case avoid the use of a simple indexical command:

5a. Min, tasé!
"Min, the bag!"

or

5b. Tasé, kono!
"The bag, there!"

instead of the briefer indexical (used, for example, to a younger sibling):

6a. Kono!
"Over there!"

or (uttered with impatience as well as urgency)

6b. Kono! Tasé!
"Over there! The bag!"

The general principle here might be summarized as "who interprets?" reflecting the locus of responsibility for specifying the task to be performed. In unstylized interaction, the unelaborated indexical may be the only clue to the specific assistance requested, and additional clarification ("The bag! Get it!") is provided as a kind of concession. In contrast, even minimally polite or stylized task-oriented utterances will specify either the object of the action or the action itself:

7a. Min, tasé!
"Min, the bag!"

or

7b. Min, njupukna!
"Min, pick (it) up."[8]

Minimal politeness is achieved here not by any increase in the length of utterance but by the implied effort of specificity. More fully polite task-oriented utterances are thus more complete, specifying both the action and the object and adding expressive particles or a vocative term as well.[9] Interestingly, however, even though such an utterance may be syntactically complete, it is delivered using the intonation of punctuate phrase structure that I have already described as characteristic of close politeness. Thus, instead of

8a. Tasé kono mbok njupukna.
"Please take the bag there." (literally, the bag there please take [imp.])

one might hear

8b. Tasé kono Min! Mbok njupuk ya?
"The bag there Min! Please take (it), okay?"

This effect may also be achieved by the use of punctuate intonation with no additional lexical elements: *Tasé kono! Mbok njupuk!"*

Verb forms: imperative, passive. The subject of verb formation in Javanese grammar is too complex for adequate explication here, but some general points should be noted.[10] First, the passive verb form is not simply a stylistic alternant of the active form but is grammatically required (as a general rule) whenever there is a specified recipient of the action; to put it crudely, the passive form is the norm wherever it is a logical possibility. This means that the passive construction is not (as in English) a way of diffusing a described action or deemphasizing its agent; in effect, the grammar already obligates deemphasis of the agent. (On the contrary, to use an active verb form where there is a specified object of the action places marked emphasis on the agent.)

Second, the passive construction is so much the normal or unmarked verbal form that it is grammatically prescribed even in the imperative mode if the object of the action is specified. For passive verb forms the imperative suffix is *-(n)en* instead of the basic active imperative suffix *-a*. (There are other forms of imperative as well: the causative imperative [active and passive], expressed by the suffix *-na*, and the locative imperative [active and passive], *-ana*.) The passive imperative is, again, not available as a stylistic device; it is a grammatical construction distinct from the third-person passive used as a stylized imperative (discussed later).[11]

There are numerous ways of avoiding either the active or the passive imperative verb form, including the use of the narrative (nonimperative) passive verb forms. This, too, is a complex subject, since the passive forms include distinct first-, second-, and third-person forms. Both the second- and the third-person forms can function in avoiding or softening an imperative. (The first-person passive is dealt with in sec. 4.4.4.)

The imperative forms may be thought of as the unstylized, most direct form of request. In close (familial and close-polite) interaction, the verb may in fact be omitted altogether (as illustrated in the preceding section). If specified, it may be presented as additional information, so that emphasis is on the object of the action:

9. Min, tasé kono, jupukna!
   "Min, the bag there, pick (it) up." (Literally, let it be made to be picked up [passive causative imperative].)

The third-person passive (represented by the prefix *di-*) is a standard substitute for the imperative form, with the sense "let x be performed"; it is appropriate in a range of distant-polite contexts and may co-occur with polite lexicon (madya level).

10. **Mriku enten** tasé, dijupuk **mawon.**
"The bag **over there, just** pick it up." (Literally, over there there is the bag, [let it] be picked up just.)

The third-person passive is by no means the most polite form of request possible, but in Suriname-Javanese usage it perhaps sounds more polite than it does in Central Java, where it serves as a "milder imperative" form (Keeler 1984:227-28). The passive construction—as the normally unmarked style—has none of the stilted sound in Javanese that it carries in English; the third-person passive is simply a way of avoiding both the imperative verb form and the second-person form.

The second-person passive prefix, *mbok-* or *kok-*, may also be used as a mild imperative. (In standard orthography, the hyphen is often omitted, forming a second-person particle rather than a prefix.) In many cases, the grammatical structure of such usage is ambiguous, though the meaning is quite clear; this is because there exists a homonymous form (*mbok*) with the meaning "please" (in the sense of requesting assistance). In standard Javanese the ambiguity is eliminated by the use of appropriate verb endings, as well as by the use of *kok-* as the preferred second-person prefix, but in Suriname Javanese it is difficult to distinguish precisely which form is meant. In the previously cited example,

4a. Tasé kono, mbok jupuk ya.
"The bag there, please pick (it) up, okay."

mbok jupuk has two possible interpretations. It can be interpreted as "please" (*mbok*) plus the passive imperative verb form, eliding the imperative verb ending (*jupuk* instead of *jupuken* or *jupukna*).[12] Alternatively, it can be understood as the second-person passive construction, used as a mild imperative (*mbok-jupuk*). Although their meanings are essentially the same, these two structures are stylistically distinct: *mbok* ("please") can also co-occur with polite lexicon, whereas *mbok-* (*kok-*), as a form of familiar second-person pronoun, does not. These two stylistic structures therefore have distinct distant-polite transformations:

4c. Tasé **mriku**, mbok dijupuk **mawon.**
"The bag **over there**, please **just** pick (it) up." (Literally, . . . please [let it] be picked up **just.**)

In this case, *mbok* ("please") is retained and the imperative is changed to a third-person passive verb form.

4d. Tasé **mriku**, mbahé jupuk **mawon**.
"The bag **over there, just** (let) (you) grandparent pick (it) up."

In this case, the second-person passive is retained, but the kinship term *mbah* ("grandparent") is substituted in place of the pronominal form *mbok-*. (The definite article ending [-é] also serves to soften the second-person reference.)

At the risk of overburdening this one-syllable morpheme, one can interpret the stylistic ambiguity of example 4a as an ambiguity of close versus distant politeness. In example 4c stylization is in the direction of distant politeness, with the use of third-person passive; in 4d it has a definite element of close politeness, with the use of the kinship term as a second-person passive marker. The use of *mbok* as a first-level stylization element can thus be interpreted as implying either close-polite stylization (second-person passive) or potentially distant-polite stylization ("please").

Interrogative forms of directive. Another formulation in imperative contexts is actually a case of what Brown and Levinson (1978) call indirection. This is the use of an interrogative construction, well known as a form of polite imperative or directive (Ervin-Tripp 1972; 1976b). In this case, the element of indirection is rather minimal, and the imperative implication is fairly strong.

In Suriname Javanese there are two ways of using interrogatives in imperative contexts. The first is the simple question *"Ora x?"* turning the simple verb into a negative interrogative: "Aren't you x-ing?" For example, *Ora mélok?* "Aren't you coming with (me)?" implies an affirmative response and effectively requests compliance.

The second interrogative formulation of an imperative I heard only slightly less frequently. This is the positive interrogative *Arep x?* "Are you going to x?" or "Do you want to x?" For example, *Arep tuku jeruk?* "Are you going to buy oranges?" is a way of suggesting to a friend that it is his or her turn to provide some refreshment from a roadside fruit stand. Both *ora* and *arep* are used to children in making directives or invitations.

Both of these interrogative forms are associated with close-polite interaction, more polite than an imperative but not sufficiently indirect for distant interaction, even if transposed to a polite lexical form. The closest English gloss for *"Ora x?"* might be "Why aren't you x-ing?" with its strongly exhortative quality. In the domestic setting, both of these forms take on the character of stereotypic greetings or invitations.

Just as a polite imperative may be presented as a question, a close-polite invitation is often, conversely, presented as an imperative ("Go on! Help yourself!").

Material requests. The indirect requests/imperatives I have just discussed are associated with interaction between equals and with downward interaction. There is also a special category of task-oriented interaction that is characteristically directed upward, from junior to senior: the request for some material good (as opposed to service or assistance). (It is worth noting that Indonesian as well as Javanese distinguishes formulaically between requests for goods [Indonesian: *Saya minta,* "I ask for"] and requests for services [Indonesian: *Tolong,* "Help," or *Coba,* "Try to"].)

The material request formula, characteristic of children's best-behavior speech, is straightforward:

11a. Aku njaluk [direct object]
 "(I) ask for [direct object]"

often shortened to

11b. Njaluk [direct object]
 "I ask for [direct object]"

As in other contexts, the fuller utterance is more polite.

This material request formula has its exact analogue in polite lexicon:[13]

12a. **Kula nuwun** [direct object]
 "**I ask for** [direct object]"

again, often shortened to

12b. **Nuwun** [direct object]
 "**(I) ask for** [direct object]"

In this polite lexical variant, the formula has the effect of placing the speaker in the metaphoric position of a child requesting something from a parent; the use of polite lexicon serves to establish the actual social distance and thus underlines the metaphorical, "as-if" quality.

4.3.4 Summary

Task-oriented interaction is the implied background for much of Suriname-Javanese politeness stylization. In distant-polite contexts, the implied background is suggested by the fact that the task-oriented lexical items—deictics, interrogative words, affirmatives, and negatives—are the first lexical items to shift to polite form. This lexical shift in effect redresses the strongly directional quality that task-oriented interaction has in its home context, the domestic setting. A similar effect is achieved by the use of the third-person passive verb form as a form of directive, even without any lexical shift.

In close-polite contexts, the stylistic marks of close politeness—ellipsis, particles, vocatives—generally emphasize the element of connectedness while modifying the strong directionality of task-oriented interaction. Ellipsis, however, takes a modified form: instead of a simple indexical, close-polite stylization calls for a more specific elliptical formulation (specifying the verb or the object of the action).

As the next section demonstrates, the background of task-oriented interaction can take on a more positive aspect by serving as the model for the domestic politeness formulas that enact the visitor's incorporation into the life of the household in a quasi-insider relationship. In this context, the interrogative formulations of task-oriented interaction have particular prominence.

4.4 Domestic Politeness Formulas

Politeness formulas have been studied by Goffman (1967), Firth (1972), Goody (1972), Ferguson (1976), Irvine (1974), and Ervin-Tripp (1976b). The term is taken from Ferguson and covers a rather broader range than the more commonly used term "greeting."

The domestic formulas I describe here might indeed be termed "greetings," if that term is understood in the broad sense of formulas that enact social recognition. They are not, however, restricted to initial exchanges—that is, opening an interaction—but are equally likely to occur as intermittent exchanges that frame shifts of activity or movement from one domestic arena to another. Such "greetings" occur between members of the same household (typically in downward-directed interaction) and also between household members and other insiders—visitors whose connection with the household is socially close.

In form, the domestic greeting is indistinguishable from the close-polite, interrogative forms of task-oriented interaction previously discussed. In general, such greetings take two forms, which I refer to as the "invitation" and the "agenda question," both phrased as interrogatives. In either case, the content of the utterance may be less significant than the social recognition it conveys; the hearer's response may be a perfunctory return recognition rather than a substantive answer. Nevertheless, the task-oriented background association is probably an essential ingredient of the message. Whereas distant-polite interaction with outsiders specifically avoids directional, task-oriented utterances, interaction with insiders and quasi-insiders consists largely of exchanges regarding the concrete particulars of household and personal activity. The domestic greetings transform unstylized task-oriented interaction into close-politeness formulas, which communicate that the visitor is "as if" an insider to the household, fully included in its workings but nevertheless exempt from its chain of command.

The domestic greeting has a directional character similar to that of task-oriented interaction. A greeting is apt to be issued by the senior party, whether the host or the visitor. If the former, it will take the form of an invitation ("Aren't you eating?"); if the latter, it will take the form of an agenda question ("Have you already cooked?"). In fact, one can sometimes observe a kind of politeness contest, in which the guest and the host compete to seize the initiative in presenting such questions or invitations. This is the obverse of the Alphonse-Gaston mutual deference competition with which we are familiar in Western cultures. It might be called a mutual "indulgence" competition, with each party adopting the "parenting" role in the parent-child relationship model (see sec. 4.4.3).

It is precisely this sort of mutual politeness competition—whether of deference or indulgence—that establishes the analytic distinction between what I have termed "directionality" and the more commonly used term "asymmetry." Such a competitive exchange is symmetrical and perhaps even equal in substance, but the form of each utterance is decidedly directional—that is, enacting a metaphorical inequality of relationship.

The social category of insider includes a wide range of kin, quasi-kin, and neighbors, whose inclusion is determined more by factors of circumstance and personality than by clear rules of role relationship. Indeed, it is likely that the transition from outsider to insider status is mutually negotiated, by degrees, precisely through the shift to close politeness. The meaning of a domestic politeness formula, then, lies not solely in its semantic or referential content but also in the choice of a close-polite rather than a distant-polite formulation; that is, it has a stylistic meaning.

4.4.1 The Domestic Agenda

The content of the domestic greeting formulas is usually stereotypic, reflecting a culturally shared agenda for daily activities. For example, if it is late morning, a woman entering a house to visit with the female househead will greet her with the question, "Have you already cooked?" (*Wis masak?*).[14] A late afternoon visit is the occasion for the question

"Aren't you sleeping?" (*Ora turu?*), in reference to the customary midday siesta. The host will usually ask the visitor either "Where are you coming from?" (*Sak'endi?*) or "Where are you going?" (*Arep nandi?* or *Nyang ndi?*), depending in part on the precise time of morning or afternoon, which serves as an indication of whether the visitor is setting out on his or her errands or coming back from them.[15]

These questions are not primarily requests for information. Even the questions "Where have you been?" and "Where are you going?" are understood as the sort of perfunctory recognition that many English-speakers intend by the formula "How are you?" It may be that the visitor has an anecdote or some news to report that will be elicited by these questions; equally likely, the visitor will offer a minimal response ("From town"; "To the store") that is understood not necessarily to be factual. These particular questions are common not only in insider interaction but also between casual acquaintances, and it seems that the degree of detail expected in response is a function of the closeness of the relationship. In my own experience, I felt I had responded inappropriately both when I offered excessive detail to a casual interlocutor and when I offered too brief an answer to someone I knew quite well.

The category of domestic greeting that seems more clearly a mark of insider interaction has to do not just with predictably scheduled daily activities but with specifically domestic and even personal functions: eating, bathing, and sleeping typically provide the content for such insider domestic greetings. It will be readily understood that bathing and sleeping are activities not normally subject to discussion in casual or formal contexts; for Javanese, eating is similarly a personal activity, as is discussed more fully later.

4.4.2 Invitations

In form, insider greetings are identical to the polite forms of task-oriented interaction. There seem to be two main types of insider greeting. The invitation, which is interrogatively phrased, echoes the close-polite form of interrogative imperative; the announcement, which is an affirmative statement of intention, is similar in form to the material request from a child to an adult. Both types of insider greeting in effect affirm the participants' joint involvement in the domestic routine by orchestrating the core domestic and personal functions of eating, sleeping, and bathing in their appropriate time slots.

The most typical insider greeting, heard at almost any time of day, is the question *Ora mangan?* ("Aren't you eating?" or "Won't you eat?"). This form of invitation—almost an imperative—is appropriate only to an insider and is used chiefly with reference to "rice meals." To eat a rice meal at someone else's house is itself a mark of insider status in that household. (Indeed, one greeting I frequently encountered when visiting a household where I was an insider was the question "Where did you eat?"—which I interpreted both as a gentle reproach for having eaten elsewhere and as a way of determining what other households I frequented on an insider basis.) Nonrice dishes, or snacks, are served to formal visitors, but in a more formal style: the dish is set before the guest with the distant-polite invitation *Mangga* ("Please"). An informal visitor may also be served snacks, which may be placed before him or her with an informal invitation such as *Nyoh! Mangan bakmie!* ("Here! Eat [some] noodles!"). Such informal visitors included, in one household, a friend of the family's college-age son, and in another household, a "boat-mate" (*djadji*) of the householders.

In contrast, the interrogative invitation *Ora mangan?* ("Won't you eat?") is essentially an instruction to the visitor to serve himself a meal of rice in the kitchen. This is identical to the appropriate manner of instructing a child to go and eat. Only a true insider will actually comply with the invitation, certainly on the first issuance. If the invitation is repeated (and it may not be, if it was intended merely as a gesture of hospitable closeness), its imperative character becomes more pronounced: *Ora mangan?? Mangana!* ("Aren't you eating?? Go and eat!"). Eventually the reluctant guest may be led to the kitchen and handed a plate heaped with rice and its accompaniments.

The formula "Aren't you eating?" is one of a set of domestic activity invitations. A visitor who is treated as an insider, especially an overnight guest, will be invited to nap (in the afternoon) or to bathe (in the early evening): *Ora turu?* "Won't you sleep?"; *Ora ados?* "Won't you bathe?" The routine of the household can continue only by absorbing such visitors into its patterns. With children or young adults, such invitations have the force of an imperative.

The formulaic invitations have variant forms as well. Commonly heard are *Wis mangan?* ("Have you already eaten?") and *Durung ados?* ("Not yet bathed?"). Variants using *wis* ("already") seem to anticipate an affirmative response: *Wis* ("[I] already have"). Such an invitation has a more perfunctory character and a less imperative effect than the other variants—though this form, too, may be repeated several times in an urging tone, with elaborations: *Ora mangan meneh?* ("Eat again!"). Variants using *durung*, "not yet," have a more emphatic and almost reproachful tone, as if the guest were indeed a child and were expected unquestioningly to comply.

Though the form of such invitations echoes the strongly directional queries and imperatives of task-oriented interaction, their function is unquestionably polite. The model for such formulaic invitations is less the task-oriented model of parent-child interaction than the almost equally common (in Javanese culture) relationship of host to visiting junior kin. Older children and young adults are readily absorbed into related households, temporarily or permanently, providing household assistance in exchange for whatever advantages of location or relative wealth the host household may offer (see H. Geertz 1961:36-37). In this situation, the host family is expected to train the visiting youngster in the ways of the household in quasi-parental fashion.

4.4.3 Parent-Child Interaction Model

I have mentioned that these formulaic invitations are identical to the sorts of instructions given to children of the household. Indeed, they seem to be modeled on adult-child interaction: it is unusual to hear adult members of a household invite or instruct one another in domestic activity in this manner. It is rather assumed that each member of the household will suit him- or herself, within a generally understood agenda of activities. Invitations, instructions, or reminders between members of the household thus have a clearly directional character, issued by the senior to the junior.

On one occasion, when I had come to feel almost a part of the household, I used the formulaic invitation *Ora mangan, mbah?* ("Aren't you eating, grandmother?") to the grandmother as I served myself the midday meal.[16] She did not reply with the standard response, *Mengko* ("Later"), but instead answered that she ate when she felt like it—in effect correcting me for presuming to invite her to eat in her own home. In interaction with the younger members of the household, however, similar invitations by me were responded to in the standard formulaic way.

All greeting behavior may, as previously suggested, be considered as having an element of politeness, if only in the sense of taking note of the presence of the addressee and expressing a positive interest in his or her activity. In the case of parent-child interaction, however, the emphasis on politeness would be quite misleading. What is primarily affirmed in this context is a relation of responsibility and authority. The greeting formulas when used by parent to child have the character of instructions or, more precisely, of ongoing indirect supervision (avoiding simple imperative constructions). Between adults of whatever relation, the politeness factor becomes more prominent, though the element of defining responsibility and authority does not necessarily disappear.

The contrast between the polite character of greeting interrogatives (in interaction between adults) and their supervisory aspect (in parent-child interaction) is operationally reflected in the contrasting forms of response in each case. An adult will respond with a brief "later" (*mengko*) or "already" (*wis*), indicating that no further concern or action on the part of the questioner is required. (The one-word response is softened by the addition of the appropriate kinship term, in vocative use, except between siblings and close friends of the same age.) A child, however, will frequently not respond verbally but will clearly acknowledge the imperative character of the question by either obeying it or shrugging it off. The appropriate verbal response for a child is simply the response required in imperative contexts generally: "Yes, Mom" (*Ya, mak*), for example.

4.4.4 Announcements

The interrogative invitation formulas represent only one aspect of insider politeness. A complementary type of formula, also based on the agenda of personal activities, is the affirmative announcement.

An announcement formula takes the form *Aku arep* . . . , "I'm going to (eat, bathe, sleep, etc.)." Such an announcement is used to mark a shift of activity or movement from one area to another. In effect, it serves as a sort of leave-taking formula, announcing the speaker's intention to disengage from a current or potential social interaction. The specificity of the announcement emphasizes the closeness of the relationship: the acknowledgment of such personal functions is obligatory in insider interaction but inappropriate in formal interaction.

The customary response to an announcement formula is some kind of affirmative: *Iyo!* ("Yes!"). This response recognizes the leave-taking message by granting permission to go and perform the mentioned activity. Nevertheless, directionality is not as pronounced in the case of announcement as in the case of invitations. My impression is that such leave-taking formulas are characteristic of junior-senior interaction (as from a teenager to an aunt or uncle) but that they may also be used by the senior to the junior or by the host to a guest to mark similar shifts of activity. In senior-junior interaction, the response of the junior kinsperson will be a respectful affirmative that expresses compliance rather than grants permission: *Ya tante* ("Yes, aunt").

A special category of announcement is the *pamitan*, a literal leave-taking performed when leaving the house. This is perhaps the most strongly emphasized of all aspects of politeness. Unlike the domestic greetings, the *pamitan* is obligatory not only in insider interaction (that is, between "as-if" family members) but also in formal interaction (from guest to host and from one guest to another, especially to a senior). It is also used within the domestic group. Within the family, the directionality of the formula is especially clear: junior household members must announce their departure to senior household members, but the reverse is not the case. A junior household member, noticing that a senior householder is about to go out, is quick to ask, not as a polite greeting but out of interested curiosity, *"Arep nandi* [kin term]?" ("Where are you going?"). The same question uttered by a senior household member to a junior has a definite air of reproach, as if suggesting that the *pamitan* should already have been offered.

4.4.5 Task-Oriented Analogues

The interrogative invitation formula is syntactically identical to the close-polite interrogative form of imperative utterance. To take one example, the sentence *Ora ados?* ("Aren't you taking a bath?") might be used equally by a parent instructing a child to bathe or by a host to an overnight (insider) guest as a way of inviting the guest to have a bath.

Similarly, the affirmative announcement formula is syntactically identical to the form commonly used by a child in requesting assistance. The sentence *Aku arep mangan* ("I will/want to eat") might be either a way of excusing oneself from social interaction or, spoken by a child to an adult, a request for food.

A subtle distinction exists, however, between the announcement and the request, as seen in the way ellipsis tends to operate in each case. In a *task-oriented request*, the pronoun *aku* ("I") is frequently omitted as understood: *Aku arep mangan* ("I want to eat") becomes *Arep mangan* ("[I] want to eat"). In an *announcement*, the close-polite stylistic message is underlined by specifying the pronoun, while the auxiliary *arep* ("will" or "want to"), with its insistent or demanding overtone, is often omitted. Thus, *Aku arep mangan* ("I will eat") becomes *Aku mangan* ("I [will] eat").

In fact, the auxiliary verb *arep* has two meanings that are distinct lexical items in contemporary English. In its unemphatic use it serves simply as a future-tense marker, like the English "will" or, more colloquially, "is/am/are going to." But *arep* can also be used as an independent verb with the meaning "to want." In this sense, it may, for example, occur as a one-word question, addressed to a child and referring indexically to an item of food: *Arep?* "Do you want some?" In task-oriented usage, *arep* represents an emphatic use and is not omitted in ellipsis; in this usage, the statement represents an expressed wish rather than an announced intention. In formulaic usage, *arep* is a simple tense marker and may be omitted.

Finally, in announcements as in general discourse, a more complete utterance demonstrates greater distant politeness. Thus the domestic greeting, which is itself a gesture of insider relationship, may be subtly adapted to emphasize either the closeness of the relationship (by means of ellipsis, intonation, etc.) or the metaphorical character of the insider relationship (by distant-polite devices, such as completeness). In fully complete form, an announcement would include a term of address (kin term [KT] or personal name [PN]) and an expressive particle, most commonly *ya*:

13. Aku arep mangan ya (name)?
 "I want to eat, okay, PN?"

The recurrent use of the pronoun *aku* ("I") in domestic announcement formulas presents a striking contrast with distant-polite style as well as with unstylized task-oriented interaction. Owing to the prevalence of ellipsis in Javanese syntax, the first-person pronoun is very frequently omitted as understood. Indeed, to specify the first-person pronoun unnecessarily is perhaps a violation of distant-polite stylistic norms (regardless of lexical level employed). In direct contrast to distant-polite style, it seems to be a feature of respectful usage (at least in the domestic context) that the first-person pronoun is used with marked frequency in junior-senior interaction. In fact, the respectful response to hearing one's name called is simply the first-person pronoun *Kula* ("I," polite lexical form). (The senior party, in contrast, is likely to use a kinship term in self-reference, just as in English a parent may use "Mommy" or "Daddy" in self-reference in addressing a young child.)

Thus, not only do the formulaic announcements in junior-senior interaction usually specify the pronoun "I," but there is also a tendency to focus on the speaker's personal activities or state: "I'm hungry, grandmother"; "I've just been in town, uncle"; "I'm sick"; "I love movies." The central theme is connectedness, echoing child-parent interactions in which the child is asked about his or her likes or volunteers statements of immediate needs. (Recall also the close-polite form of material request, *Aku njaluk x* ["I want x"].)

The prominence of the first-person pronoun in respectful domestic interaction goes along with not only the complete avoidance of the second-person pronoun but the avoidance even of any substantive comment on the senior person's activities or state. That is, whereas some term of second-person *address*—the vocative-function kin term—is obligatory in respectful speech, second-person *reference* is virtually nonexistent. A few formulaic references ("Have you eaten?" "Where are you going?") are exceptions to this principle, but even these are more likely to be heard in slightly distant relationships than in respect relationships with close kin. For example, a child who sees his grandmother leaving the house is likely to get a more favorable response by using a first-person statement

14a. Arep mélok mbah!
"[I] want to come too, grandma!"

than by using a second-person question

14b. Mbah, nandi?
"Grandma, where (are you going)?"

This restriction on reference is one example of a substantive requirement in directional interaction that cannot be remedied by the careful selection of stylistic devices.

By specifying the first-person pronoun in either familiar or polite lexical form, the speaker conveys a clear sense of connectedness and (in appropriate styles) respect. The explicit use of the first-person pronoun contrasts not only with the avoidance of second-person reference (in respect relationships) but also with the impersonal, object-focused phrasing of task-oriented interaction. The frequent use of passive constructions in task-oriented interaction eliminates the need for either first- or second-person pronouns: *Lawangé ditutup* ("[Let] the door be closed"); *Dipangan* ("[Let it] be eaten," i.e., "eat this"); *Tak-pangan* ("[Let it] be eaten by me," e.g., "I'm going to eat my lunch"). Against this background of routine, impersonal task-oriented formulations, the full subject-focused announcement formula has the effect of calling attention specifically to the actor and the activity as belonging within both the culturally prescribed domestic agenda and the socially relevant circle of inside participants.

Figure 4.1 illustrates the relationship between the task-oriented utterance and the announcement formula. (Many additional stylistic options could have been included in this array.) The basic utterance (option 1), *Tak-pangan,* might be translate as "Let me eat"; it is a passive first-person formulation that deemphasizes the actor. Option 1 can be stylized in two different directions: as an upward-directed utterance (2a and 2b) it would normally be a request to be served or offered food; as a downward-directed utterance (3a and 3b) it would more likely be an announcement of the intention of eating, a conventional way of excusing oneself temporarily from social interaction. As in all upward-directed interaction, option 2 uses the obligatory kin term as a vocative coda. Whereas the upward-directed request consistently uses the first-person pronoun (familiar form, *aku*) and may elide the auxiliary verb,

Figure 4.1 Announcements and task-oriented styles.

Request
(Option 2,
to senior)

Option 2b
Aku arep mangan, [kin term].
"I want to eat, [kin term]."

Option 2a
Arep mangan, [kin term].
"(I) want to eat, [kin term]."

Option 1
Tak-pangan.
"Let me [just] eat."

Option 3a
Aku mangan, ya?
"I'll eat, okay?"

Announcement
(Option 3,
to junior or equal)

Option 3b
Aku arep mangan, ya?
"I will eat, okay?"

Less Stylized... More Stylized

the downward-directed announcement may omit the pronominal subject but uses the auxiliary verb (*arep,* with the strong sense, "want to").

As discussed in chapter 7, the first- and second-person pronouns have very different resonance. Use of the first-person pronoun establishes a quasi-dependent relationship vis-à-vis the hearer. This relationship can be very close but always maintains its directional character; the senior is less likely to make consistent use of the first-person pronoun but may freely use the second-person pronoun, which the junior must consistently avoid. The directionality of the relationship in no way diminishes its closeness for Javanese, even though the junior may offer little in the way of gestures of concern or support for the senior. The respect the junior communicates is itself a positive *and close* attitude.

4.5 SUMMARY

The domestic politeness formulas (invitations and announcements) are related to their task-oriented analogues as stylized versions. Whereas the task-oriented content of these formulas communicates a relationship of personal connectedness, the element of stylization mutes this message; the politeness formula is thus not a statement of actual household membership but rather a statement of "as-if" membership.

The domestic politeness formula is not only the commonest form of task-oriented interaction with "as-if" insiders, such as overnight guests, it is also the only appropriate form of greeting in such contexts. The more distant or more casual forms of greeting, appropriate in outsider interaction, are inadequate for relationships of closer involvement. (These include the conventional queries "Where are you going?" and "Where are you coming from?" which provide a middle ground of stylized close-polite interaction: unlike domestic greetings, they do not refer to personal activities but rather to public comings and goings. The conventional distant-polite greeting is the equivalent of our "Good day," *Slamet* or *Wilujeng*—literally, [be] safe or well.)

A marked feature, then, of both the politeness formulas and task-oriented interaction is their directional quality—the implied contextualization of the utterance as either senior-junior or junior-senior. The term "directionality" is used here in preference to "inequality" because it avoids the suggestion of material status (rather than role) differences; it is preferable to the more restricted term "asymmetry" because these directional formulas may in fact be reciprocally exchanged without losing their upward or downward implication.

This "home-context" of task-oriented directionality probably contributes to the sensitivity of interaction stylization in Javanese culture. Even in the Suriname setting, where Javanese status differences are relatively narrow and have little political significance—in contrast to the hierarchical structure of traditional Indonesian Javanese society—a minimal level of social competence requires some degree of stylistic sophistication. Even in the absence of the aristocratic/political model of status stylization, the Suriname-Javanese speaker must nevertheless control the evocation (and the avoidance) of the domestic model of directional interaction.

The strongly directional quality of domestic interaction is an essential framing element in interpreting the stylistic distinction between formal and respectful politeness. A directional element is inherent in respectful politeness but not in formal politeness in Javanese. But respect style is also a style of close as opposed to distant politeness. It is this cluster of contextual associations that dramatically differentiates the concept of directionality, as I have used it to describe domestic interaction, from the more distantly hierarchical forms of social inequality conventionally associated with the phenomenon of Javanese speech levels. Kinship relations for Javanese present the ideal model of interpersonal closeness, but at the same time they present also the defining context for directional interaction codes—that is, for stylized *social inequality*. Even more unexpected from the point of view of the Western observer is the corollary association: *equality* is here a concomitant of social distance rather than closeness and is expressed stylistically as formal (distant) politeness. The factors of closeness, distance, and directionality interact in sometimes subtle ways to affect lexical usage generally (chap. 6) and particularly the use of pronouns and pronoun replacement forms (chap. 7).

NOTES

1. By "task-oriented interaction" I refer to interchanges directed toward accomplishing an immediate task or obtaining specific information. Such interchanges make frequent use of such elements as interrogatives, deictics, and direct responses (affirmative and negative). Other sorts of interaction, of course, also occur in the household context.

2. Of course, polite lexicon may be asymmetrically exchanged, but this is rare in Suriname-Javanese usage (outside of close-polite, respect contexts). The standard content of distant-polite conversation includes, as well as narrative statements, formally phrased interrogatives (often used as greetings) and recitals of, for example, the names of persons attending a recent social event or the dishes prepared for it.

3. Nevertheless, silence in the form of "not speaking" (*satru*) is a well-known form of negative social sanction, as described by H. Geertz (1961:117-18).

4. For imperative and passive verb forms see section 4.3.3. In fact, for Suriname Javanese, as perhaps for rural Javanese generally, the passive imperative is not commonly used. The more likely imperative form is the causative imperative construction *Lawangé tutupna* ("the door be-made-closed"). The elaboration of imperative verb forms in Ngoko probably has more relevance for Javanese town dwellers with traditionally large domestic staffs than for villagers.

5. The participation of a child (either as speaker or as addressee) also affects interaction style.

6. To a junior, the speaker might use the kin term *dik* (short for *adik*, "younger sibling"), *nak* (short for *anak*, "child"), *cah* (short for *bocah*, "boy"), or *wuk* (short for *bawuk*, "little girl"); to a senior, *mas* or *kang* ("elder brother"), *yu* ("elder sister"), *oom* ("uncle"), *bik* ("junior aunt"), *tante* ("aunt"), *wa* ("senior aunt or uncle"), *pak* ("father"), or *mbah* ("grandmother or grandfather"). (I never heard the term *mak*, "mother," used in this metaphorical extended way, though the honorific form *bu* [short for *ibu*, "mother"] may be so used.)

7. As presented here, this utterance is grammatically incomplete: the verb *jupuk* is actually the basic root form of the verb. Unless the word *mbok* is understood as the second-person passive prefix, the root should be completed with some form of imperative suffix plus (if active) the active prefix *n-*. In practice, however, the imperative suffix is often elided, and the active prefix, when used, is difficult to discern in rapid speech. This utterance is therefore

an adequate depiction of normal usage in Suriname Javanese. (In fact, the commonly heard variant of *jupuk*, in this and other dialects, is *jikuk*.)

8. Imperative forms used in these examples are not necessarily the standard Javanese forms; see the discussion of imperative verb forms in the next section.

9. It is a general rule of Javanese style that an utterance is more polite if it is more complete (even in the direction of redundancy). See Keeler (1984:13).

10. Verb formation in Javanese is fully discussed in Horne (1961) and Keeler (1984).

11. In Suriname Javanese the use of imperative forms is not as elaborate as textbook accounts suggest. A preferred form seems to be the causative imperative (-*na*) (with or without the active verbal prefix), with the sense of "Make (the action) done." This may be less a stylistic preference than a phonological tendency toward nasalization such that the simple imperative suffix -*a* tends to be transformed to -*na*; the sense, in other words, may be better represented as a simple imperative than a causative one.

12. The active imperative is formed using the active prefix, in this case *n*-, plus the imperative suffix -*a* or the causative imperative suffix -*na*. The active prefix is never dropped, though it can be difficult to discern aurally; it is properly speaking not a prefix but a nasalization of the initial phoneme of the verb root. The imperative suffix may be elided: one can hear simply *"Jupuk!"* or, in Suriname-Javanese dialect, *"Jikuk!"*

13. Standard Javanese distinguishes between *nuwun* and *nyuwun*, but in Suriname Javanese and other nonstandard dialects both are pronounced /nuwun/; usage is here entirely formulaic.

14. All formulas are here given in ngoko style of lexicon. In respect contexts, polite lexicon may also be used.

15. *Sak'endi?* means literally, "From where?" *Arep nandi?* is literally glossed as "Want (to go) to where?" A variant form is *Nyang ndi?* "To where?" (*Nandi* is a contracted form of *nyang ndi*.)

16. Readers familiar with usage in Java might well be shocked at the use of the familiar form *mangan* (to eat) in addressing a "grandparent." In the Suriname context, however, that form seemed entirely appropriate to this relationship, and the honorific would have seemed stilted or even mocking, as more appropriate for a ceremonial context.

CHAPTER 5

Speech Levels in Javanese

5.1 Introduction

The Javanese system of lexical alternants is widely cited as a case of elaborately style-inflected language. Lexical marking of social style is, of course, highly developed in Asian languages generally: Japanese and Korean (Martin 1964); Hindi (Jain 1969) and Tamil (Schiffman 1986); Thai, Burmese, and Vietnamese (Cooke 1970).[1] However, not only the complexity of the Javanese system but also the cogency of Geertz's brief description (1960:248ff.) has made it the most often analyzed and anthologized case of lexical alternation (see, e.g., Fishman 1968; Burling 1970; Keesing 1971:165; Pride and Holmes 1972; Silverstein 1979).

All style-inflected languages exhibit a relatively broad range of lexicon in which stylistic choice is obligatory, so that most utterances force the speaker to "say" something about the social context of the utterance and particularly about the speaker-hearer relationship. Exactly what is being "said" stylistically presents a challenge for cross-cultural interpretation.

For Suriname-Javanese speakers, the system of lexical variation takes its place as an element, perhaps attenuated, within the broader structure of stylistic meaning described in chapter 2. Nevertheless, the Suriname-Javanese style system cannot be described without at least a general understanding of lexical levels as they work in standard Javanese.

5.2 Review of the Literature

The most familiar description of the Javanese system of speech styles in the literature of sociolinguistics is Clifford Geertz's (1960) brief account, anthologized repeatedly since its initial appearance as a section of his ethnographic study *The Religion of Java*. In its original context it is subsumed within the discussion of "*priyayi* belief and etiquette" — pertaining, that is, to the aristocratic rather than the peasant cultural tradition. This treatment is eminently logical in the context of an account of religion, for it is only within the aristocratic tradition that etiquette takes on articulated spiritual significance.[2] From the point of view of language use, however, a gap is thereby created: one wants to know to what degree this "peculiar obsession" with speech style is incorporated within the life-style of the Javanese villager, whether or not its use is associated with a religious world view.

Field studies of rural Javanese speech style are virtually nonexistent, though there are very useful accounts that either are more general or that pertain to elite speech style. Poedjosoedarmo (1968) provides a comprehensive description of the system of lexical styles that outlines systematic differences in the stylistic usage of elite and non-elite speakers, augmenting the very broad distinctions suggested by Geertz (discussed in sec. 5.5). Uhlenbeck (1970) analyzes selected occurrences in modern Javanese fiction that demonstrate style shifts and style combinations. Suharno (1974) offers a markedly original analysis of Javanese grammar, including style alternation, from a transformational point of view. Silverstein (1979) analyzes the primary source material to place the system within the framework of linguistic theories of reference. Keeler's (1984) "cultural approach" to teaching Javanese is an invaluable general resource, not only for the clarity of the introduction but also for the ethnographic description and cultural insights that abound in the notes following each of the lessons.

Bax's (1974) field study of a semirural community "just outside Yogyakarta" documents the rather formal styles elicited in tape-recorded conversation sessions.[3] Smith-Hefner (1981) gives an insightful account of the Tenggerese dialect, one that is possibly more remote from standard Javanese than that of Suriname. Wolff and Poedjosoedarmo (1982) present a sophisticated investigation of casual domestic and social interaction, based on tape recordings made by Javanese research assistants in their own (generally urban or elite) social settings. J. Errington (1982; 1985) provides a detailed account of the historical development of speech styles, including the contemporary range of usage, focusing on elite speech styles in the Surakarta area.[4]

5.3 THE SYSTEM OF LEXICAL LEVELS

It is difficult to exaggerate the complexity of the Javanese system of lexical variation. The system is based on sets of precisely ranked, or style-coded, morphemes that are semantically equivalent but stylistically contrastive. A reader unfamiliar with the system may equate it, initially, with our own use of stylistic variants: for example, a residence is the same as a home, but the former word is Latin derived and therefore more formal.[5] Even the brief account provided here should suffice, however, to establish the difference. The English synonyms are not semantically interchangeable in the same way as the Javanese variants. In Javanese, the hobo joke is impossible—the monologue in which a shabbily dressed derelict speaks with high-flown pomposity about his own situation, including his residence or domicile. This is because (apart from the honorific vocabulary, discussed later) the style of utterance has no implied referential significance but is strictly determined by the immediate social context of the utterance, especially the relationship of speaker and addressee. Moreover, in the Javanese context, far from being inappropriate, it is frequently obligatory for persons of humble status to use the more elevated styles of speech (but see sec. 5.5 for a discussion of social dialects).

5.3.1 Style Repertoires

The Javanese speech styles are not social dialects; it is not the case that elite speakers employ exclusively "high" style and non-elite speakers "low" style, though there are indeed class-associated differences in style repertoires. For any speaker on any given occasion, the styles represent options whose selection and manipulation are determined according to contextual factors: the relative social status of the person addressed; the participants' degree of acquaintance and relative ages; and the requirements of the social setting, that is, its degree of "formality."

It is appropriate to think of the style system as a vastly expanded version of the European alternation of second-person pronoun (*tu/vous, du/Sie*, etc.). As in that case, the Javanese style system has a dual significance, analyzed by Brown and Gilman (1960) as "power" and "solidarity." Like the European pronouns, the style system exhibits both symmetrical exchange (an index of solidarity versus social distance) and asymmetrical exchange (an index of power, with the politer style directed "upward").

The enormously greater complexity of the Javanese system has the structural effect of disambiguating the areas of message conflict arising from this dual significance (see secs. 7.1 and 7.2). In place of a simple binary signal, the Javanese lexicon provides a range of polite forms signaling either "deference" (Brown and Gilman's "power") or "formality" (social distance, nonsolidarity). The result is an array of distinct repertoires for insider and outsider interaction for both elite and non-elite speakers.

5.3.2 The Javanese Lexicon: Paradigms

At the heart of the Javanese style system is the binary discrimination between "ordinary" (or *ngoko*) and "polite" (or *krama*) vocabulary.[6] The first-person pronoun "I," for example, is rendered as *aku* for purposes of addressing one's younger brother or sister but *kula* when addressing one's parents or grandparents. Hundreds of vocabulary items exhibit this sort of binary discrimination.

The terms "ngoko" and "krama" are traditionally used to refer not only to the style of particular lexical forms but also to the overall style of utterance (what Errington terms "sentential" as distinct from "lexical" style); thus, one is said to be "speaking Ngoko" or "speaking Krama," almost as if separate languages were involved.[7] As mentioned in chapter 2, in describing observed Suriname-Javanese usage I use the terms "formal" and "ordinary" to refer to the overall lexical style of an utterance, reserving the terms "ngoko" and "krama" to refer to the style of particular lexical alternants; however, where the Javanese terms must be used, as in the detailed descriptions of this chapter, the capitalized form (e.g., Ngoko) refers to style of utterance (sentential style) and the lowercase form (e.g., ngoko) to the style of individual lexical variants.

Two additional features of the system greatly increase its complexity. First, most utterances are neither "pure Krama" (that is, krama plus neutral vocabulary) nor "pure Ngoko" but rather are composed of a judiciously assorted mix of lexical levels. The need of speakers for stylistic compromise is so pervasive that a third category of lexical style—*madya*, or "middle"—exists to fill the need. (Again, the term "Madya" is used to refer to the overall style of an utterance that is neither Ngoko nor Krama.[8]) As Errington (following Uhlenbeck) emphasizes, there is no unitary Madya style of utterance but rather a continuum of stylistic mixes, in which a varying ratio of krama to ngoko is combined with the madya vocabulary.

The second source of stylistic complexity is the use of honorific vocabulary—polite lexical forms that are used to express honorific reference and are therefore, in principle, independent of the overall style of an utterance. As discussed later, their use in reference to the addressee does in effect enhance (or even define) the overall style of utterance.

To form a picture of the Javanese lexicon it is necessary to think in terms of lexical paradigms—semantic items that may be realized morphologically in two or more stylistic alternants. Thus, the first-person pronoun is a semantic or lexical item having (for Suriname Javanese) two stylistic alternants, *aku* and *kula*, that is, a binary lexical paradigm.

The Javanese lexicon is made up of paradigms comprising from one to four stylistic alternants, as diagramed in figure 5.1

For the vast bulk of the very rich lexicon of Javanese, no stylistic variants (in the strict sense) exist, but only the sort of connotative nuancing with which English speakers are fully familiar (Uhlenbeck 1970; Poedjosoedarmo 1968). This huge, stylistically undifferentiated vocabulary is usually included within the term "ngoko." Because this term is used to refer to those "ordinary" lexical forms that do have

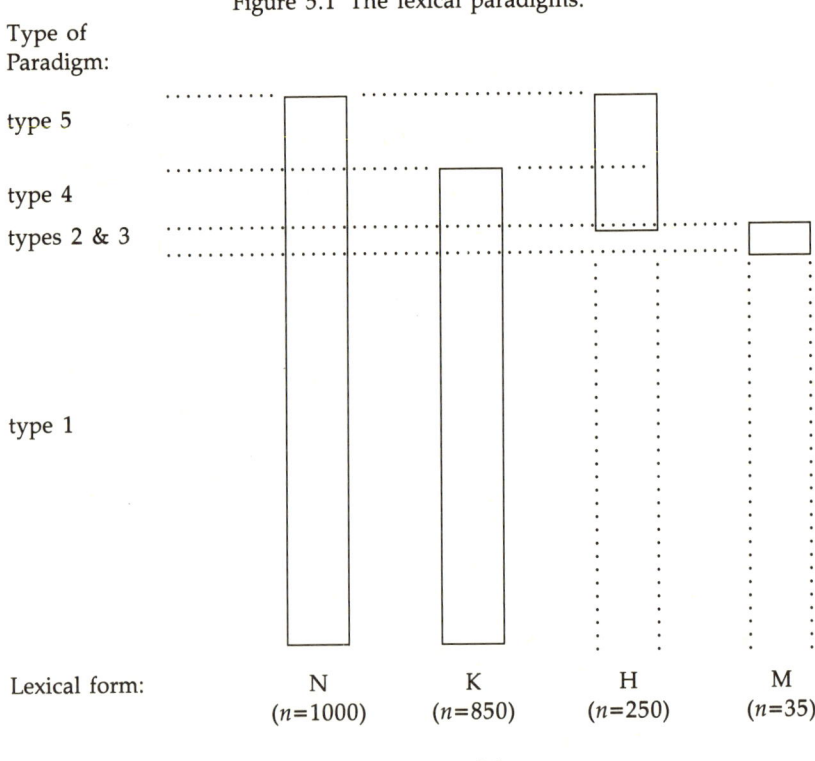

Figure 5.1 The lexical paradigms.

Types of paradigm:

1 = N/K   (n=715)
2 = N/M/K   (n= 25)
3 = N/M/K/H   (n=10)
4 = N/K/H   (n=90)
5 = N/H   (n=150)

Lexical forms:

N = ngoko (excluding neutral vocabulary)
M = madya
K = krama
H = honorific (krama inggil)

Sources: Poedjosoedarmo (1968:64-67; 1969: passim); Uhlenbeck (1970: 450-51). By extrapolation; numbers are approximate.

polite variants, I use the term "neutral" to refer to stylistically undifferentiated vocabulary (following Suharno 1974:168-71).

About a thousand lexical items exhibit stylistic alternation. For most of these items, stylistic differentiation is limited to the basic binary contrast between ordinary (ngoko) and formal (krama) variants. Uhlenbeck's and Poedjosoedarmo's numerical data indicate a total of 715 simple ngoko/krama contrasts (Uhlenbeck 1970:450-52; Poedjosoedarmo 1968:64-67).

5.3.3 The Madya Styles

In addition to these 715 lexical items, there is a numerically small (n = 3) but stylistically potent group of morphological elements (affixes) that also exhibit binary ngoko/krama stylistic differentiation. In effect, much of the flexibility of the spoken style system arises from the use of these morphological variants. Whereas literary style (excluding dramatic representations) is normally either entirely ngoko or entirely krama (plus neutral) vocabulary (Uhlenbeck 1970), spoken conversation achieves a broad range of differentiation through the combination of polite (madya or krama) lexicon with ordinary (ngoko) affixes. This is the hallmark of the Madya range of speech styles.[9]

The Madya styles of utterance also make use of a relatively small (n = 35) group of lexical items in which a third, intermediate (madya) lexical variant exists along with the basic binary ngoko/krama alternation. In figure 5.1, the set of madya variants is seen as a minute island of complexity within the general picture of binary krama/ngoko alternation. Nevertheless, because the madya variants include such frequently occurring items as indexicals, they have a disproportionate impact on the overall style of utterance.

In order to speak Javanese, then, the speaker must make appropriate selections within this framework of lexical paradigms. Not surprisingly, there are definite restrictions on combining elements of different paradigmatic status—co-occurrence restrictions, or rules of syntagmatic organization. A great deal of flexibility exists: it is not that one may not combine x and y', but rather that the combination has stylistic significance different from either $x + y$ or $x' + y'$. (There are, of course, combinations that are simply unacceptable, particularly of krama forms with certain frequently used ngoko forms.)

Other subtleties of co-occurrence arise in the adjustment of Madya speech style, because some lexical items shift to polite (madya) form before other items do. For example, the affirmative response *iyo* takes the krama form *inggeh* (often shortened to *nggeh*) in *any* level of polite (Madya or Krama) speech style. As Uhlenbeck (1970:450ff.) notes, there are about fifty such items for which the ngoko variant is systematically avoided in Madya styles, including most of the specifically madya-inflected paradigms.[10] These items constitute minimal markers of polite style (Bax 1974): the use of the ngoko (ordinary) form signals that the utterance is not even minimally formal.

The Javanese speaker thus may call on a broad range of stylistic differentiation based solely on the alternation among three lexical levels (ngoko, madya, krama). To this picture must be added the obligatory use of appropriate honorific vocabulary.

5.3.4 Honorific Vocabulary

The honorifics constitute a category of polite lexicon having particular personal reference—to personal actions, possessions, and parts of the body. Unlike the formal (*krama*) variants for these items, the honorific (*krama inggil*) terms indicate that the designated action or object (and hence its agent or possessor) is accorded particular respect. The stylistic function of the honorific vocabulary is thus referential rather than contextual, providing a source of verbal humor on the model of the "hobo jokes" mentioned above.

Used with reference to a third person, the honorific vocabulary is exempt from any co-occurrence restrictions and does not expand the repertoire of speech styles. Stylistic complexity arises because honorifics are required in some contexts to refer to the addressee—that is, for second-person reference. Second-person application of honorifics becomes an integral element of the overall style of an utterance, fully obligatory: it does indeed expand the stylistic repertoire, with decisive effects on both its structure and its social function.

5.3.5 Style Selection and Interpretation

In one respect, any systematic catalogue of the speech styles will be a defective representation of their application. Since very few items exhibit four-way stylistic contrast, the stylistic significance of a particular lexical form is shaped not strictly by its place in the overall four-level system but rather by its own particular paradigmatic contrasts; thus, a krama variant for which there is no honorific counterpart may sound "higher" than one belonging to a complete paradigm. (The verb "to change clothes," for example, has a krama but no honorific form; the krama form will inevitably occur in honorific second-person reference.) Similarly, a ngoko variant that stands in opposition to an honorific but not to a krama variant will sometimes be used in formal contexts and will therefore have a less familiar sound than other ngoko forms. And in paradigms that have a madya variant as well as ngoko and krama forms, the ngoko will sound more familiar and the krama more formal than otherwise.

The extraordinary complexity of the Javanese style system achieves correspondingly impressive precision in stylistic communication. Both social distance and inequality (or deference) can be finely shaded by the careful combination of lexical variants. The resulting transparency of stylistic communication—the ease of decoding—goes along with a formidably demanding task of *encoding*. The lack of ambiguous stylistic forms and of vague contextual categories means that the speaker must decide quite narrowly among the available stylistic options. When one considers also that these stylistic forms entail a social status component—that is, they communicate the degree and direction of social inequality—it will be appreciated that even a simple utterance can be "heavy" (*abot*) in sensitive settings. Clearly, these lexical paradigms carry weight as well as meaning.

5.4 Lexical Levels: Examples of Styles

Notwithstanding the small proportion of the lexicon affected by stylistic differentiation, spoken Javanese gives the impression of pervasive lexical transformation. This is because, as every commentary points out, the most frequently used lexical items are generally subject to differentiation. Perhaps the commonest of all is the group of stylistic markers mentioned above, which includes pronouns, prepositions, and such items as "yes," "there is/are," and "only, just" (Uhlenbeck 1970:452). Moreover, the lexical items of greatest personal relevance are likely also to have honorific forms, which serve as stylistic markers of another sort.

5.4.1 "To Come"

For a specific example, let us look at a lexical item that presents all four stylistic variants (ngoko, madya, krama, honorific): the verb "to come, arrive" (here presented in the Suriname-Javanese paradigm).

	ngoko	madya	krama	honorific
"to come:"	teka	dugi[11]	dhateng	rawuh

The verb can be combined with one of the stylistically variable affixes previously discussed. Javanese is an "agglutinative" language, in which syntax requires the frequent use of affixes, especially the stylistically variable forms. The possessive suffix has distinct ngoko and krama forms:

	ngoko	krama
"his/her:"	-(n)é[12]	-(n)ipun

The verb and the possessive are combined according to stylistic co-occurrence restrictions, as follows:

	ngoko	madya	krama	honorific
"to come"	teka	dugi	dhateng	rawuh
[possessive] "his/her"	-(n)é	-(n)é	-(n)ipun	---
coming"	tekané	duginé	dhatengipun	rawuhé, rawuhipun

5.4.2 "Yesterday He Came Late."

To glimpse the scope of the system we can place this compound morpheme within a simple utterance. The sentence "Yesterday he came late" (literally, "Yesterday his coming was late morning") has only two additional variant elements, and it avoids the question of second-person address. The separate components may be arrayed as in figure 5.2. (The word *wingi* "yesterday," because it lacks polite variants, is stylistically neutral.)

Figure 5.3 presents the resulting variety of possible utterances. For each *basic style*, lettered "a," the same utterance is presented with *honorific* third-person reference, lettered "b." Third-person honorifics are, however, extraneous to the overall stylistic level of an utterance. (This example shows three basic Madya styles; for a longer utterance, in which the overall proportion of krama vocabulary could be finely tuned, there would be at least four.)

Very roughly, the Ngoko styles are used either to a close friend or to a servant.[13] The Madya styles are used (by elite speakers) to address non-elite individuals of varying status: low Madya to an elderly servant; middle Madya to a young shop assistant; Madya to an older "farmer-neighbor or fruitseller" (Poedjosoedarmo 1968:60).[14] The Krama styles

Figure 5.2 Stylistic components.

	ngoko	madya	krama	honorific
(past time)	dèk	—	kala	—
"yesterday"	wingi	—	—	—
"his coming"	tekané	duginé	dhatengipun	rawuhé *or* rawuhipun
"late morning"	awan	—	siyang	—

Figure 5.3 Example: "Yesterday he came late."

Speech Style		"Yesterday he came late."
Ngoko	1a.	Dèk wingi tekané awan.
	1b.	Dèk wingi rawuhé awan.[a]
Madya	2a.	Dèk wingi duginé awan.
	2b.	Dèk wingi rawuhé awan.
	3a.	Kala wingi duginé awan.
	3b.	Kala wingi rawuhé awan.
	4a.	Kala wingi duginé siyang.
	4b.	Kala wingi rawuhé siyang.
Krama	5a.	Kala wingi dhatengipun siyang.
	5b.	Kala wingi rawuhipun siyang.

[a] 1b and 2b happen to be identical for this example.

are used to address lower status individuals who are not familiar acquaintances and all nonintimate acquaintances within the elite. Non-elite speakers use polite (Madya or preferably Krama) style in all interaction with the elite.

5.4.3 Honorific Address: Examples and Contexts

At this point we can examine the effect of introducing second-person honorific reference. Poedjosoedarmo (1968) stresses that honorifics are used strictly in address directed *toward* a member of the elite (*priyayi*) social class. The ambiguity created by the dual function of polite speech style—encoding both interpersonal distance and status respect—is in theory eliminated by the obligatory use of honorifics as a mark of status respect.

Poedjosoedarmo's account implies that this is the only context of use for second-person honorifics—that they are not used by non-elite speakers in interaction with one another but only in address (and reference) to an elite individual. J. Errington (1985:61) confirms this as the norm, but reports a trend to extend honorifics within the class of non-elite speakers.[15] I observed only two honorific forms in common Suriname-Javanese (i.e., non-elite) usage, *dhahar* ("eat") and *tindak* ("go, walk"), both used in formulaic utterances.[16] On the whole, the use of honorific address seems to create a boundary of class affiliation, not in the sense of different social dialects but in the sense of different rules of polite recognition.

If we revise the previous example ("Yesterday he came late") to include an element of second-person reference ("Yesterday *you* came late"), the honorific factor will have an impact on the style of the utterance as a whole (its level of politeness). That is, the use or omission of the honorific verb, since it now refers to "you" rather than "he," has implications for the speaker's attitude toward the addressee and must be taken into account along with the "stylemic" level of the utterance.

The resulting array of stylistic variants is shown in figure 5.4. Because the second-person honorific is an integral part of stylistic level, there are particular contexts (indicated by dashes) in which the honorific form cannot be used—namely, in utterances of any level addressed to a non-elite hearer. Conversely, there are contexts in which the honorific is obligatory—namely, in an utterance of any style addressed to an elite hearer who is not close enough and equal enough to be referred to using the familiar form. (To put it a different way, there is no occasion for the use of krama instead of honorific address in addressing an elite hearer; if he or she is not close enough for ngoko, the honorific is required.)

The previous example ("Yesterday he came late") can be used without lexemic alteration to mean "yesterday you came late" (literally, "yesterday your coming was late morning"); the use of a third-person verb is a commonly used and somewhat polite device for referring to an action of the addressee. This example illustrates, incidentally, the semantic burden that may be placed on stylistic elements; the ambiguity of reference is eliminated, in many contexts, precisely by the use or omission of the honorific.

Figure 5.4 Example: "Yesterday you came late."

"Yesterday you came late."

Speech Style	To Non-Elite	To Elite
Ngoko	Dèk wingi tekané awan.	Dèk wingi tekané awan.
With honorific address	—	Dèk wingi rawuhé awan.
Madya	Kala wingi duginé siyang.	—
With honorific address	—	Kala wingi rawuhé siyang.
Krama	Kala wingi dhatengipun siyang.	—
With honorific address	—	Kala wingi rawuhipun siyang.

Honorific address (second-person reference) thus creates three additional levels, one each in the Ngoko, Madya, and Krama styles. (Recall that the use of honorifics in *third-person* reference did not create any distinct stylistic levels.)

Of the six styles represented in figure 5.4, *only the first style—plain Ngoko—can be used to address a member of either social class*. The use or omission of honorific address in all other cases creates a clear distinction of appropriateness along a social class boundary, detailed in the next section. And in the case of plain Ngoko, the possibility of ambiguity is completely eliminated by the fact that its connotations are so different in interclass and intraclass contexts. Between members of the same class (and in particular among elite speakers) Ngoko connotes intimacy; between members of different social classes, Ngoko implies maximal social distance (downward) and is reciprocated upward by maximal politeness.

This double significance of the simple Ngoko style is thus the only area in the style system as a whole that requires disambiguation, and the differences of context are so great as to eliminate any uncertainty concerning the speaker's intention. Throughout the remaining range of contexts, interaction is gauged in degrees of distance that are clearly differentiated stylistically. Social distance entailing status respect (Brown and Gilman's "power semantic") is conveyed by stylemic formality (madya or krama) plus honorific address. Social distance without status respect (an option absent in the western European pronominal system) is conveyed by stylemic formality *without* honorific address.

5.5 Social Context and Social Dialects

Part of the determining context of politeness style is, as these comments indicate, the social class of the speaker. Errington (1985:45) speaks of the "structurally distinct type of speech level repertoire" of commoners as opposed to *priyayi* speakers in describing the criteria for use of Madya styles. Not only do speakers of different social classes have somewhat different linguistic repertoires, but they also use their shared repertoire somewhat differently. These differences in repertoire application may be summarized as reflecting the (necessarily) mutually opposed definitions of inside and outside class membership of elite and non-elite speakers respectively, or what Errington (1985:42) has called "in-group" versus "out-group" usage of each class.[17] The use or omission of second-person honorifics gives a clear illustration of this difference in repertoire. (This discussion of social dialects pertains only to speech styles in Java; there is no elite class of Javanese speakers in Suriname.)

5.5.1 The Social Class Boundary of Honorific Address

Poedjosoedarmo (1968:59, 74) makes it clear that the use or omission of honorific address reflects a single aspect of the social context of utterance—namely, whether or not the addressee is a member of the elite social class. The contextual factor of relative social distance thus comes to be treated as an absolute social class boundary; this boundary is in general what is referred to, implicitly, in the use or omission of second-person honorifics.[18]

It might be argued, of course, that style *always* has some semantic or referential significance—that its function is to "say something" about the context of the utterance. In this generalized sense, the use of honorifics is usually identified as a signal of respect. This is perhaps adequate as a description of their use in third-person reference, and it describes their use in second-person reference within a close range of acquaintance for the elite speaker. To the extent that second-person honorifics serve as a sign of recognition of class affiliation, however, the respect message is superseded by this more narrowly referential function.

A comparable (though extreme) example is the use of "Your Majesty" as a form of second-person pronominal reference to the Queen of England. Syntactically equivalent to the ordinary second-person pronoun, the phrase "Your Majesty" nevertheless has particular referential significance. It means not "you" but "you, the queen," and it cannot adequately be described strictly in terms of style, as simply the most polite form of the pronoun. In the Javanese case, the second-person honorific means something like "you, hereby recognized as a member of the elite class." Its stylistic meaning may be glossed as deference or respect, provided that the term is understood to include the sense of "as-if" deference.

5.5.2 Differences in Elite and Non-Elite Usage

The use of honorifics for second-person reference is central to the distinction between inside and outside class membership. As in the case of any binary-coded signal, it is not only the use of honorifics that is significant but also their omission. The signaling (class-affiliation) function of second-person honorifics serves to reorient the entire ladder of styles around a social status boundary.

Both elite and non-elite speakers have honorific vocabulary in their style repertoires (the former more extensively than the latter), and both classes tend to reserve the use of second-person honorifics for addressing members of the elite community (Poedjosoedarmo 1968:69). For an elite speaker, the use of honorific address is an expression of insider relationship, if only to the extent of shared class affiliation; for the non-elite speaker, their use establishes a definitive outsider relationship. For the non-elite speaker, the combination of honorific address with ordinary (Ngoko) style is thus an impossibility—a contradiction in terms—because it would combine outsider with insider stylistic markers.

The use of madya, as Errington (1985) observes, presents a similar difference in repertoire structure. For all speakers, plain Madya (without honorifics) is used to address *only non-elite* individuals; its stylistic significance may be expressed as "intermediate social distance." The precise significance, however, differs sharply between speakers of different classes. For the non-elite speaker, the absence of honorifics indicates that the addressee is an insider with respect to class affiliation, whereas the use of some degree of madya vocabulary indicates the lack of a close personal relationship. For the elite speaker, conversely, the absence of honorifics indicates outsider class affiliation. (The use of madya in place of either krama or ngoko may imply personal acquaintance coupled with some regard, whether for age or for social position; Poedjosoedarmo's [1968:60] example is "a farmer-neighbor or fruitseller who is older than the speaker.")

Elite and non-elite speakers have different style repertoires not so much as a matter of differential competence but rather as a reflex of different rules of appropriate co-occurrence. The term "repertoire" clearly takes on a special meaning when it reflects not so much the linguistic competence of the speaker as the attributed class affiliation *of the addressee*.

A closer look at the two types of repertoire reveals a basic difference in their structures. Figure 5.5 gives the array of lexical styles available to non-elite speakers. (I have adopted level numbers, names, and notation from Poedjosoedarmo [1968]; style 9 is bracketed to indicate its absence from most *wong cilik* [non-elite] repertoires.) The restriction of the use of honorific address to interaction with elite speakers has an interesting consequence for the non-elite style repertoire taken as a whole. For non-elite speakers, the division between insider and outsider codes subdivides the ladder of styles as a threshold of social distance—at the point, that is, when increasing social distance becomes outsider interaction, at the boundary of class affiliation. The non-elite repertoire of lexical style thus conforms fairly closely to the conventional four-level style model—Ngoko, Madya, Krama, Krama Inggil.

Figure 5.5 Non-elite repertoire

	Speech Style	Level	Vocabulary	Affixes	Honorific Address
In-group	Plain Ngoko	(1)	N	n	
	Madya Ngoko	(4)	M, N	n	
	Equal Madya	(5)	M	n	
Out-group	Madya Krama	(6)	M	n	H
	[Young Krama]	(9)	K	k	H

Notes: N = use of ngoko vocabulary
n = use of ngoko forms of affixes (*di-*, *-(n)é*, *-aké*)
M = use of madya vocabulary, with krama where madya forms are lacking
K = use of exclusively krama (and neutral) vocabulary
k = use of krama forms of affixes (*dipun-*, *-(n)ipun*, *-aken*)
H = use of honorific for second-person reference
Source: Adapted from Poedjosoedarmo (1968:58-61).

The picture is not so simple for the elite repertoire of styles (fig. 5.6). In this case, the area of status respect occurs within the domain of insider interaction, that is, within the elite speech community itself; the area of maximal social distance, or outsider interaction, specifically excludes the deferential honorific styles. Social distance and deference are in this case structurally separate, rather than coincident, stylistic categories. The elite speaker's repertoire does not constitute a ladder of increasing politeness with increasing social distance but is rather an assortment of contexts, each with its own scale of politeness. If we wish to construct a ladder of styles for the elite speaker's repertoire, it will have to take the form of a double ladder, distinguishing clearly between interclass interaction (outside) and intraclass interaction (inside). The result is shown in figure 5.7.

The striking difference between the unified ladder of non-elite usage and the double ladder of elite style repertoire points to a difference in the role of honorific address between the two social dialects. For the elite speaker, the use of honorifics in second-person reference is not simply an index of class affiliation, though it is that; it also reflects a degree of distance (whether symmetrical or asymmetrical) in the personal relationship. The omission of honorifics is not necessarily a statement of outsider class affiliation but may have to do instead with the closeness of the personal relationship. The use or omission of second-person honorifics in elite usage thus plays a role precisely analogous to the western European choice of pronoun in the two-semantic phase described by Brown and Gilman. For the elite speaker, lexical politeness

Speech Levels in Javanese   135

Figure 5.6 Elite repertoire: contexts of use.

Speech Style	Addressee Is:	
	Elite	Non-Elite
1. Plain Ngoko N	close *or* younger	inferior
2. Antya Basa N + H	close, high status	—
3. Basa Antya N, K + H	close, very high status	—
4. Madya Ngoko M, N	—	slightly lower and younger or much lower and older
5. Equal Madya M	—	slightly lower and older
6. Madya Krama M + H	occasionally, if some intimacy	—
7. Old Krama K (k)	elder to younger (polite)	inferior and older
8. Equal Krama K	—	stranger, not very low status
9. Young Krama K + k + H	equal or superior, usually not close	—

Notes: N = use of ngoko vocabulary
M = use of madya vocabulary, with krama where madya forms are lacking
K = use of exclusively krama (and neutral) vocabulary
k = use of krama forms of affixes (*dipun-, -(n)ipun, -aken*)
(k) = use of some krama affixes
H = use of honorific for second-person reference

Source: Adapted from Poedjosoedarmo (1968:58-61).

Figure 5.7 Elite repertoire: ladders of style.

Inside (interaction with elite speakers)	*Outside* (intraction with non-elite speakers
1. Plain Ngoko	1. Plain Ngoko
2. Antya Basa	4. Ngoko Madya
3. Basa Antya	5. Madya
6. Madya Krama	7. Old Krama
9. Young Krama	

is differentiated into the components *respect* (signaled by the use of honorifics) and *formality* (signaled by the use of polite stylemes in addition to honorifics).[19] Honorific vocabulary participates in *both* these stylistic-semantic functions.

What is peculiar to the elite style system is that all these subtleties of relationship are encoded in the obligatory selection of appropriate lexicon, yielding the complex structure of figure 5.7. Taking a broader view, however, we can see that this double-ladder model of lexical levels is structured along essentially the same lines as the three-way model of speech style presented in chapter 2: that is, "ordinary" style (level 1, Plain Ngoko) is contrasted independently with "formal" style (level 7, Old Krama) and "respect" style (level 9, Young Krama), as diagrammed in figure 5.8.

From this point of view, the elite style system constitutes a lexicalized version of the style system I have depicted for Suriname Javanese. If (as the comments of several respondents suggest) we can take the model of Suriname Javanese as broadly representative of non-elite Javanese usage as well, the basic three-way model becomes the underpinning structure of Javanese speech style in general, expressed in lexical variation by elite speakers and in prosodic contrasts (as well as lexicon) by non-elite speakers.

Lexical variation does have an important place in the speech style of non-elite Javanese speakers, including those in Suriname. The material in the following chapter illustrates its role and at the same time indicates the very broad range of individual differences in the use and omission of polite lexical forms.

Figure 5.8 A three-way model of elite lexical usage

```
Formal Style                              Respect Style
  level 7                                    level 9

         level 5                   level 6

              level 4         levels 2 & 3

                    Ordinary Style
                       level 1
```

NOTES

1. Refer to Brown and Levinson (1987) for more complete bibliography.
2. A *priyayi*-born friend, when she first comprehended the gist of my project,

compared it with a textbook of Javanese grammar by saying, "That is religion—your project is real life."

3. Apart from the inherently formal atmosphere of these recorded conversations, several factors make the present study not easily comparable with Bax's material. The Suriname dialect has unquestionably been influenced by close contact with both Dutch and Sranang, but it has also been isolated from the postwar influences on Indonesian Javanese: the rise of Bahasa Indonesia as the national language, the expansion of technical vocabularies in both languages, and the spread (particularly in the Yogyakarta area) of formal education in Javanese. Bax reports that Javanese speakers born since the war exhibit markedly more formal usage than their elders, reflecting both the effect of education and the expanding range of urban influence. The Suriname community thus represents, in some respects, a more conservative and rural sample than that studied by Bax.

4. These two field studies, like Keeler's textbook, were unfortunately not available at the time of my own fieldwork.

5. For definition of the term "formal" see chapter 2.

6. "*Ngoko*" means literally "to use *kowé* (the familiar second-person pronoun)." In fact, there are many occasions when speakers use only the ngoko vocabulary but nevertheless avoid the familiar second-person pronoun (see chap. 7). "*Krama*" (pronounced approximately as "kromo") means simply "manners," possibly deriving from the affix *ke-* plus *rama* ("father," honorific form).

7. Siegel (1986), taking a philosophical rather than a structural view, speaks of "translation" between the two "languages" (Ngoko and Krama). For Central Javanese, this act of translation no doubt does amount to a form of bilingualism, but a structuralist approach must insist that this is a bilingualism imposed by the structure of the speech code itself and therefore is more precisely referred to as "diglossia"—two codes rather than two languages.

8. In describing Suriname Javanese I will dispense with the term. Even the most formal styles of utterance fall within what in Java is considered Madya speech style, in effect displacing the full Krama style. Suriname-Javanese speakers normally distinguish only two overall styles of utterance: *omong*, "(ordinary) talk," and *basa*, "(polite) language," though many are aware of the possibility of a third, more formal style, which they term Krama Inggil.

9. For detailed descriptions of the structure and use of Madya see Uhlenbeck (1970:452-53) and Errington (1985:chap. 4).

10. For other items that lack a madya form, it may be the ngoko form that is invariably used in a Madya utterance: Errington (1985:10), for example, notes that the relative pronoun (*sing*) shifts to krama (*ingkang*) only in fully formal (Krama) utterances and never in Madya.

11. Suparlan (personal communication) points out that *dugi* is not in fact a madya form but a regional (non-Mataramese) variant of krama. The Suriname Javanese evidently consider the Mataramese variant, *dhateng*, as "higher" because it is the form used by Javanese visitors (e.g., Indonesian consulate or

embassy personnel); the two regional krama forms have thus been paradigmatically ordered.

12. The initial (n) occurs allomorphically following an open syllable.

13. Other contexts of Ngoko are to children, from teacher to student, and between neighbors (Siegel 1986).

14. Some traditionalists still refuse to use the Madya styles at all, viewing it as simply inferior polite speech; conservative (elite) speakers reserve it for out-group use, that is, to non-elite addressees (Errington 1985:51-54, 103-4).

15. C. Geertz (1960:253-54) observes that non-elite speakers use krama forms in intraclass interaction as if they were honorifics. Uhlenbeck (1970) disagrees with this point, but it is certainly true of the second-person pronoun as used in Suriname Javanese. Errington (1985:67) notes such usage for Surakarta only for lexical items that lack an honorific (krama inggil) form—though this restriction does not apply in the case of the second-person pronoun. (He notes also [1985:72] that this use of the second-person pronoun is reported for East Java.)

16. Also heard, but far less commonly, were the honorific forms *siram* ("bathe") and *saré* ("sleep").

17. The terms "elite" and "non-elite" require some clarification. The core membership of each of these speech communities is easy to identify: the *priyayi* (aristocracy), on the one hand, and the *wong cilik* ("little man": villagers and urban proletariat), on the other. In contemporary Indonesia, however, the elite class is constituted, for social purposes, primarily by educational level. Something similar is true of Javanese society: an elite speaker should perhaps be defined as someone who uses elite speech style. (For Suriname, the problem of definition does not arise, for there is no elite speech community for Javanese language.)

18. This statement applies only to nonintimate interaction. An intimate relationship (familial or quasi-familial), even in the elite social context, may dispense with second-person honorifics.

19. These are the terms used by Poedjosoedarmo (1968:61) regarding plain ngoko, who says that it "expresses neither formality nor respect."

CHAPTER 6

Individual Styles of Lexical Politeness

6.1 INTRODUCTION

Individual styles of formal lexicon use (madya and krama) range broadly in Suriname Javanese, from virtually no use, as among urban adolescents, to routine conversational use, particularly among first-generation immigrants. Even within a given social category there is wide variation among individuals in terms of lexical competence and performance.

This degree of variability fundamentally distinguishes the Suriname-Javanese style system from that of Java. It is likely that the basic three-way model of style (figure 2.1) describes the structure of both systems equally well; but whereas in Java the calibration of madya and krama lexical forms conveys varying degrees of formal politeness and formal respect, for Surinamers the most minimal of formal markers may suffice, in most contexts, to render the intention of formality. The formal dimension of the Suriname-Javanese style system thus approximates a binary code (polite/nonpolite, or *basa/omong*). (The overall model of speech style is, of course, not binary but triadic—the three-way model described in chap. 2.) On certain occasions, however, minimal formality does not suffice; in discussions of public affairs or on formal social occasions, a group of men will maintain consistently formal lexical style.

In observing everyday interaction, the clearest predictor of the degree of stylistic formality was not context or topic or even social relationship of participants but rather the evidence of that particular speaker's past performance. Some of the individuals I saw frequently were adept at using formal style and used it invariably in certain contexts (though none used any degree of formality in addressing me directly).[1] Others used no formal lexicon in any of the conversations I observed, even in contexts that elicited formal style on the part of other (same-generation, same-sex) speakers.

This chapter gives examples of the usage of individual speakers in a single setting: all are instances of informal interaction in my Paramaribo host family's house, with one or both of the grandparents participating. Besides showing the variation among speakers, these examples show variation in the usage of each speaker—even, on occasion, within a single utterance. I indicate in each case any discernible factors motivating a switch in speech style. This chapter does not give examples of usage by speakers who never used formal lexical style, although there were several such individuals of widely varying ages.

All the examples given here come from notes written at the time of the conversation, in some cases supplemented by tape recording. I made only sparing use of the tape recorder, because its presence made many speakers uncomfortable except on occasions of structured interaction (such as interviews or *slametans*). Note taking, too, required some discretion. For the most part, I felt comfortable writing detailed notes only of those conversations involving the members of the family with whom I lived, because it was clear that they understood the usefulness to me of both written and taped records of conversational usage. Other people were understandably disconcerted by my note taking; interestingly, the presence of a member of my host family seemed to allay their discomfort.

By the time these particular conversations took place, I was able to focus on elements of lexical (and sometimes intonational) style without being distracted by an unfamiliar name or vocabulary item, and I had developed a method of abbreviating the most common lexical markers. When conversational speed was rapid, I omitted from my note taking those lexical items that were irrelevant to the matter of stylistic level. For example, if the complete utterance read, "now his hair is white" (*saniki rambuté puteh*), in my notes I omitted "hair" (*rambut*), because it is stylistically neutral in the Suriname dialect. In transcribing my notes, I have adhered to the rule of making no insertions, even of stylistically neutral items, preferring to retain the ellipsis as a tolerable annoyance.

The Paramaribo household in which I lived was headed by an elderly couple, both originally from west Central Java. The "grandfather," whom I call Ba Pèn, was active in neighborhood religious affairs and was well known also for his expertise in traditional Javanese ritual medicine. He was knowledgeable about Javanese culture generally, including the art of linguistic etiquette, and so, though he lacked any claim to socioeconomic prominence in the community, he was generally treated with respect as an elder. His wife, Ba Nom, was an unassuming individual whose circle of acquaintance was restricted for the most part to friends in the downtown market where she had for many years worked as a food seller. In conversations where both were present, she usually took a much less prominent part. Her speech was somewhat affected by the loss of front teeth, which may have caused her some embarrassment in conversation; she was not as adept conversationally as Ba Pèn or some of the visitors, such as Ba Min (see sec. 6.3).

The visitors to the household were quite varied. Regular Sunday visitors were the set of close friends (including *djadji*, or boat-mates) of the elderly couple. On weekdays several young women would arrive during the early morning to drop off their young children to be cared for while the women worked and to be picked up in the late afternoon or early evening. In addition, there were a number of men who came on mosque business or other official business for more or less formal discussion with the grandfather. Occasionally, a friend or two of the elder foster daughter (Sita, twenty years old) would visit, and there were occasional visits from members of her very large extended (natural) family. Within each category of visitor, however, there was a considerable range in the degree of linguistic politeness, varying with the individual rather than with any contextual determinant.

Notwithstanding the wide variation in individual speech styles, it is nevertheless possible to suggest some general co-occurrence guidelines governing lexical variation.[2] As described in the following section, there were systematic co-occurrences of discrete sections of the polite lexicon, which could be arranged into a series of superposed levels of lexical politeness. Individual variation generally took the form not of random admixture of polite forms but rather of differential application of these fairly distinct levels.

6.2 Lexical Co-Occurrence

If a set of co-occurrence rules were to be written for Suriname use of Javanese speech styles, it would have to specify the interaction of prosodic with lexical features, as well as to distinguish distinct functions of certain lexical items (formulaic greeting, polite "punctuation," etc.). I do not attempt to construct a comprehensive set of rules on the basis of my limited data but rather indicate the sort of problem to be considered.

Toward the end of my fieldwork, I constructed the following provisional outline of lexical co-occurrence, based on my general impressions as well as on my notes. The outline (fig. 6.1) shows five levels

Figure 6.1 Levels of lexical co-occurrence.

Level	Syntax	Polite lexical markers			
1	P	mboten	"no"[a]	kula wangsul	"I'm going home"[b]
		inggeh	"yes"[a]	mboten ènten	"there isn't"[a]
		sinten	"who"	empun	"already"[a]
2	P	kula	"I"	mboten	"not"[c]
		ajeng	"will"[b]	dhahar (honorific)	"eat"[b]
		mangké	"later"	dèrèng	"not yet"
		wau	"just now"	mawon	"only"
		pinten	"how much"	pundi	"where"[b]
		setunggal, kaleh, etc. (cardinal numbers)			
3	D	ajeng	"will"[c]	damel	"make"
		griya	"house"	wangsul	"go home"[c]
		pukul	"hour"	sedaya/sedanten	"all"
		tumbas	"buy"	sami-sami	"likewise"[b]
		mlampah	"walk"	kirangan	"I don't know"[a]
		sakmangké	"after"	sakdèrèngé	"before"
		énjéng, siyang, etc. (times of day)[b]			
4	D	sampéyan	"you"	piyambak	"oneself"
		purun	"want"	ngertos	"understand"
		wonten	"there is"	waged	"can"
		kaleh	"with"	mbénjéng	"tomorrow"
5	D	dangu	"long time"	ngantos	"until"
		kala	"past"	lajeng	"then"

Notes:
P = punctuate syntax; D = discursive syntax.
(Punctuate syntax makes use of short phrases and elliptical constructions, possibly punctuated with vocative address or expressive particles. Discursive syntax employs fuller constructions and connective phrases with few punctuative particles or vocatives. See chap. 3.)
[a] direct response (no punctuative or discursive function)
[b] formulaic function
[c] discursive as well as formulaic or response function

of polite lexicon, related serially (that is, each level adding on the specified items to those of the preceding levels). Levels 1 and 2 co-occur with the elliptical or punctuate phrase structure syntax I have identified as characterizing ordinary and respect style; levels 3, 4, and 5 co-occur with the discursive syntax of formal style. (Note that the use of honorifics is not a distinguishing feature of any of the styles; only a single honorific [krama inggil] form is indicated—*dhahar*, "eat"— and that occurs exclusively in formulaic invitations.) I have treated standard and substandard forms alike, as not distinguished by this speech community.

The functions indicated by superscripts in figure 6.1 require some amplification. "Direct response" refers to one- or two-word responses to any direct question or invitation: "yes," "no," "already," etc. Use of polite forms in this context does not necessarily imply the use of the polite form of the identical items in other contexts. *Inggeh,* "yes," is used also both as a punctuative response (that is, punctuating the speech of another speaker rather than responding to a specific utterance) and as an expressive particle; in these functions it may appear in the familiar form *Iyo,* even though in direct response (even within the same utterance) the polite form is used. Similarly, *mboten,* "no, not," and *empun,* "already," function as verb modifiers in discursive utterances in addition to their function as direct responses; polite form in the latter function does not necessarily imply polite form in the former.

"Formulaic functions" are associated with the items appearing in such formulas as leave takings, interrogative greetings, and conventional time-of-day greetings ("Good morning" etc.). Again, these items may occur in polite form in this formulaic use but in familiar form when used in other contexts (e.g., "tomorrow morning").

Items in the third category appear in their polite form in all functional contexts, discursive as well as responsive or formulaic. It is difficult to imagine a context in which any of the polite markers would occur in discursive use but not in direct responses or formulas. The responsive and formulaic functions are thus minimal politeness contexts.

Figure 6.1 by no means presents the entire range of polite lexicon in Suriname usage. It shows only those items that occurred with sufficient frequency and predictability to be identified, provisionally, as markers of politeness style.[3] Not every speaker was competent in all five levels, even in the minimal form represented here. It is probably safe to say that every adult and near-adult speaker would understand all the vocabulary here, certainly up to level 4, and every speaker would be able to produce the vocabulary of levels 1 and 2. (The polite pronoun *sampéyan,* "you," is a special case: probably every child knows the word, but only the more distant-polite contexts require [or permit] its use; see chap. 7.) The repertoire presented in this chart is that of the older-generation speakers, particularly those born in Java. Most of the younger-generation speakers use the vocabulary of level 2 as a *maximally* formal style, whereas for their elders it constitutes a *minimally* formal style.

There is thus no regular correlation between context and level, except within the usage of an individual speaker. The array of levels, insofar as it represents the system accurately, implies only that an utterance that includes a polite form from level 3, for example, will probably include the polite rather than the familiar forms of the other items of level 3 (as well as those of levels 1 and 2).[4]

6.2.1 Exceptional Items

The array of levels does not, however, provide a complete picture of stylistic repertoire—even apart from the idiosyncratic use or omission of polite vocabulary and the extensive additional vocabulary available to most older-generation speakers. Several items of polite vocabulary, though very frequently heard, were omitted because they did not seem to behave as markers in the way the other items did, while one or two familiar lexical variants did seem to serve as markers of polite style, just as if they were polite lexical variants.

To take the second point first, two lexical markers included in my notes (but omitted from figure 6.1) are actually *familiar* rather than polite variants; these are *mengko*, "later," and *durung*, "not yet," which appear in my notes at level 1. These are very common one-word responses to formulaic questions and invitations. In familial interaction (level 0, we might say) they occur in abbreviated form, as single syllables: *Ngko, Rung*. In their more fully articulated form they serve (in my interpretation) as a mark of politeness. In other words, at level 1 these items shift not to a madya or krama variant but to their fully enunciated ngoko form, and the shift to the formal lexical variant occurs at the next level. In this and some other instances, then, enunciation serves as a marker of minimal politeness. (Level 0, as the prelexical level of style, must be thought of as complexly structured in its own right. We have already seen that the features of respect politeness come into play before any lexical shift is entailed. It may be that enunciation constitutes a prelexical feature of formal politeness.)

Of the commonly heard polite variants omitted from the chart, one was so frequently heard, even in isolation, that it scarcely served as a marker of style. This is the one-word polite greeting *Wilujeng*, obligatory in any encounter with an elder-generation acquaintance. (It occurs in more formal interaction in expanded formulas coupled with a time-of-day indicator, which are then also in polite lexical form.) A subtle issue that cannot be dealt with here is the alternation between this essentially deferential greeting and the use of an interrogative greeting in polite form, which perhaps suggests greater formality and less deference. Another very frequent item was the word *Inggeh* or *Nggeh* ("Yes") used as a one-word punctuative response acknowledging another speaker's discursive utterance. The use of this item was unpredictable in terms of co-occurrence, seeming to reflect the momentary relationship of audience to performer rather than an overall level of formality.

6.2.2 Connectedness Marking: Familiar Lexical Variants

Two other polite lexical variants, though frequently heard, proved too elusive to be described in terms of co-occurrence rules. These are the simple indexical (or deictic) words *niku,* "that one," and *mriku,* "to that place." (These two may be taken as emblematic of the entire series of related indexicals.) These items occur so frequently that they should indeed be considered as markers of minimal formal style. Nevertheless, on several occasions the familiar variants of these items co-occurred with a range of polite lexical variants. The resolution of the puzzle lies in the distinction between formal and respectful politeness. I suggest that the indexicals behave differently from other lexical items because they participate both as *markers of formality* (or distant politeness) and as *markers of connectedness* (or close politeness). That is, the polite variant *niku,* "that one," serves as a marker of formal style, whereas the familiar variant *iku* serves as a marker of connectedness style. In contexts of respect, some level of lexical politeness (say, level 2) may co-occur with the use of the familiar forms of these indexical items.

This point is illustrated in a comparison (drawn up toward the end of the fieldwork period) between two speakers' usage in roughly comparable contexts. Context 1 was Sita's visit to the head of her natural family, a very aged and much-respected villager whom she saw rarely but who stood in the relationship of natural grandfather to her.[5] Unlike most of her urban friends, Sita had a ready command of polite lexicon (possibly as far as level 4 of fig. 6.1). She clearly felt great fondness as well as deep respect for the grandfather, and her speech style expressed this in a combination of level 2 lexicon with familiar-style deictics.

Context 2 is the speech of Mini, a woman somewhat older than Sita (perhaps in her late twenties or early thirties), addressing the "grandmother" of my host household in Paramaribo. There was no kin relationship of any sort between them, but the grandmother and grandfather had daily charge of Mini's two-year-old son while she worked. (Mini's usage is more fully described in the following section.) Mini, too, had an unusual command of polite lexical style, certainly including level 5. Her style in addressing the grandmother was normally one of formal respect, using level 4 vocabulary with a few exceptions.

Figure 6.2 shows the usage of these two speakers, Sita and Mini, with the respective grandparents. The items included are those that

Figure 6.2 Lexical markers (formality vs. connectedness).

Polite Markers		Context 1: Sita to grandfather	Context 2: Mini to grandmother
inggeh	"yes"[a]	+	+
mboten	"no"	+	+
mangké	"later"[b]	+	+
(em)pun	"already"[b]	+	+
dèrèng	"not yet"[b]	+	+
mangké	"later"[c]	–	+
(em)pun	"already"[c]	–	+
dèrèng	"not yet"[c]	–	+
mboten ènten	"there isn't"	–	+
kula	"I"[b]	+	+
kula	"I"[c]	–	+
sampéyan	"you"	–	+
sinten	"who"	+	(+)
pinten	"how many"	+	+
pundi	"where"	+	+
kaleh	"with"	+	(+)
niku	"that one"	–	(+)
mriku	"(go) to that place"	–	+

Notes:
[a] affirmative function
[b] formulaic function
[c] discursive function
( ) indicates item alternates between polite and familiar form

occurred in both contexts (in either familiar or polite form) and that were among the more or less consistent markers of Mini's style.

The polite markers included in figure 6.2 are only a subset of the polite lexicon used by Mini in context 2, whereas for Sita in context 1 they constitute the full range of polite usage. Mini's style was normally level 4 in that context, and her intonation and syntax were relatively formal, but with fairly consistent use of the kin-term vocative. Sita's style in context 1 was a good example of level 2 politeness, with punctuate syntax and crooning intonation. The deictic items serve in distant-polite contexts as minimal markers of polite lexical style; here, however (as in other close-polite contexts), they occur in familiar form as markers of connectedness. Other items on the chart show a similar effect, notably the second-person pronoun. (Sita used not only the kin term *mbah*, "grandfather," but also the familiar pronoun *kowé*, "you," for second-person reference in this context.)

Figures 6.1 and 6.2 should not be interpreted too rigidly. They are illustrative rather than definitive, but the points they illustrate are important. Figure 6.1 illustrates the interaction of prosodic and lexical elements of style: at the point at which a speaker shifts into more complete lexical formality (level 3), she or he also shifts into formal syntactic and intonation patterns. (Speakers who are not competent in the more polite lexical levels [levels 3 through 5] are not likely to use the formal prosodic elements. Recall, however, that the younger-generation speakers are fluent in Dutch, which they use in school and business contexts. For them, Javanese is essentially a domestic and close-polite code.)

In figure 6.2 we see that the addition of polite lexical items is not simply a matter of increasing politeness along a ladder of expanding lexical repertoire. Certain items may shift to polite style while other, possibly more common items are nevertheless retained in familiar style. The crosscutting politeness norms of connectedness and formality affect the use of lexicon as well as the use of the prosodic elements discussed in chapter 3.

6.3 Co-Occurrence and Admixture: Ba Min

The greater difficulty in constructing a set of co-occurrence rules is not technical but fundamental. This is the problem, mentioned in chapter 1, of distinguishing between unmarked (routine or "presupposed") and marked ("creative") uses of lexical alternation. As every observer of stylistic phenomena has noted, the rules of style are subject not only to manipulation but also to momentary lapses. In the case of Suriname Javanese (and perhaps in non-elite Javanese speech generally), stylistic admixture is sufficiently common that the concept of stylistic rules must be very loosely applied.[6] The ranking of progressively more formal levels of lexical shift (fig. 6.1) does represent a realistic picture of stylistic usage, but departures from that pattern, in the form of admixture of advanced level polite forms with more basic level familiar forms, are readily accommodated by speakers as idiosyncratic usages and are not necessarily regarded as violations of a norm.

This sort of idiosyncratic usage is illustrated by the speech style of a woman who visited the house only twice during my stay. Ba Min (as I call her) was an expert in Javanese massage, a curative technique, and she had been summoned to treat an ailment of Sita's. Though apparently several years younger than Ba Pèn or Ba Nom, she was a *djadji* (boat-mate) of the grandfather, which constituted a bond of virtual kinship between them.

Ba Min was an energetic woman and a lively speaker, and she discoursed about a range of matters throughout both massages, addressing herself primarily to the grandfather and sometimes to the grandmother. Her dramatic speech style liberally used expressive particles. Her use of lexical politeness was almost randomly varied: every utterance included some formal lexical items, but no rule of co-occurrence could predict which items of the utterance would be in formal style and which in familiar.

A few extracts illustrate the pattern of lexical admixture. My notes necessarily omit a great deal of Ba Min's rapid speech and in most cases show only the relevant markers of formal or familiar lexical style; consequently, most of the utterances are fragmentary. Ba Min's conversation was largely a report on local domestic happenings, with Ba Pèn or Ba Nom providing an occasional comment or interrogative (using ordinary style, as appropriate in addressing a younger person). These nine utterances are given in the sequence they occurred; the gist was that someone, whose name was not mentioned, was mistreating his family and generally going to ruin. (I was probably the only person present who didn't know the entire story already, but I adhered to my rule of refraining from asking questions in order to minimize the effect of observation on speech style.)[7]

I indicate lexical style as follows: **boldface** indicates the use of a minimal marker of *polite style* (level 1 or 2 of fig. 6.1); <u>**underlined boldface**</u> indicates the use of a more advanced polite form (level 3 or higher). Conversely, single angle brackets ⟨ ⟩ indicate a form in *ordinary style* for which the polite variant is well known in Suriname Javanese (level 3 or 4) and that therefore sounds informal; double angle brackets ⟪ ⟫ indicate a form in ordinary style that serves as a minimal marker in its polite variant (level 1 or 2) and that therefore sounds especially familiar.[8]

1. Mboten <u>**sanjang piyambaké**</u>, ⟨anaké⟩ ... **mawon**.
   "<u>**He**</u> didn't <u>**say**</u>, his ⟨child⟩ **only** ..."

2. **Kula mawon.** ⟨Omongé wong⟩ sing ⟨wédok⟩... **sinten?** ⟨Déwé⟩.
"**Just me.** ⟨They say⟩, his ⟨wife⟩ (literally, ⟨female person⟩)... **who?** ⟨Himself⟩."
3. ⟨Omongan⟩ **niku**... ⟨Aku⟩ mikir **ènten** bojo.
"That ⟨talk⟩... ⟨I⟩ think **there is** a girlfriend."
4. Masih ⟨ènèk wong⟩, lha ⟨wongé⟩.... Lha, **inggeh mriku,** ngono ⟨waé⟩!
"Still ⟨there is someone⟩, well, ⟨that person⟩... well! **indeed (to) there,** ⟨just⟩ like that!"
5. ⟨Durung⟩ **sampéyan.**... ⟨Aku⟩ ngono.
"**You** ⟨haven't yet⟩.... ⟨I⟩ (said) that."
6. **Niku nggéh wonten. Mriko,** lha **saniki**... puteh.
"**That indeed there is. Over there,** well, **now**... white."
7. Lha bengi.... Soréné ⟨omong-omong⟩, benginé mati!
"Well in the evening.... That afternoon (he was) ⟨talking⟩, in the evening (he was) dead!"
8. ⟨Nang kéné⟩... **sampéyan**... **wonten.**
"⟨Here⟩....**you**... **there (it) is.**"
9. **Tiang** niko, **tiang** ombé, ⟨wongé⟩! Lha **inggeh!**
"That **person,** a **person** (who) drinks, ⟨that person⟩! **Indeed!**"

Within this brief extract there are no fewer than seven items that appear in both their polite and familiar forms; four of these are items that in general occur so frequently in polite form as to be considered minimal markers. Figure 6.3 lists these seven items, together with (in parentheses) the lines in which they occur in each form.

Throughout Ba Min's interaction with the grandfather, as recorded in my notes, there are only six items that appear always in polite form and never in familiar form. Two of these are relatively uncommon

Figure 6.3 Lexical admixture (Ba Min).

Item	Familiar Form	Polite Form
"I"	aku (3, 5)	kula (2)
"just, only"	waé (4)	mawon (1, 2)
"here"/"there"	nang kéné (8)	mrika (4, 6)
"there is"	ènèk (4)	ènten (3)
		wonten (6, 8)
"speak"	omong (2, 3)	sanjang (1)
"person"	wong (2, 4, 9)	tiang (9)
"self"	déwé (2)	piyambak (1)

items, each of which occurs here only once: **dugi** (krama for *tekan*), "up to," and **kaleh** (krama for *karo*), "with." The remaining four items are common enough to suggest a function as minimal politeness markers: **sampéyan,** "you"; **sinten,** "who" (with only one occurrence, however); and **mboten,** "no," and **inggeh,** "yes," both as used in response (rather than discursive) contexts.

Interpretation of such an idiosyncratic use of lexical politeness is difficult for an outsider. Several aspects suggest themselves as a first-order approximation. First, the speaker is clearly communicating not only distant politeness but also close politeness, or connectedness: the dramatic intonation and use of expressive particles are evidence of this. The use of lexicon may also participate in this dual politeness message, as in the case of Sita, reported in the previous section. Here, however, it is not a particular item whose familiar variant serves to mark closeness but rather the use of familiar variants of almost every item. One example is particularly revealing. In line 9, the speaker twice uses the polite variant for "person," **tiang**, and follows it with the familiar variant, ⟨*wong*⟩. The final (familiar) occurrence of the item is, syntactically, an example of a coda: the phrase-final particle, vocative, or (as in this case) topic-marker characteristic of close-polite utterances. This sort of coda goes along with the punctuate phrase structure of ordinary (rather than formal) style. It is natural enough, though not inevitable, that the speaker would shift to familiar lexical style in employing this syntactic device. In this example, then, the initial topic-marking occurrence, **Tiang niko**, expresses distant politeness while the final topic-marking occurrence, ⟨*wongé*⟩, expresses close politeness.[9]

Of the four lexical politeness markers of Ba Min's style, three are associated with the category of task-oriented domestic politeness.[10] These are the affirmative and negative responses (*inggeh* and *mboten*) and the interrogative "who" (*sinten*). (The other interrogatives occurred either not at all ["where"] or in both familiar and polite forms ["what," "how many"].) These three may well constitute a core of lexical politeness for domestic (insider) interaction; compare level 1 of figure 6.1.[11]

If these three were the only items occurring in polite form, there would be nothing in Ba Min's style to suggest that she was other than a visiting family member. The fourth marker, however, together with the range of randomly occurring polite lexical forms, gives her speech a distant-polite quality. The fourth lexical marker, *sampéyan*, "you," is most unusual in relationships of close respect, even where there is significant use of polite lexicon (as in the example of Sita's visit to her natural grandfather, cited above). As an alternative to a kinship term, the polite second-person pronoun is a gesture of equality as well as of social distance. One might say that Ba Min participated as an insider to the household but not as an intimate acquaintance of the grandfather, giving lexical acknowledgment of "proper" social distance but omitting any element of stylistic respect.

Finally, Ba Min's use of polite lexicon was only slightly broader than is reflected in this extract. The entire interaction with the grandfather included, on her part, only about twenty-five items in polite form. Unlike one or two other visitors to the house, Ba Min was not one who cultivated formal speech style; her use of polite lexicon—if a guess may be permitted—was an accommodation to the grandfather's style rather than a reflection of her own speech habits. This judgment does not rest on any evidence of her usage in other contexts (which I did not have occasion to observe) but rather reflects an observed contrast with the tendency of certain other visitors to take the opportunity of conversation with Ba Pèn, at least initially, as an occasion for the maximal display of formal vocabulary. Ba Min's style might be summed up as a variant of ordinary style—lively, expressive, and discursive—sprinkled with polite lexical markers to acknowledge social distance as well as, possibly, Ba Pèn's position as a local cultural authority.

The counterpoint between close politeness and distant politeness is nicely illustrated by Ba Min's use of leave-taking formulas. On one occasion she poked her head in the door of Sita's room to say goodbye, first to Sita and then to Sita's half-brother, a young man of about twenty who cultivated an urbanely formal lexical style. Her goodbye to Sita used a style of close-politeness—a crooning, indulgent formula of downward deference:

10. ⟨Aku⟩ tak ⟨muleh⟩ ⟪ya⟫ nuuk!
    "⟨I'm⟩ ⟨going home⟩, ⟪okay⟫, honey!"

The deliberately elongated final vocative (*nuuk*), a term of affection used to little girls, establishes this as a style of "as-if" intimacy. The syntactically superfluous first-person passive particle (*tak*) serves, however, to underline the stylized "as-if" character of the intimate tone; by elaborating the syntax it mediates the utterance, creating a degree of stylistic distance and acknowledging that the addressee is indeed an adult and not a child.

To Sita's half-brother, Ba Min on this occasion used a style distinctly more formal than this, though not completely formal:

11. ⟨Aku⟩ sing **mantuk**, PN.
    "⟨I'm⟩ **going home**, (name)."

This was not crooned, but the final vocative suggests close-politeness phrasing. The polite lexical form is used for "go home," ⟨*muleh*⟩/ **mantuk**, but not for "I," ⟨*aku*⟩/**kula**. The syntactically superfluous relative conjunction *sing* ("who"), like the passive particle of the previous example, is an element of stylistic distance.

In both of these leave-taking formulas, the speaker combines elements of close politeness with elements of distant politeness or stylistic distance; in example 10 the emphasis is on close-politeness ("as-if" intimacy), whereas in example 11 the emphasis is on stylistic distance. For comparison, we can construct the following examples of more distant-polite leave-taking formulas, which are not fully formal and which have little or no element of respect. The message here is simple social distance of varying degrees:

12. ⟨Muleh⟩, **inggeh**.
    "(I'm) ⟨going home⟩, **okay**."
13. **Ajeng wangsul**.
    "(I'm) **going to go back**."

In examples 10 and 11, Ba Min specifies the first-person pronoun, which by itself establishes a sense of personal involvement. Examples 12 and 13 not only use additional polite lexical markers, they omit the pronoun altogether, thus shifting from close politeness to distant politeness.

A very different way of combining close and distant politeness is suggested by the example of Mini's interaction with the grandparents, described in the next section. Her usage was almost invariably a polished example of formal respect, the relationship of a noninsider to a much older acquaintance. Close politeness here is conveyed by the element of respect (the vocative kin-term and use of short phrases); lexical style is more or less consistently polite (that is, formal).

6.4 FORMAL RESPECT STYLE: MINI

Of the women whose children were cared for in the household, Mini used markedly more polite lexical style than the others. Nevertheless, she also participated more frequently in informal visiting in the household than the others, and she seemed in some ways a "member of the family," as we would say. I once remarked on her use of polite vocabulary to Ba Pèn, who explained that she was better educated in Javanese style because she came from a village rather than the city. It was therefore of great interest to me to observe, on attending a *slametan* at her mother's home in the village, that neither Mini nor the other women of her family used any degree of polite vocabulary in addressing

Individual Styles of Lexical Politeness   153

their elder-generation kin, including one great-grandmother. The difference between Mini's usage in her own family and in the household in which I stayed seemed to me to illustrate the difference between genuine family membership and other kinds of insider status, which I term "as-if" kinship.

Mini's speech style also illustrates the variability in applying the "style model" presented in chapter 2. For the most part, her usage combined formal and respectful politeness. Her utterances were modulated almost to a murmur (making observation often difficult), but the even, clipped quality had no hint of "crooning" and suggested formal rather than respect style. Nevertheless, her phrasing usually incorporated the vocative-function kinship term, a clear mark of respect style.

Some examples of her speech illustrate the combination of polite vocabulary (of varying degrees) with the vocative-function kinship term:

1. **Pundi** mbah? **Mboten**. . . . ⟨digawé⟩ **sinten** mbah?
   "**Where**, grandmother? **No**. . . . ⟨made by⟩ **whom** grandmother?"
2. **Sinten**, mbah? **Ènten** dansi **teng pundi** mbah?
   "**Who**, grandmother? **There's** a dance **where**, grandmother?"
3. **Pinten** sasi **niku** mbah?
   "**How many** months (old) is **he**, grandfather?"
4. . . . tanggal **pinten**, mbah?
   "... **what** date, grandmother?"
5. **Nopo** mbah? **Kados** bubur, mbah?
   "**What** is it, grandfather? **Like** porridge, grandfather?"
6. **Kaleh** (name), mbah? **Tiang jawi mboten ènten**, mbah?
   "**With** (name), grandfather? **Aren't there** (any) **Javanese people**, grandfather?"

All of these examples conform to the punctuate phrase structure associated with the interrogative greeting formulas discussed in chapter 6. In general, respectful interaction with a senior individual consists largely of such interrogatives, as well as responses to interrogatives.

In interactions between Mini and the grandparents there was almost no symmetrical exchange of polite vocabulary. There is only one instance in my notes of one of the grandparents using polite vocabulary in addressing the young woman. The grandfather was beginning a discussion about his personal history and immigration and used the following phrases:

7. **Mangké** ⟨wongé⟩ nesu. Mbah **kula**...
"**Later** ⟨those people⟩ were angry. **My** grandfather..."

In this case, the content of the utterance, a serious discussion of historical circumstances, probably influenced the style. In the case of the pronoun *kula* (polite for "I," "my," etc.), there is perhaps the additional factor (discussed in chap. 7) of asymmetric self-reference.

6.4.1 Interrogatives and Responses

Some examples of initial (greeting) interrogatives illustrate Mini's consistently respectful syntax, with some variation of lexical level:

8. **Mboten** <u>siram</u> ⟨iku⟩ mbah?
"**Hasn't** ⟨he⟩ had his **bath**, grandmother?"

(This question was in reference to another of the children, not to the speaker's own child, and was therefore not a task-oriented interrogative but merely a conversational opening.)

9. (Indistinct) ⟨turu⟩, mbah?
"(Isn't he) ⟨sleeping⟩, grandfather?"

(This question did refer to the speaker's own child; however, it also is not a task-oriented interrogative, because it implies no purposeful action but is rather a comment on the uncooperativeness of young children.)

Mini often omitted any initial greeting, simply entering the house as a "member of the family." In that case, a simple conversational interrogative might serve to initiate the interaction as a form of delayed greeting, as in these examples:

10. ⟨Tuku⟩ ⟨nandi⟩, mbah?
"⟨Where⟩ (did you) ⟨buy⟩ (it), grandmother?"

11. Didom **sinten**, mbah?
"**Who** sewed (it), grandmother?"

It was my impression, borne out also by these examples, that the level of vocabulary was not as consistently polite in these greeting interrogatives as it was in other conversational interrogatives or in task-oriented speech (of which some examples appear below). One example in my notes illustrates this lexical contrast particularly well. On this occasion, Mini was later than usual in picking up her child after work, having attended a party in the evening. Addressing both the grandparents, she used familiar vocabulary in her initial interrogative greeting, immediately followed by a statement and a response using polite vocabulary:

12. Soré ⟨turu⟩ ⟨opo⟩ mbah?
    "This afternoon ⟨did⟩ (he) ⟨sleep⟩, grandparent?"
    Yogané kancané 'verjari.' **Empun**, mbah.
    "The **child** of my friend had a birthday. **Already**, grandparent."

To some extent, then, it seems that the use of polite lexicon makes the use of respectful phrasing less necessary. There are many examples in my notes of this speaker's use of polite vocabulary without respectful phrasing, that is, without the vocative-function kin term. In responding to interrogatives, this speaker tended to omit the vocative kin term, as in these examples:

13. **Mboten** èntoq 'frij.' **Mboten ènten**.
    "(I) **don't** have a holiday. **There isn't** any."
14. **Kaleh** (place name), ngétan **maleh**.
    "(Compared) **to** (place name), it's **more** eastward."
15. **Mboten**. ⟨Sesok⟩ kerja. **Sedinten** tekan?
    "**No**. ⟨Tomorrow⟩ (I) work. In **one day** (you) can get there?"

6.4.2 Task-oriented Utterances

A type of utterance that, in Mini's usage, frequently omitted the vocative phrasing was the category of task-oriented speech, both interrogative and affirmative. (These are the requests, questions, commands, and correctives that imply some needed action, presumably on the part of the addressee; responses to these are also "task-oriented.") Mini's level of vocabulary in this type of utterance was almost without exception markedly polite, as in examples 16 and 17, both addressed to the grandmother:

16. <u>**Sampéyan**</u> **mboten** <u>**gadah**</u> (indistinct)?
    "**Don't** <u>**you have**</u> a (indistinct)?"

The grandmother's response provided a nice illustration of asymmetrical exchange of lexical style, using (as a one-word response) the familiar form of "have," ⟨duwé⟩, in return for the polite form, <u>**gadah**</u>.

17. **Pun ajeng** anu—!
    "(It's) **already going to** you know—!"

This was called out from the kitchen to the grandmother, informing her that the pot on the stove was about to boil; the speaker left out the main verb, possibly because she couldn't stop to think of the polite form.

Some other examples of brief task-oriented utterances follow. These are responses by Mini to task-oriented questions initiated by the grandmother on three different occasions. (Example 18 was a response to a question about an occurrence outside; 19 answered a question concerning the whereabouts of one of the children; and 20 followed up on an instruction to fetch something for the grandmother.)

18. **Mboten nopo-nopo** sing **mriku**.
    "(There) **isn't anything there**."
19. **Kaleh** (name), **nèng** dalan.
    "**With** (name), in the street."
20. **Teng mriku?**
    "**Over there?**"

Because (as described in chap. 4) task-oriented interaction for Javanese is inherently directional, that is, asymmetrical, it is necessary to make quite clear that one identifies oneself as the junior in the interaction. This can be accomplished through stylistic devices quite apart form the actual content of the utterance. Mini provided one very clear example of deferential style combined with nondeferential content. She had not appeared with her child for two days, and when she next came she was asked by the grandmother where she had been: ⟨*Nandi mau*⟩? "⟨Where⟩ (were you) ⟨lately⟩?" She responded in polite style:

21. **Teng pundi** mbah, **mboten** kerja.
    "**Where** (should I have been), grandmother, (I) **didn't** work."

To be polite in content (rather than style), the response should have been either more specific ("I was at home." "I was visiting.")—without necessarily being accurate, however—or else apologetic ("Don't be angry." "Excuse me."). If transposed into familiar vocabulary, even with the kin-term vocative, the actual response would be quite abrupt and nondeferential: ⟨*Nandi mbah, ora kerja*⟩! In effect, the grandmother was being told, albeit deferentially, that Mini's whereabouts were her own business.

6.4.3 Lapses

Mini also provided an occasional example of stylistic revision. In one instance, addressing the grandfather, she revised the lexical style of the utterance in midsentence:

22. ⟨Pirang⟩ sa—**pinten** sasi **niku** mbah?
    "⟨How many⟩ months—**how many** months is **he**, grandfather?"

In another instance, the kin-term vocative was added to a lexically polite utterance, apparently as an afterthought:

23. Saitiq-saitiq **sedanten**—mbah.
"Little by little **all** (of them)—grandfather."

It seemed to me that the speaker had lost the rhythm of the respectful phrasing in focusing on polite lexical style. (*Sedanten* is actually a substandard krama variant, and Mini may have been deliberating between that and the standard krama, *sedoyo*.)

An interesting departure from respectful style involved a momentary switch from Javanese into Dutch. In this case, in an adaptation of a fairly standard sort of interrogative domestic greeting Mini substituted Dutch for Javanese lexicon and omitted the kin-term vocative:

24. 'Slaape?'
"Are you sleeping?"

This was addressed to the grandfather, who was lying down on the couch in the front room in the late afternoon. Two points are worth bringing out. First, the omission of the kinship vocative suggests a separation of the two cultural frameworks (the Javanese household and the Dutch-speaking outside world). Second, the use of the Dutch word perhaps reflects Mini's uncertainty regarding the lexical level appropriate for this case. The lexical item "to sleep" is one of a small number for which two distinct politeness styles exist—the formal and the honorific—both of which variants are widely known (if not widely used) by Suriname Javanese. Certainly Mini was familiar with both forms. In addressing the grandfather and in referring to one of the children, she alternated between the familiar form, ⟨*turu*⟩, and the (formal) polite form, **tilem**. With reference to the grandfather himself, however, she may well have felt that the honorific form, **saré**, might be appropriate, and that the use of the formal **tilem** would register as a refusal to use the honorific. However, the use of honorifics in Suriname Javanese is extremely restricted, and indeed it is likely that this speaker had almost never had occasion to use the honorific form of "to sleep"—especially because, as already noted, familiar lexical style was freely exchanged within her own family. The use of Dutch in this case is thus a way of avoiding the use of too low a lexical style in Javanese without undertaking an unaccustomed stylistic performance. However, the effect of the Dutch was not to elevate the style; in urban circles (including, to some extent, the elderly couple themselves) Dutch is the preferred language for addressing children. The question "Slaape?" sounded almost like nursery talk.

To some extent, Mini's lexical style seemed to be influenced by the spatial setting of the interchange. In conversing with one or the other grandparent in the backyard area, her speech sometimes seemed to be markedly familiar in lexical style. I noticed in particular that the subfamiliar form of the negative appeared in the backyard context, in striking contrast to her habitual use of the polite negative in front-room interaction. For example, in speaking to the grandmother, she used the phrase (referring to her own child):

25. ... ⟪nggak⟫ ⟨gelem⟩ medun.
"... (he) ⟪doesn't⟫ ⟨want⟩ to get down."

Ordinary style would require the negative ⟨ora⟩ instead of ⟪nggak⟫.

The backyard setting was the only context in which I heard this speaker use the subfamiliar negative in addressing the grandfather. I have only one instance of this in my notes, but one that is quite dramatic in that the negative occurs as a one-word response rather than as part of a verbal phrase. She had been asked a question by the grandfather and responded:

26. ⟨Opo⟩ mbah? ⟪Nggak⟫.
"⟨What⟩, grandfather? ⟪Nope⟫."

It is quite possible that the content of the question had an influence on the style of her response, quite apart from the spatial setting. The question had reference to an event I knew nothing about, but it seemed to annoy her.[12]

The abruptness of the one-word negative response is very striking to a Javanese speaker, for the negative response is probably the first category of utterance to undergo lexical shift both in respectful *and* formal speech styles. Moreover, the use of the vocative coda in respectful style, although it may be omitted for longer or discursive utterances, is absolutely obligatory in the case of a one-word response (other than a crooned **inggeh**, "yes"). To use the subfamiliar negative response without a kinship-term vocative is thus completely nonrespectful. (In a sense, the omission of the vocative is necessarily entailed by the use of the subfamiliar negative, whose phonological features [flat vowel and final glottal] are incompatible with even the minimal crooning intonation associated with the use of the vocative.)

There occurs in my notes only one other instance of markedly nonrespectful usage on the part of this speaker. In this case, Mini was addressing the grandmother. (The interaction took place in the front room, but not as part of a social visit: the young woman was attending to her child, squatting on the floor.) Her tone clearly seemed to indicate annoyance:

27. ⟨Dèk⟩ ⟪sopo⟫ ⟨iki⟩ 'bubblegum'??
"⟪Whose⟫ bubblegum is ⟨this⟩??"

Again, respectful style would call for the use of a vocative in any direct interrogative utterance such as this, either as a coda or as punctuation between the two phrases (*Dèk sopo, mbah, bubblegum iki?*). In Mini's usage, any utterance using familiar lexical style would normally be phrased in respectful syntactic style, with the kinship-term vocative.

6.5 COMPARISON OF STYLES: MINI AND BA MIN

Mini's style of formal respect contrasts clearly with the partially formal (and not respectful) style described for Ba Min. The prosodic character of the two styles differs markedly: lively, discursive, and dramatic for Ba Min; generally modulated, using short phrases (often interrogative) and vocative kin-terms for Mini. And though neither of the two speakers used completely formal lexical style, the difference in lexical patterns was quite striking.

In all of Mini's interactions with the two grandparents that I recorded (in writing), I observed occurrences of forty-one variable lexical items (that is, items that have a madya, krama, or krama inggil variant). Of these items, twenty-six occurred only in their polite form; just six occurred only in their familiar form. Nine items alternated between polite and familiar form, either routinely or in the form of the occasional lapses described in the preceding section.

In Ba Min's usage the pattern is quite different. Of forty-seven variable lexical items noted, just six occurred only in the polite form and nineteen occurred only in the familiar form. Twenty-two items alternated between polite and familiar style. Figure 6.4 presents these overall patterns of contrast.

Note that certain items in figure 6.4 were counted separately in distinct functions: **inggeh**, "yes" (as response), and **inggeh**, "indeed"

Figure 6.4 Formal respect (Mini) and partial formality (Ba Min).

	Mini (formal respect)	Ba Min (partial formality)
Total variable items	41	47
Polite form only	26	6
Alternating	9	22
Familiar form only	6	19

(in discourse); **mboten**, "no" (as response), and **mboten**, "not" (in discourse); **mboten ènten**, "there isn't" (as response), and **ènten**, "there is" (in discourse). Certain other items were combined as a single variable item: **nika**/⟨*iki*⟩, "this," and **niku**/⟨*iku*⟩, "that"; **mriki**/⟨*nang kéné*⟩, "here," and **mriku**/⟨*mrono*⟩, "there." Deictics are not consistent with standard Javanese.

It is of interest also to note that the much shorter total period of observation of Ba Min's speech produced a larger number of lexical items (forty-seven). This, I think, reflects a difference between respectful and nonrespectful style (as well as, possibly, an individual difference in interaction styles): the respectfully brief utterances that characterized Mini's interaction with the grandparents utilized a fairly repetitive vocabulary, centering usually on the immediate events of the domestic setting, whereas Ba Min's discursive conversation ranged widely over the local scene.

With such a large number of items occurring only in polite form (twenty-six), another requirement was needed to distinguish lexical markers in Mini's speech. In most cases, each item occurred only once or twice throughout the recorded interactions. For seven items, however, four or more occurrences (of the polite variant) were recorded. These seven can be tentatively identified as markers of formal respect style in Mini's usage (see fig. 6.5). To describe Mini's usage more precisely it is necessary to distinguish between her usage with the grandmother and with the grandfather (with whom she interacted far less frequently). Only two of the seven markers occurred frequently enough in interaction with the grandfather to appear as markers: **sinten**, "who," (four occurrences) and **teng**, "to," (two occurrences). The other five items occurred only once in interaction with the grandfather, with the ex-

Figure 6.5 Formal respect markers (Mini).

Item		Occurrences
kula	"I"	6
pundi	"where"	5
mboten ènten	"there isn't"	5
sampéyan	"you"	4
mrika (-u)	"there"	4
sinten	"who"	7
teng	"to"	5

ception of **sampéyan**, "you," which did not appear at all. Interestingly, these two markers—**sinten** and **teng**—are the only two that were *not* consistently used in polite form in addressing the grandmother; instead they alternated between polite and familiar form. They are therefore set apart from the rest of the list: the five markers of Mini's interaction with the grandmother are shown above the dotted line, and the two markers of interaction with the grandfather are shown below the dotted line.

This list of polite lexical markers can be compared with the markers identified for Ba Min's speech. There were only six items in Ba Min's speech that occurred invariably in polite form. Two of these are generally infrequent (**dugi**, "up to," and **kaleh**, "with") and occurred only once in the observed interaction. The other four items were identified as minimal markers for this speaker:

inggeh	"yes" (response)
mboten	"no" (response)
sinten	"who"
sampéyan	"you"

In Mini's usage, however, the first two items (*inggeh* and *mboten*) occurred only once or twice and so were not included in the list of markers for her speech. Moreover, the negative response **mboten**/⟨*ora*⟩ occurs, in one instance, in subfamiliar form (example 25). The last two items are indeed markers in Mini's usage, in two different categories: **sinten** is a marker in utterances directed to the grandfather, and **sampéyan** is a marker in addressing the grandmother. The numbers of occurrences in each case are too small to permit generalization beyond the simple observation that, even at the level of minimal politeness, lexical markers appear to require case-by-case consideration and interpretation.

In discussing the partially formal style of Ba Min, I suggested that her use of lexical variants entailed an element of close-politeness marking (using familiar forms) as well as distant-politeness marking (using polite forms). Comparison of her style with that of Mini shows, beyond the difference in overall categories, that several relatively commonly heard polite forms were used consistently by Mini but not at all, or not consistently, by Ba Min. The following five items were used only in polite form by Mini and only in familiar form by Ba Min:

nopo-nopo/⟨*opo-opo*⟩	"anything"
pun/⟨*wis*⟩	"already"
dinten/⟨*dina*⟩	"day"

griya/⟨*omah*⟩ "house"
sedanten/⟨*kabeh*⟩ "all"

There were no converse instances, that is, items used only in polite form by Ba Min and in familiar form by Mini, with the exception of the subfamiliar negative already mentioned (example 25).

In addition, some items appear only in the polite form in Mini's speech but appear both in polite and in familiar form in Ba Min's speech. One of these is the first-person pronoun, for which Ba Min alternated between **kula** and ⟨*aku*⟩. The other cases are the affirmative and negative existentials: "There is," **ènten**/⟨*eneng*⟩; "there is not" **mboten ènten**/⟨*ora eneng*⟩.

The difference between the styles of these two speakers is not, however, adequately described as a difference in lexical level. The overall style of speech differed as well. There is ample evidence of this difference in overall style; most obvious is the use of the vocative coda. In Mini's usage, as already pointed out, the vocative kinship-term coda is a pronounced feature, particularly of interrogative utterances. In the speech of Ba Min, however, only four instances of vocative coda appear—three of them addressed to the grandmother,[13] one to the grandfather:

1. **Pinten**, mbah?
   "**How much**, grandfather?"
2. Sumuk ⟨yo⟩ PN?
   "It's hot ⟨isn't it⟩, (name)?"
3. Eh, yu, nèk **kula sanjang** ⟨wongé⟩ nesu.
   "Yes, older-sister, if **I said** (anything) ⟨they⟩ were angry."
4. **Wangsul** ⟨yo⟩ bik!
   "(I'll) **go home** ⟨okay⟩ aunt!"

Examples 2 and 4 are types of politeness formulas, that is, a type of utterance most likely to use the vocative coda. Example 1 is also fairly typical, for the single-word interrogative is an utterance very likely to be softened by the use of a vocative.

Ba Min's conversation was relatively free of the conversational interrogatives that tend to co-occur with a vocative coda. (Example 2 was in fact an initial greeting to the grandmother.) Ba Min's conversation, unlike that of Mini, consisted of discursive narrative rather than interrogatives and responses. Instead of the vocative, then, we find a consistent use of expressive particles, which are virtually absent in the speech of Mini. Also in contrast to Mini's speech, Ba Min followed the conversational pattern of interjecting a polite "Yes," *Inggeh*, as a punctuative response to the other speakers' utterances. This is a conversational device usual even in the most formal contexts and is in fact the stereotypic collective response of the participants in a *slametan* responding to the invocation. In Ba Min's speech, the polite interjection is frequently modified by the addition of an expressive particle, with the meaning "Yes, of course!" or "My word, yes!":

Lha **inggeh**!
Inggeh kok!

6.6 Formal Discursive Style: Lexical Shifts

Within a single conversation, the overall level of lexical politeness can vary considerably. It is affected by interruptions and ongoing activities, by the presence and departure of other speakers, by topic of conversation, and apparently also by the duration of the interaction (tending to become less polite).

One recorded conversation exhibits several fluctuations of lexical level, reflecting all these factors. The participants were people I saw frequently during my stay—the elderly couple themselves and two of their regular visitors. One of the visitors was an elderly woman who had come over on the same ship with the grandmother (the *djadji* relationship); the other was a woman only slightly younger, who, I had many occasions to note, spoke Krama more consistently than most visitors.

The visit began at a rather formal lexical level. It was my impression that the grandfather of the household tended to elevate the lexical level when I was present (though he exclusively used Ngoko in addressing me, as a "daughter" in the household). This was not a matter of showing me respect or even of impressing me but rather of assisting my education in correct, polite Javanese.

1. Mriki . . . mboten wonten. Mriki niku, ⟨siji loro⟩ **tiang gadah nggèn**.
   "Here . . . there isn't. Over here, ⟨one or two⟩ **people own homes**."

In this example, only the idiomatic phrase "one or two" is in ordinary lexical style; although it could certainly be transposed into polite form, **stunggal kaleh**, this would sound quite formal and perhaps ceremonial.

The lexical level became less formal rather quickly, and the style of conversation became more animated, as in the following sentences from the same speaker:

2. Ngentèni **piyambaké** montoré. Montoré ⟨ora⟩ kétok lho!
   "**She** was waiting for a ride. The ride ⟨didn't⟩ show up!"

The first and second sentences of this utterance contrast considerably in lexical style, even though only two lexical items are stylistically significant. (Two other items, which appear here in ordinary [ngoko] form, do have polite variants; however, these are used only in very formal settings.) In the first sentence, the use of the polite third-person pronoun **piyambak** is more than minimally polite lexically, for one frequently hears the ngoko form in moderately polite utterances; moreover, the pronoun can be elided or substituted by a polite indexical (**niku**, "this one").[14] In the second sentence, the use of the ordinary negative ⟨*ora*⟩ indicates *less* than minimal lexical politeness, because the negative (unlike the third-person pronoun) is among the first lexical items to shift into polite style.

The same speaker's subsequent utterances continued at this less than minimally polite lexical level. At this point he was describing the scene of a traffic accident and "sketching" the situation with a forefinger on the tabletop in front of him:

3. ... ⟨kéné⟩. ⟨Iki⟩ 'brugi,' ta, ⟨iku⟩ montor.
   "... ⟨here⟩. ⟨This⟩ is the bridge, you see, ⟨that⟩ is the car."

The use of the ordinary forms for the indexicals ("here," "this," "that") characterizes a markedly familiar style of speech, because these are among the first items to shift into polite form in discursive formal utterances. In this case, the style resembles that of a teacher addressing his pupils; possibly the activity of diagraming influenced the speech style in this direction. In the next sentence, minimal lexical politeness is reintroduced:

4. ... ⟨réné⟩ ta? Ngetèketèk-ketèketèk terus **mawon**.
   "... (it) ⟨comes⟩, okay? Chug-a-chug **just** straight ahead."

In this case, the use of the ordinary form of "just," ⟨*waé*⟩, would perhaps lower the lexical level even more than the use of the indexicals noted above, because the use of *waé* in final position has the effect of an expressive particle or even of a directive. The other participants at this point maintained the slightly formal character of the visit by using the polite form "yes," **inggeh,** as an occasional conversational punctuation. (Kin terms and other vocatives were not used at any point.)

The next stretch of conversation tended to remain in ordinary lexical style, with only occasional use of such polite markers as indexicals, negatives, and existentials. Even these, however, were not consistently in polite form: two instances of the familiar negative ⟨*ora*⟩ appear in my notes.

The conversation then split up, as the older woman visitor and the grandmother went into the kitchen and proceeded to converse entirely in ordinary style (Ngoko). The younger woman visitor stayed in the front room, where she and the grandfather began to speak in a more polite style than they had used with the others present. It is possible that this lexical shift provided a way of counteracting the more familiar setting of a tête-à-tête (though I was present as well). The Suriname Javanese tend, however, not to be as particular about avoiding (or hedging) male-female interaction as is reported for Java, and in this case the age of the participants (particularly of the grandfather) might have been sufficient to alleviate embarrassment. My impression was rather that these two people took a certain pride and pleasure in their command of polite speech style, and they used this opportunity to indulge that taste in the absence of the "nonplayers." Unfortunately, my note taking was disturbed at this point, but one example may suffice:

5. **Mboten <u>kaleh</u> mriki niku** . . . jam **<u>skawan</u>**.
   "**Not <u>with</u> that one over here** . . . **<u>four</u> o'clock**."

The boldface underlined forms indicate that more than minimal lexical politeness is observed. (There is one ngoko form in this utterance, *jam*, "o'clock," but the polite variant is only rarely heard in Suriname Javanese and would constitute a further level of formality.)

The level of lexical politeness fluctuated several more times. The front-room conversation became less formal, but when the other women rejoined the conversation (having served all present a bowl of soup), the lexical level became more formal once again. One example is of interest because of an internal shift in lexical level. (The speaker is the slightly younger woman visitor, well versed in polite style.)

6. a. **Kula mrika, mboten <u>kraos</u>** . . . **kula <u>sanjang</u>**.
   b. **Kula <u>wangsul</u> mriku**, terus **<u>kiyambaké</u>** (name) . . .
   c. **Mboten <u>ènten</u>** ⟨omongé⟩. ⟨Aku ora gelem rono⟩. . . . ⟨Aku mbesok nek⟩ . . .
   d. **Ingkeh mboten ing ngriki** . . . **kula**.

   a. **I went there, wasn't <u>happy</u>** . . . **I <u>said</u>**.
   b. **I <u>went back</u> there**, then **<u>he</u>** (name) . . .
   c. ⟨He said⟩ **there wasn't** (any). ⟨I don't want to go there⟩. . . . ⟨Tomorrow if⟩ . . . ⟨I⟩ . . .
   d. **Yes, not here** . . . **me**.

The first two lines display a consistently polite style. Four vocabulary items occur in more than minimally polite style: **kraos**, **sanjang**, **wangsul** (discursive use), and **kiyambaké** (a dialect form of **piyambaké**, "he"). The complete absence of ngoko forms is itself a mark of more than minimal politeness.

In this context, the occurrence of a sentence (6c) exclusively in ngoko—and particularly as it includes a pronoun, a negative, and an indexical—constitutes a very striking shift:

6c. ⟨Aku ora gelem rono⟩.
"⟨I don't want to go there⟩."

This is the same phrasing and lexical style that a child might use (though a child would probably use the substandard negative, *nggak*). In my recollection (though not reported in my notes) this sentence was indeed uttered almost as an outburst of annoyance at having to go somewhere so inhospitable. In the following line, the speaker recovers her polite speech style to announce that tomorrow she will be away.

6.7 Polite Performance

Polite lexical style serves a number of different functions. For some speakers, as just described, formal speech style is almost an art form, whose cultivation and exercise give pleasure and satisfaction. Of greatest interest, however, are politeness functions that are obligatory and not simply a matter of individual taste. In Suriname Javanese, polite lexical forms still serve (in some social circles) as a form of minimal recognition of social distance, as well as an obligatory marker of certain formal occasions.

Even those individuals who do not cultivate lexical competence for its own sake must master the system of levels to some minimal degree. I was present on one occasion when the grandparents of my Paramaribo household received a formal visit from a middle-aged woman, the elder sister of a close neighbor. The visit took place at the time of general visiting that marks the end of the Moslem fasting month (called *Bada* by Suriname Javanese). The visit was conducted entirely in ordinary style, without use of polite lexicon even at leave taking and without even the minimal polite lexical markers (such as *inggeh*, "yes," and *mboten*, "no"). Nevertheless, at the end of the visit the visitor made a formal statement of the purpose of the visit, presented entirely in polite lexical style (Madya); though ceremonial, the statement was not simply formulaic, as, for example, the stereotypic formal invitation to a *slametan*. Having completed this ceremonial statement, the visitor asked permission to depart using a minimally respectful style and familiar lexicon, as if addressing her own grandparents:

1. ⟨Aku muleh⟩ ⟪ya⟫ mbah. Suwun.
   "⟨I'm going home⟩ ⟪okay⟫ grandmother. Thanks."

Even apart from such ceremonial functions, polite lexicon of at least level 2 (see fig. 6.1) is an expected component of adult social interaction in dealings with individuals who are either substantially older or very slightly known. At any bus stop or roadside stand frequented by Javanese, a bystander can hear an apparently obligatory exchange of polite lexicon, especially levels 2 and 3.

The selection of lexicon in even brief encounters seems to carry great significance, at least for some individuals. It was striking to me that the lexical level of a conversation was invariably specified by direct quotation in its retelling: my impression was that to relate an encounter with no quotation of polite lexicon would imply that the encounter had been entirely in familiar lexical style.

The grandmother, Ba Nom, on returning from a marketing excursion, habitually repeated even brief exchanges with socially significant individuals. In one case, she recounted a chance meeting with a distantly related and relatively highly placed village official. She quoted, with evident satisfaction, the greeting he had offered her:

2. **Kepripun,** bik!
   "**How** (are you), aunt!"

Kepripun is the polite lexical variant (madya) for *kepiyé*; it is usually shortened to *pripun*, and in its unshortened form it is the politest variant in the normal Suriname repertoire. As there were rather few individuals in the grandmother's social circle who were both competent in formal speech style and willing to accord her formal politeness, she made a point of recounting such exchanges, however brief.

On another occasion, the grandmother was reporting a substantive conversation with Mini, who normally used at least a minimal level of formal respect with both the grandparents. She quoted Bik ("Aunt") Mini's response, first using familiar respect style and then correcting to formal respect:

3. ⟨Ora⟩ mbah! **Mboten** mbah!
   "⟨No⟩, grandmother! **No**, grandmother!"

The correction may have been Mini's own self-correction, or it may have been the grandmother's way of properly encoding the relationship (as I interpreted it at the time).

Most interesting is the example of Sita, the foster daughter of the family, quoting a conversation with her "boss" (who was Creole). Her supervisor had asked, in Sranang, if she wanted more money, and Sita had responded in the negative, interpreting the question as a suspect offer. In reporting the conversation to the grandparents she used Javanese for her own part of the conversation:

4. **Mboten**, ⟨ngomong ora⟩.
 "**No**, (I) ⟨said no⟩."

Here she used the polite variant *mboten* as a direct quotation and the familiar variant *ora* as a (redundant) indirect quotation. (The familiar style was the only style she used with the foster grandparents.) In this case, there was no question of literal accuracy, because she had certainly not used Javanese with her Creole supervisor. My guess is that she had used Dutch (rather than Sranang) in responding to his question, and it was this shift that Sita represented using the device of lexical shift. (It would be interesting to discover whether the two common Suriname languages, Sranang and Dutch, function in general as high and low speech styles.) Equally possibly, the polite Javanese rendition may have been Sita's representation of the relationship itself rather than of any specific linguistic element.

A further demonstration of the deeply ingrained observance of lexical politeness occurred at the end of fast (*Bada*). Seven or eight local men, ranging from twentyish to middle-aged, had been drinking till late in the evening at a neighbor's house and had launched a round of respectful visits at that point. They visited the grandfather (one of the local religious elders) in a boisterous group, calling him by his respectful-familiar epithet ("Ba Pèn! Ba Pèn!") as they approached the house.

Entering the house, the gathering was transformed into a formal social occasion. The men intoned a formal request to enter, **Kula nuwun**, as they crossed the threshold, and each shook the grandfather's hand and murmured a brief greeting that I took to be the stereotypic *Bada* greeting, though the words were indistinct. One of the men then made a brief speech to the grandfather, using polite lexical style and formal intonation. The most voluble of the group was a young man studying to be a *kaum* (religious official). He greeted me with "Happy new year," in the (expected) Ngoko, and discoursed at length explaining the occasion to me, still in familiar style. But when he interrupted himself to ask the grandfather for help in interpretation, it was in polite lexical style:

5. **Pripun** mbah?
"**How** (do you say it), grandfather?"

Though his speech was less than perfectly coherent, the compartmentalization of styles was absolutely clear.

NOTES

1. This is in sharp contrast to the experience of researchers in Central Java, who report having trouble finding people with whom to exchange Ngoko.
2. The term "co-occurrence" is adopted from the work of Ervin-Tripp (1972) as a way of representing speakers' implicit rules of usage.
3. The term "marker" is used here (following Bax [1974] and Errington [1982]) to indicate those polite lexical variants whose use is obligatory within a given level of politeness.
4. Note that a conventional phrase tends to shift as a unit, even though it may combine words of differing stylistic sensitivity (a lexical marker with a nonmarker or an item from a three-way paradigm with one from a binary paradigm—see example 25, sec. 6.4.3).
5. He was actually her cousin's grandfather, but Sita's natural family—a large kinship network—had treated him as its head since the death of her own grandfather.
6. Alton Becker (personal communication) reports that the same sort of random lexical admixture occurs in Javanese speech in Indonesia.
7. This material is presented not as a text for semantic analysis but as an example of the use of lexical variants as markers of a relationship or functional context. There may also be semantic influences on lexical style, as I have noted in one or two examples elsewhere in this chapter.
8. These indicators, like the levels of figure 6.1, do not represent the conventional lexical categories (madya, krama, krama inggil).
9. There is also the element of implied disapproval, as the coda "*wongé*" is characteristically used. Here I think it is less a matter of a referential function of stylistic level (which is normatively, at least, *not* a factor) than of the "ordinary-style" context associated with negative gossip. In other words, formal style conversation is not an appropriate context for savoring scandal, so a disapproving exclamation "calls for" ngoko rather than madya. (I am grateful to Penelope Brown for raising this issue.)
10. I use "task-oriented" to refer to interaction that communicates a request, instruction, question (other than a politeness formula, discussed in sec. 4.4), or correction, as well as the response to any of the foregoing. See section 4.3.
11. The other three markers listed as level 1 (fig. 6.1) are items that did not occur in the function specified in Ba Min's speech, as recorded. (She bade good-bye only to the grandmother, as the grandfather had already retired.)
12. P. Brown (personal communication) suggests that the use of respectful style would make it impossible to convey irritation. This strikes me as quite plausible, for this speech community at least.

13. Note the use of three different forms of address—personal name (PN), elder-sister (*yu*), and junior-aunt (*bik*)—all addressed to the same individual.

14. Here there is the possibility that polite reference was intended. The person referred to was myself, and it is possible that in my presence and with this interlocutor the grandfather might have wanted to underline my status as a foreign visitor, even though he (naturally enough) would not have addressed me using second-person honorifics. If polite reference is indeed a factor, it would constitute a case of using a krama form as an honorific, a phenomenon discussed in Errington (1985:67).

CHAPTER 7

Pronoun Selection and Replacement

The phenomenon of ranked lexical paradigms, so characteristic of Javanese, is familiar to Europeans in the context of pronominal variation—usually as the binary stylistic opposition of familiar/formal. In Javanese as well, despite its pervasive and complex lexical variation, the selection of pronoun forms occupies a special place.[1]

Pronominal variation in Javanese appears to be a more sensitive stylistic element than the general system of ngoko/krama lexical variation. Unlike other lexical items, pronouns have specific reference to the principals in the social relationship. For that reason, perhaps, *the pronouns are arguably the first items to shift out of familiar style*—though not necessarily first to shift *into* polite style: first and second person must be separately discussed. The gap between shifting out of familiar style and shifting into formal style is filled in with a variety of pronoun replacement forms, including zero-replacement.

The ease of pronoun replacement gives a stylistically marked character to the use of actual pronominal forms, particularly in familiar style, but to some degree in formal style as well. For first-person reference, use of the pronoun—*whether in familiar or formal lexical style*—seems to label an utterance as close polite (either ordinary or respect style).

The case of Suriname Javanese is especially revealing, because general lexical formality is much less prevalent here than in Indonesian Javanese. This broadens the scope for the use of pronoun replacements outside the ngoko/krama paradigms. The selection or avoidance of pronoun forms constitutes a very sensitive stylistic index that considerably elaborates the overall style model presented in chapter 2.[2]

7.1 BROWN AND GILMAN: THE "METAPHOR" MODEL

The classic and seminal analysis of the European system of pronoun alternation is that of Brown and Gilman (1960), who show that the binary contrast of familiar/formal (T/V) masks a complex interaction of semantic determinants. Two distinct semantics are entailed in the European choice of second-person pronoun—the semantics of "power" and "solidarity." (I prefer to use the more abstract terms "inequality" and "social distance.") The use of a single stylistic contrast to represent two independent semantic dimensions produces two areas of conflicting usage determination, as the Brown and Gilman model shows (fig. 7.1)

The European pronominal style system was originally an honorific system, with an elevated second-person pronoun—characteristically, the plural form—used in addressing higher ranking individuals. This honorific system serves only one semantic function and hence entails no conflicted usage. As Brown and Gilman point out, the gradual inflation of polite usage and the eventual extension of the honorific pronoun for use in virtually all nonintimate relationships allowed the introduction of a second and increasingly dominant semantic function of the polite pronominal form, that of expressing social distance.

This dual semantic function can be described as a system of stylistic metaphor (as Silverstein [1979] has done): the use of an existing style code to express a second semantic distinction represents a metaphorical or conceptual identification of the two semantic dimensions. The symmetric exchange of what was originally a honorific form becomes, metaphorically, an expression of simple social distance—the "Alphonse-Gaston" reciprocal deference. In present-day European usage, conversely, as the social distance semantic becomes the dominant one, social inequality may be expressed metaphorically as the asymmetric maintenance of social distance: the inferior party expresses a greater degree of social distance than the superior party.

Figure 7.1 European pronominal variation.

Social Distance

Inequality	− (T)			+ (V)	
upward (V)	superior and solidary	V/T*		superior and not solidary	V
equal	equal and solidary	T		equal and not solidary	V
downward (T)	inferior and solidary	T		inferior and not solidary	T/V*

* Areas of conflicted usage
Source: Adapted from Brown and Gilman (1960).

As Clifford Geertz makes clear, a similar metaphorical identification of inequality as asymmetric social distance operates in the Javanese system of ranked lexical levels. Geertz invokes the image of a "wall" constructed by the use of politeness forms, a wall that is centered on the individual addressee. The inferior party to an interaction is obliged to construct a more substantial wall around the superior party than the inferior expects to receive in return (C. Geertz 1960:255-57).

Unlike European languages, Javanese provides both the option of metaphorically encoding inequality (as asymmetrical social distance) and also stylistic options that specifically encode *deference* as distinct from simple *distance*. The honorific vocabulary, including the honorific second-person pronoun, is such a deference code (although it is also used symmetrically in elite speech style to express mutual deference, that is, social distance). And beyond the lexical style code, the overall respect style (described in chap. 2) conveys a specifically deferential attitude without implying social distance. The pronoun system—even in the extended paradigm of pronoun replacement forms discussed in this chapter—does not carry the entire weight of style encoding. Nevertheless, the selection of pronoun form is as sensitive a stylistic issue in Javanese as it is in the European system.

7.2 PRONOMINAL PARADIGMS IN JAVANESE

The basic lexical variants of the pronominal paradigm can be presented simply:

	First-Person	Second-Person
Honorific:	(dalem)[3]	(panjenengan)
Formal:	kula	sampéyan
Familiar:	aku	kowé

The parentheses reflect the fact that in Suriname Javanese the honorific forms are used rarely (in second-person reference) or not at all (in first-person reference). This lack of honorific forms seems to suggest that the Suriname system is essentially the same sort of binary signal as the European pronominal system; nevertheless, the system is in fact much more flexible and more complex than the lexical paradigm by itself indicates. An implied option in all Javanese pronominal reference is zero-replacement, which is so common as to constitute the normal form in many contexts. Thus, the use of *any* nonzero pronominal form has the force of a marked stylistic option. Moreover, the interpretation of these stylistically marked options is very different for first- and second-person reference, as is discussed in detail in the following sections.

7.2.1 The Second-Person Paradigm

The conventional three-level pronominal paradigm (familiar/formal/honorific) must be revised considerably to reflect the actual range of pronoun replacement options. Second-person reference admits both the zero-replacement option and kin-term replacement of the pronoun; the latter is the normative form in respect contexts (i.e., upward but not distant—Brown and Gilman's "superior and solidary" category). The resulting paradigm eliminates the encoding conflicts identified by Brown and Gilman for second-person reference (see fig. 7.2).

There is nothing rigid about the stylistic options presented here; zero-replacement and other forms of substitution are available in almost any social context. What is strictly observed, however, is the *avoidance* of particular forms in certain contexts: the familiar *kowé* is generally unacceptable in any upward-directed or distant-polite interaction, and the formal and honorific forms would be absurd in either close-polite interaction between equals or downward interaction. (For many speakers, the honorific *panjenengan* is not an available option, and the formal *sampéyan* is thus used in all distant-polite contexts, upward as well as equal.)

The sheer number of options tends to ameliorate the stylistic conflict Brown and Gilman describe; *the speaker is never faced with the simple choice between polar contrasts (familiar versus honorific)*. In the European model, as in any binary code, polar contrasts are also adjacent options. To put it another way, an individual deciding whether to use the kinship term or the formal pronoun *sampéyan* (in addressing an older person not closely acquainted) would have to take the decision far more seriously if those two options also had to perform the functions that are performed respectively by the familiar pronoun *kowé* and the honorific *panjenengan*.

Figure 7.2 Javanese second-person pronominal options (non-elite usage).

Inequality	Social Distance (+/−)	
	−	+
upward	[Kin term]	Honorific (panjenengan)
equal	Familiar (kowé)	Formal (sampéyan)
downward	Familiar/[zero]	[zero]

7.2.2 The First-Person Paradigm

For first-person usage we can construct a similar diagram. No honorific first-person pronoun exists in Suriname Javanese, so the options (in this first approximation) are four: familiar (*aku*), formal (*kula*), the kinship term used in self-reference, and zero-replacement. (See sec. 6.3 for an explanation of the notation used in fig. 7.3.)

The kinship term used in self-reference is a mark of downward respect, complementing the kinship term used for second-person reference in upward-directed respect. (The pattern is similar to the American usage in which parents address their young children using the same terms to refer to themselves as the child uses: "Give Mommy the pencil.")

The prominence of zero-replacement in distant interaction reflects the fact that any form of first-person pronoun is in effect a stylistic mark of connectedness or deference. The first-person pronoun, in either lexical form, can be described as having almost a "confessional" quality, in the literary sense of self-revelation.

The pronoun style system, by providing options (and obligations) of specifically deferential politeness, eliminates the areas of *encoding* conflict identified by Brown and Gilman (1960). However, the problem of *decoding* ambiguity remains, especially given the possibility of metaphorical stylistic usage—of using distant forms to indicate deference and deferential forms to express polite distance. Here, the overall style of utterance (formal or respectful) serves to disambiguate pronominal style choices.

7.2.3 First-Person and Second-Person Connotation

The availability of optional replacement forms for the pronouns (including the option of zero-replacement) has definite consequences for the stylistic significance of the pronominal forms themselves. The formal second-person pronoun, *sampéyan*, is affected not only by the

Figure 7.3 Javanese first-person pronominal options (non-elite usage).

Inequality	Social Distance	
	−	+
upward	⟨aku⟩/**kula**	**kula**
equal	⟨aku⟩	[zero]/**kula**
downward	⟨aku⟩/[kin term]	[zero]

availability of an honorific form to express formal respect but also by the general use of the kinship-term option to express close respect. As a consequence, the formal *sampéyan* has some implication of nonrespect, conveying simple social distance without deferential overtones. By contrast, in the absence of an honorific or kin-term option, the formal first-person pronoun, *kula*, must serve in formal respect style as well as formal style. Unlike formal "you," formal "I" has a definite connotation of deference.

Accordingly, the omission or replacement of the pronoun form carries different stylistic implications in first-person and second-person reference. In general, to omit the first-person pronoun in an otherwise formal lexical style suggests a deemphasis of the formal pronoun's *respect* connotation, whereas to omit the formal second-person pronoun suggests a deemphasis of its *distancing* effect. The stylistic significance of zero-replacement thus depends critically on the overall style of the utterance.

7.3 Zero-Replacement

The ease of ellipsis in Javanese syntax and the consequent availability of zero-replacement for pronominal reference give the use of *all* pronoun forms a marked or emphatic character. Because, unlike in the European case, the overall lexical style of a Javanese utterance is established by the use of other items (deictics, interrogatives, negatives, affirmatives), the pronouns perform the more specialized function of characterizing the personal relationship with some specificity.

Zero-replacement of the pronoun may thus be regarded as a kind of avoidance device—a means of avoiding the specification of personal relationship implied in the use of the pronoun in any form. This avoidance device has different implications depending on the pronoun being omitted as well as on the overall style of the utterance.

7.3.1 Overall Formal Style of Utterance

In an overall formal style of utterance, the selection of the formal variant is implied by simple co-occurrence with an overall formal level of lexicon. The pronouns are among the first items to shift out of familiar lexical style, so the use of *any* item of formal vocabulary rules out the use of a familiar pronoun form. Omission of the pronoun presents a sort of stylistic compromise.

For second-person reference, for example, a formal utterance may be modified in the direction of greater connectedness and less distance by omitting the pronominal subject, "you" (*sampéyan*), and adding a kinship term as a vocative coda. An implication of slight respect is thereby conveyed, though less than by the use of the kinship term as a pronoun replacement and far less than by the use of the honorific pronoun.

In first-person reference, in contrast, omission of the formal *kula* renders the style less than fully formal *or* respectful, because *kula* is the appropriate form in all contexts of distant politeness. It is my impression that speakers in a relation of equality avoid specifying the first-person pronoun in formal utterances, perhaps to avoid the implication of respect that is associated with *kula*. (See also sec. 4.4.)

7.3.2 Overall Ordinary Style of Utterance

Zero-replacement works somewhat differently in the context of ordinary speech style. In the case of the first-person pronoun, the formal variant, *kula,* is appropriate even in relationships of close respect and even at a minimal level of formal politeness. In some utterances, therefore, the omission of the pronoun in an otherwise familiar lexical style might be interpreted as a "first level" of polite (formal or respectful) style—on the assumption that the familiar form, *aku,* has been avoided as excessively familiar.

This politeness implication of zero-replacement is still more pronounced in the case of second-person reference. The familiar "you," *kowé,* is possibly the first lexical item to be avoided in styles of minimal politeness (formal or respectful). The more polite second-person options, however, may also be avoided as markedly distant (the formal *sampéyan*) or markedly respectful (the kinship-term replacement form). Simple avoidance of second-person reference is thus almost an integral part of minimally polite speech styles. In an overall familiar lexical style (ordinary style), omission of the second-person pronoun is a definite mark of first-level politeness.

One stylistic hallmark of ordinary style is the use of the coda sentence structure—that is, the addition of an expressive particle, an affirmative, or a vocative at the end of the sentence or phrase. The use of the coda establishes an overall style of connectedness that ameliorates the element of social distance associated with omission of the pronoun. The overall stylistic message is one of connectedness or close politeness, which nevertheless avoids excessive familiarity or intimacy. In the case of the vocative coda (either a kin term or nickname), the message is made more explicit: the personal relationship with the hearer is affirmed even though the pronoun is omitted. (Of course, the pronoun need not always be omitted in a coda structure utterance.)

A revealing example of this usage is the omission of the second-person pronoun as the subject of a sentence combined with a vocative coda using the second-person pronoun; that is, the pronoun is removed from its normal position as sentence subject and added in the more marked position as a vocative coda. For example, in downward-directed utterance (especially to a child), instead of the standard syntax,

1. Kowé wis mangan?
   "Have you eaten?"

one might hear the somewhat stylized

1a. Wis mangan, kowé?
    "Already eaten, you?"

(The latter example is better rendered with the southern American close-polite "you all" as a vocative coda.) This kind of stylization affirms that the use of the familiar pronoun is an intentional stylistic feature and not simply taken for granted, so that the utterance expresses not merely an absence of polite distance but rather a positive relation of connectedness.

7.3.3 Overall Respect Style of Utterance

In respect style there is a marked difference between upward- and downward-directed usage in pronominal reference (in spite of the potential mutuality of the overall style). There is also a difference in the use and avoidance of first-person and second-person pronominal forms.

In upward-directed utterances, the speaker is likely to avoid the use of the familiar second-person pronoun, *kowé*, even if the relationship is too close to permit the use of formal vocabulary. (The avoidance of *kowé* in such interaction is far less strictly observed, however, than in Indonesian Javanese.) In contrast, the familiar first-person pronoun, *aku*, might well be used in the same utterance; indeed, its omission— in the absence of other stylistic respect markers—might be taken as excessively aloof. The familiar first-person pronoun has a special overtone of personal closeness, perhaps carrying a connotation of a childlike role vis-à-vis the senior.

Downward-directed utterances show the opposite tendency. The senior is much more likely to use the familiar second-person *kowé*—again, perhaps, echoing in quasi-kin relationships the usage of parent to child— but only rarely uses the familiar first-person *aku* (even though there is no question here of a potential shift to polite vocabulary). This basic nonreciprocity suggests that both parties are careful to maintain a minimal degree of distance toward the senior and, conversely, to emphasize the closeness of the junior party. Here again we can see inequality expressed as asymmetrical distance.

A similar nonreciprocity may be seen in the differential use of kinship terms and the vocative coda. The junior party will use the appropriate kinship term both as the normative second-person pronominal form and as an obligatory vocative coda. (This is true regardless of other elements of overall style, which may exhibit marked ellipsis and dynamic intonation.) The senior party is less likely to use a kinship term either as a vocative or in second-person reference, but he or she may use a kinship term as a form of first-person pronominal reference. A vocative coda in downward-directed interaction is used only in the context of overall respect style, with crooning intonation, and then it is more likely to be a nickname, pronoun, or term of endearment than a kinship term.[4] In effect, both the senior and junior parties tend to reserve the use of kinship terms to refer to the senior party in a respect relationship.

The element of nonreciprocity inherent in the system of lexical levels can be seen as well in the use of the various pronoun replacement forms. Thus, although the model presented in chapter 2 for overall style—including the category of respect style—presents no inherently asymmetrical stylistic pattern, *the selection of pronominal forms—as in the case of European usage—is inherently directional.*

7.4 Other Pronoun Replacement Forms

In the speech community I observed, the style system functioned in most contexts not to express formal respect (so prominent in the accounts of Indonesian Javanese) but rather gradations of simple distance (or formality) and simple respect. My own observations centered on domestic settings and so included a rather broad range of close and quasi-close interaction styles. In this context, certain pronoun replacement forms, in addition to those included in figures 7.2 and 7.3, are especially salient.[5]

7.4.1 Second-Person Reference

For second-person reference, in relationships of equality and in downward-directed respect style, the personal name or nickname can be used in place of the pronoun. This usage is more polite than the use of the familiar *kowé*, because it avoids the overtone of unstylized or even insulting use of the familiar pronoun. Equally common (in my experience) is the use of the passive verbal prefix. Both the personal name and the passive verbal prefix are mild distancing devices, though the use of the personal name is a form of stylized (mediated) closeness. The personal name is used particularly in descriptive statements:

2a. Min kok duwor!
"You're so tall, Min!" (Literally, Min [is] so tall.)

A special case is the use of the vocative coda plus zero replacement of the second-person pronoun. In this pattern, even though the vocative coda may be the familiar pronoun *kowé*, the use of the coda form instead of the pronoun subject creates a stylized closeness:

2b. Kok duwor, kowé!
"You're so tall!" (Literally, so tall, you [are]!)

7.4.2 First-Person Reference

First-person pronoun replacement forms include a passive verbal prefix, *tak-*. Use of the prefix form eliminates the marked, confessional quality of the first-person pronoun and focuses instead on the action being accomplished: *Tak-pangan* instead of *Aku mangan*—"I'll just eat (this)" instead of "I'm eating."

In addition to the verbal prefix, there are two other forms of first-person reference that create a definite distancing or stylized effect. The first is simply the insertion of the relative conjunction *sing*, "who, which":

3a. Aku gawé wédang.
"I'm making tea."

becomes

3b. Aku sing gawé wédang.
"(It is) I who make tea."

This example was uttered by Ba Nom on one occasion as she walked past me into the kitchen. The utterance was clearly a politeness formula—an announcement—in effect, giving her reason for walking past me without stopping to talk. The use of the relative conjunction *sing* is neither necessary nor usual in this context, but it has the effect of focusing attention on the activity rather than on the performer of the activity (the speaker). It is thus perhaps especially appropriate in the context of an older person making an announcement to a younger person, because it avoids both the sense of asking permission and the expectation of indulgent personal attention that is conveyed, for example, in a child's announcement of "I am bathing" (*Aku ados*). The use of the relative conjunction *sing* in this context is a distancing device, though the result is not so distant as either zero-replacement or the polite lexical variant. (Between family members, i.e., in truly intimate speech, the entire utterance will be omitted, as the need for polite announcement does not arise in senior-junior interaction.)

A somewhat similar distancing device is the substitution of the first-person pronominal *awak déwé* for the simple first-person singular, *aku*.[6] This seems more common for some speakers than for others, possibly amounting to a kind of mannerism or affectation for some individuals. In some contexts it has an emphatic sense (the phrase means literally "the body itself"), as in the following utterance, in which Sita was commenting on the case of a policeman involved in a traffic accident: "*Nek awak déwé, disetrap!*" "If it was [you or] me, [we'd be] jailed!" In this case, the phrase has the inclusive plural connotation that it frequently carries in formal discourse (in its polite-variant form, *awak piyambak*). In another instance, a young boy who had been invited to go swimming asked whether his younger brothers and sisters were also included by asking simply, "*Awak déwé?*" "Myself?"

The pronominal phrase *awak déwé* is not necessarily either plural or emphatic; it can also be used simply to avoid using either the familiar or the polite forms of the first-person pronoun in cases where elision is felt to be inappropriate. For example, in returning from the market, the grandmother once reported to me that she had met a cousin of the family: "*Awak déwé petuk* [name], *dikon mampir.*" "I met [name] and was invited to stop in." The pronoun phrase here is in effect a polite (or perhaps slightly pompous) substitute for simple elision, which is more usual in informal conversation.

In the speech of some individuals, the phrase *awak déwé* is regularly substituted for the first-person singular pronoun. This usage has the effect of rendering the utterance more formal and less familiar than the ordinary ngoko pronoun, *aku*. I would hesitate, however, to interpret this slight stylistic shift within the framework of the ngoko/krama stylistic variation, since it bears little relation to the social context of the utterance. Rather, the generalized used of *awak déwé* seems to correspond to the hypercorrect use in American English of "myself" in place of "me" in phrases such as "come and visit Jane and myself." The implicit stylistic premise may be that the use of the simple (familiar) pronoun sounds childish or unsophisticated. In the case of Javanese, this sensitivity to the simple first-person pronoun seems to be heightened by the necessity, in formal and respectful contexts, of avoiding it in its ordinary (ngoko) variant. (In thoroughly formal Surinamese speech, as in the invocation at a mosque *slametan*, a more formal variant of *awak déwé* is used as a plural first-person pronoun, *awak piyambak:*

the ngoko variant, *déwé* ("itself"), is here replaced by the krama variant, *piyambak*.)

7.4.3 Pronominal Affixes

Grammatical categories in Javanese are in general signaled by the use of affixes. Pronominal affixes exist in two categories: the possessive suffix and the passive prefix.

The possessive suffix is the only form of possessive pronoun in familiar lexical style. The familiar possessive suffixes are as follows:

First-person	Second-person	Third-person
-ku	-mu	-(n)é
"my"	"your"	"his, hers"

The possessive suffix has, stylistically, the full force of the personal pronoun. That is to say, the possessive also conveys connectedness (especially in first-person reference) or familiarity (in second-person). A common polite replacement form for the second-person possessive is the third-person possessive suffix, *-(n)é,* understood to refer to a possession of the addressee.

In formal lexical style there is only a third-person possessive suffix, *-(n)ipun*. For first- and second-person possessives, the appropriate pronoun is used as a possessive, following the noun it modifies.

The passive verb form employs a pronominal prefix to indicate agent. The passive prefixes are:

First-person	Second-person	Third-person
tak-	mbok- (kok-)	di-
"by me"	"by you"	"by him, her"

(Syllable final *-k* is a glottal stop and may also be spelled *-q*.). In this case, too, the third-person prefix may be used as a distant-polite form of second-person reference.

The passive prefix, unlike the possessive suffix, does not have the stylistic force of the pronoun itself. The passive construction in Javanese is a syntactic device—so widely used that it might almost be thought of as the normal verb construction—that serves to place emphasis on the recipient rather than the agent of the action. For example,

    4a. Opo kowé nulis?
        "Are you writing?"

uses the active form of the verb and in effect presents the question "What are you doing? Writing?" By contrast, the passive form,

4b. Opo kok-tulis?
"Is (this) written by you?" (literally, is [it] by you written?)

focuses not on the activity but on the object acted upon. To take another example,

5a. Aku mangan gedang.
"I'm eating a banana"

is in effect an answer to the (implied or expressed) question "What are you doing/going to eat?" The corresponding passive form,

5b. Gedangé tak-pangan.
"I'm eating the banana." (literally, the banana [is] by me eaten)

answers the implied question "Who'll eat the banana?" In both cases, the active constructions presuppose a legitimate personal interest in the activities of the person referred to as taking place in the context of a domestic agenda (see chap. 4). The passive forms express no such assumption, focusing rather on the object of the action, and so may be regarded as potentially more distant or impersonal utterances.

The first-person prefix, *tak-*, and the second-person prefix, *mbok- (kok-)*, appear also in the form of particles in intransitive verbal constructions. In this form they are not merely impersonal or distancing devices but have the effect of a politely deprecating utterance. (The examples given here are not necessarily acceptable in standard Javanese.) For example,

6a. Aku mangan.
"I'm eating."

becomes

6b. (Aku) tak mangan.
"I'll just grab a bite." (Literally, I by me eat.)

Similarly,

7a. Kowé jupuk!
"You get it!"

becomes

7b. Mbok jupuk.
"Please get it" (also glossed as "by you [it] be taken").[7]

Again, the focus of the utterance shifts from the subject to the object of the activity, with the implied suggestion of accomplishing some little thing quickly (as opposed to actively participating in the culturally shared agenda of domestic activities).

7.5 SUMMARY

Pronoun avoidance and replacement are arguably central to the system of lexical alternation, constituting a very sensitive stylistic index that operates even in social contexts far removed from the elevated refinement of formal speech style. The concept of stylistic levels hardly does justice to the subtlety of pronominal variation.

Within the sphere of domestic interaction, at least among Suriname Javanese, the Javanese speech-style paradigm consists essentially of the familial, ordinary, and respect styles, with little use of polite lexical style. The use and avoidance of pronouns play a central part in this domestic style system, even without the involvement of other elements of lexical variation.

The mechanism of pronoun usage and avoidance is much like lexical variation in general: the choice of a particular variant implies a specific degree of respect and/or social distance. But the choice of pronoun has also an emphatically personal character, since pronouns refer specifically to the interacting participants. The use of a pronoun rather than a replacement form in effect "points to" the person so indicated. (Frequently, the use of the pronoun rather than the pronominal prefix also points to the current activity as an expected part of the domestic daily agenda, e.g., "I am eating.") This emphatic function applies even to the polite pronominal variants, particularly for the first-person pronoun.

The emphatic indexicality of the pronouns is reflected in the distinct stylistic ranges and associations of the first- and second-person pronouns. The *second-person pronoun* is the first to be avoided in its familiar form, in both distant-polite (symmetrical) and respectful (upward-directed) interaction, but it is only in distant-polite contexts that it shifts into formal style. In respect contexts, it is either replaced by the kin term or omitted altogether (with a vocative coda complement). The *first-person pronoun* (familiar form) is strictly avoided only in distant-polite interaction, but the formal style is reserved for contexts of formal respect; zero-replacement and other replacement forms are standard in distant-polite contexts. In respect contexts, the familiar first-person pronoun is less strictly avoided, but when it drops out it is readily replaced by the polite variant.

In the simplest terms, then, we can say that *respect* politeness is characterized by (1) the avoidance of the familiar second-person pronoun (with frequent iteration of its kin-term equivalent), and (2) the use of the first-person pronoun in *either* familiar form (close respect) or polite form (distant respect). *Formal* politeness, on the other hand, is expressed by (1) the use of the polite second-person pronoun *or* its zero-replacement, and (2) the avoidance of first-person reference even, to some extent, in polite pronominal form.

Pronouns may be said to carry the weight of emotional emphasis and personal involvement, possibly reflecting their prominence in the familial and peer-group interaction of childhood and adolescence. The pronoun "you" (familiar form), which is so studiously avoided in upward-directed or outsider interaction, is almost a hallmark of peer-group and downward-directed interaction—the focus, for example, of such expressions as "Where are you going?" (*Nandi kowé?*) and the jocular "You're nuts!" (*Kowé édan!*).

This last example provides an interesting illustration of the force of the pronoun itself. I once heard Sita tell the grandmother, teasingly, that she was crazy, using this expression but substituting the kinship term "grandmother" for the second-person pronoun: *"Mbahé édan!"* ("Grandmother [is] crazy!"). The grandmother gave no indication of being offended (nor was this remark necessarily intended as an offense, having some of the complimentary force of the then-current American phrase "wild and crazy guy"). I have no doubt, however, that the same expression using the pronoun (*Kowé édan!*) would indeed have been offensive, if only by implying an inappropriate degree of equality. To put it another way, the sentence "Grandmother is nuts"—whatever its substantive meaning—carries a *stylistic meaning* of respect because it shifts the pronoun into a third-person form of reference. The utterance might best be rendered as "You may be nuts but you're my esteemed grandmother."

NOTES

1. All three personal pronouns exhibit lexical variation in Javanese (as in other Malayo-Polynesian languages). This discussion will be restricted to first- and second-person variants, as more salient in the usage of the speakers I observed: the frequent use of ellipsis or substitution in third-person reference made the use of these pronoun forms more the exception than the norm.

2. This discussion makes no attempt to gauge frequencies of usage or to investigate contexts in detail but rather sets forth a range of stylistic options and their stylistic functions.

3. This self-deprecating first-person honorific form is absent in Suriname-Javanese usage and will be omitted from discussion here.

4. Usage in Java differs: the kinship terms *adik* (abbreviated *dik*), "younger

sibling," and *anak* (abbreviated *nak*), "child," are commonly used as downward-directed vocative codas.

5. See Errington (1982) for a discussion of pronoun replacement forms in elite usage (kinship terms, titles, etc.).

6. The first-person plural pronoun does not exist as a unitary morpheme in Javanese. Several phrases are used instead: *aku karo kowé*, "I and you" (*kula kalian panjenengan* in krama, the inclusive "we"); *aku kabeh*, literally "I all' (*kula sedaya* in krama, the exclusive "we"); and the phrase here under discussion, *awak déwé*.

7. As noted in section 4.3.3, *mbok* has two possible interpretations in contexts such as this, both translated in English as "please [plus imperative]."

PART THREE

Social Space

CHAPTER 8

Domestic Space

8.1 INTRODUCTION

Spatial terminology serves in many languages as a metaphorical device for describing social interaction: higher/lower, close/distant, open/closed, before/behind, and so on. In this work, however, the spatial model has more than metaphorical significance. Spatial analysis here has two distinct aspects:

1. Spatial setting has been widely recognized as an essential aspect of the *context* of interaction. In this case, an array of conventional spatial settings forms a contextual paradigm, broadly correlating with the repertoire of speech styles. (Nevertheless, the relation between spatial setting and speech style is not predictive or even prescriptive, but rather emblematic.) Formal speech style, in particular, may be seen as the interactional correlate of the front-region setting (much of chap. 9 fills out this tentative connection).

2. The social construction of space is seen here as based on *conceptual relationships* that are essentially similar to the conceptual relationships enacted in the selection of speech style. The structure of social space images the (conceptual) structure of the speech-style system.

Part 3 explores both the spatial setting of the speech-style system and its structural assumptions. The model for dealing with stylistic structure in this case comes not from other communicative codes but rather from the use of domestic space.[1] This choice of focus was imposed by the fieldwork process itself, in that learning how to "use" the house was a key discovery in learning the use of speech style. A further justification (if one is needed) is the fact that the Javanese speakers with whom I have discussed the model are uniformly appreciative. One Javanese anthropologist responded to my comparison of speech style and domestic space with a succinct "Of course"—to my mind, a valued tribute.

From a theoretical standpoint, there is no a priori basis for assuming that the stylistic features of language must be structured according to linguistic models. In the discussion of sociolinguistic models of chapter 1, it is argued that the Javanese use of language differs fundamentally from the contemporary Western norm in according primacy not to the information function of speech but rather to what might be termed its greeting function—the socially required recognition and "placement" of social participants. Models of language use that focus on its information function are not necessarily applicable to its socially significant (stylistic) elements. From this point of view, to look for a model of social placement in the patterns of *physical* placement of social participants is by no means an esoteric approach; it is, at least in this case, rather prosaic common sense.

8.1.1 A General Model of Domestic Space

The moment a building of any sort is completed, a boundary is created between inside and outside. This distinction has immediate social relevance, creating a corresponding distinction between the set of people who may (or must) enter and the set of people who remain outside.

In addition to the inside-outside distinction, there may be other social-spatial distinctions that emerge in the use of a building or that have been anticipated in its construction. The most relevant in the Suriname-Javanese context is Goffman's distinction between the front region and the back region. The act of entering a building, especially a dwelling, always has a social dimension: one is either host or guest, broadly speaking—a rightful insider or an outsider. The activities of guests may be restricted to a front-region setting, possibly a setting constructed or adapted for the occasion. Household settings not intended specifically as front-region areas belong instead to the back region. (All of these terms must be situationally interpreted. The household may participate in the house more as an honored guest than as an insider in the absence of other guests. Conversely, some visitors, especially kin, may take on an insider, rather than a guest, role.)

The front region may have no physical boundary at all, being marked instead by such social indicators as dress, gestural and verbal behavior, or even norms of attention and inattention. Where front region and back region are spatially demarcated, whether temporarily or permanently, there is created a secondary inside/outside boundary between the essentially private back region and the somewhat more public and accessible front region. The placement of this secondary boundary varies widely, as the comparative material of section 8.4 will show: the house itself may be identified as back region, in contrast to a purely public external space (as suggested by the Mehinaku material in sec.

8.1), or alternatively—as in the Javanese and Suriname-Javanese cases—a portion of the house may be customarily treated as a front-region space.

8.1.2 A Compartmental Model of Domestic Space

Structural complexity enters the basic social-spatial model when the back region is accorded social or ritual significance of its own, as a privileged inside domain; this is the complex structure I describe for the Suriname-Javanese house. The conceptual model of social space now embraces two countervailing oppositions: FRONT/back and outside/INSIDE. This spatial structure is identical to the compartmental model described for interaction style in section 3.5. From one point of view, the front region is the focal part of the house, the locus for receiving honored guests and for public ceremonial observances. From an alternative perspective, however, the front region is excluded from the most important ritual activities, which take place in the inside region—the area that in other contexts may be thought of as the back region.[2]

This is the same sort of structural complexity as that underlying the social values expressed in speech style (see sec. 3.5.1). The compartmental speech-style system implies a contrastive set of interaction values: the use of formal speech style presents "refinement" (*alus*) as a positive value, while the use of ordinary speech style presents the also positive but stylistically contrastive value "liveliness" (*ramé*). The use of domestic space reflects a similar conceptual compartmentalization. At an abstract level, the parallel is quite striking: the front region is the paradigmatic setting of formal social interaction, whereas the back region is paradigmatically associated with ordinary speech style. The inside region, I suggest, is the paradigmatic domain of the third basic stylistic option, which I have termed respect style.

The equation of spatial regions (front, back, inside) with specific interaction styles (formal, ordinary, respectful) is a matter of conceptual framework, not physical setting. That is, the use of formal speech style can "conjure up" a front-region interaction context even on a bus or

Figure 8.1 A compartmental model of domestic space.

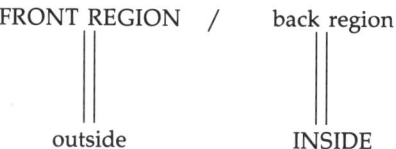

ferry. The structure of domestic space serves as a conceptual model—a paradigm—that is part of the framing context of all social interaction, even in other spatial settings. Interaction that takes place within the house can make flexible use of its settings—a formal style interaction might occur in the back region, for example—without in any way detracting from the reality of this conceptual framework (see chap. 9). (Such departures from the paradigmatic norm may be likened to the metaphorical codeswitching discussed in Blom and Gumperz [1972:424].)

8.2 SURINAME-JAVANESE "VERBS OF VISITING"

Domestic space plays an important role in Javanese social interaction. The village traditionally had no public forum, a lack that in recent decades has been remedied by the village mosque and by government-supported social welfare centers. The public spaces in the village typically were few: the streets themselves; a coffee shop; a simple shelter, which accommodated overnight travelers as well as a casual assortment of young men from the village; and the village shrine, largely ignored except for the annual village-wide observance. The rich and somewhat formal social life of the village was carried on in and around the domestic dwelling, which was at least conceptually adapted to this important function.

The Javanese house's physical structure is traditionally quite simple, as section 8.3 illustrates. Conceptually, however, the house can be understood as a complexly layered structure of social interaction. Figure 8.2 illustrates this conceptual structure in terms of what I call "verbs of visiting." These verbs reveal a multilayered structure centering on an inside region set apart from social activity. At the periphery is the most marginal social interaction, to "talk" (*omong*) without entering into the domestic arena. Slightly greater involvement is indicated by the act of "stopping" (*mampir*). (It is possible for two Javanese passing one another to hold a short conversation—to "talk"—literally without breaking their stride, that is, without "stopping" or even turning their heads.) A casual invitation for a passerby to visit may be phrased in terms of "stopping": *Ora mampir?* "Aren't you stopping?" Similarly, a casual visit at someone's home en route to another destination is described as "stopping" rather than "sitting" or "visiting."

To "sit" (*jagong*) indicates a social and not just a physical activity. "Sitting" entails an expressly undertaken visit, probably of more than minimal duration. (The house-to-house rounds of the funeral society officer, for example, are described as "stopping" rather than "sitting," since no particular house is the object of his visit.) However, "sitting"

Domestic Space

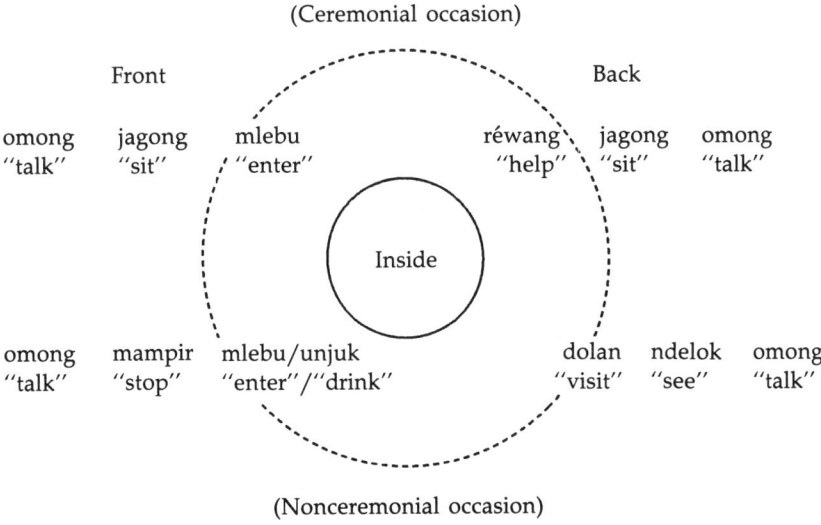

Figure 8.2 Layered social space.

does not imply that any "talk" must take place. The neighbors and friends who visit the home of the bereaved on the morning of a funeral need not actually converse with the host in order to be socially present; they may, but are not required to, converse with one another as they "sit." Such a ceremonial visit is referred to as a *jagongan*, a "sitting."

Just as "talking" need not imply "stopping," "sitting" need not imply "entering" the home. The men's *jagongan* normally takes place in the front yard and on the front porch. (Women also come to "sit," in the backyard and also in the back region of the house, if there is a passage or a room not used for sleeping.) A visit in the fullest sense requires that the guest "enter" the house (*mlebu*), normally at the invitation of the host. Once inside the house, the guest is invited to "sit" and eventually to "drink" (*ombé* or *unjuk*). The visit as a whole, however, is summed up as "entering," as in the standard exchange: "I was at Amin's house just now." "Did you go in or not?" (*"Aku mau neng nggoné Amin." "Mlebu ora?"*)

There is also a more specialized meaning of "entering" the house. For the festivities preceding a circumcision, for example, the entire front yard and backyard of the house become the scene of a party, as large as the family can afford. For the most part, the guests are served and entertained in this outside (but at least partially roofed) area. During the proceedings, however, each guest "enters" the house itself to pay respects to the boy and his parents and to discreetly hand over a gift of money. The question heard throughout the evening, from one guest to another, is "Have you gone in yet?" ("*Wis mlebu?*").

In no case is the core inside space—the sleeping room(s)—involved in adult social interaction, except of the most informal and familial kind. The verb "to go in" (*mlebu*) applies only to entering the front room of the house, not the inside region. A visitor may be invited to rest inside, but the term used is not *mlebu* ("enter") but *njero* ("inside"): "*Ayo, turu neng jero!*" ("Go on, sleep, inside!") This layered series of social interaction verbs—talking, stopping, sitting, entering, drinking—pertains only to the social space surrounding the core area.

A somewhat similar series might be constructed for interaction centering on the *back* of the house. Particularly if the house is large enough to have a side entrance, some visitors will choose to approach by avoiding the front porch, thereby signaling the visit's informal character. (Such visitors may come to a window rather than the door and hold lengthy conversations without either "entering" or "sitting.") It is quite possible, then, to "stop" and "talk" in the back region, never approaching the front or inside of the house.

On special occasions it is possible also to "sit" at the rear of the house, particularly when the preparations for a *slametan* are under way. On such occasions the backyard is invariably transformed into a kitchen area. Some women visitors, however, come not to "help" (*réwang*) with the preparations but rather to mark the occasion with a ceremonial appearance; they come to "sit" somewhat apart from the work area, even though the hostess may be too busy to join them for conversation. The verb *réwang* ("to help") thus marks a kind of "entry" into the business of the household, analogous to the front-region *mlebu*.

On nonceremonial occasions, an informal visit may vary in its duration. A brief informal visit is indicated by the verb *ndelok* ("to see"): "I went to see grandfather Pardi just now" (*Aku ndelok Ba Pardi mau*). A more substantial visit is indicated by the verb *dolan* ("to visit, to play"): "I spent some time visiting grandfather Pardi's house" (*Aku dolan neng ngonné Ba Pardi*).

Taken as a group, these verbs of visiting present a picture of domestic space as a layered enclosure, on the one hand maintaining the distinction between front-region and back-region social functions and on the other hand distinguishing degrees of social involvement in each of these social regions. This picture is represented schematically in figure 8.2.

This diagram of layered enclosures is not a map in any literal sense. Boundaries are flexible in most cases, and spaces are defined according to the social activity taking place at a given moment; informal "visiting,"

Domestic Space   195

for example, may make use of the front room as long as no formal interaction is taking place there. Some of the terms of the series are distinguished only by degree of involvement and not by any spatial boundary: "sitting" and "helping" may occur almost elbow to elbow but are easily distinguished by the different activities and dress of the participants.

The verbs of visiting are of interest as a key to the participants' map, or model, of social interaction. (The series might be extended to include the verbs associated with the inside or core region: "eating" [*mangan*], "sleeping" [*turu*], and "staying" [*manggon*].) In the following discussion I argue that this layered structure is a complex product of two alternative conceptions of domestic space: the front/back distinction places primary emphasis on the (public) front region, whereas the inside/outside distinction literally centers on the (private) inner region.

8.3 THE JAVANESE HOUSEHOLD: FRONT/BACK, INSIDE/OUTSIDE

No matter how small the structure, houses in Java have the potential for functional differentiation into back and front social settings. (A one-room house uses either the front yard or backyard, or both, as part of the social arena—as, indeed, any household does for a large-scale social event.) The simplest context for front/back differentiation is the occasion of a visit by a married couple. Typically, the men (host and male visitor) visit in the front room of the house. The women (hostess and female visitor) may initially join the men, the hostess soon withdrawing to fetch some sort of refreshment. At some point, however, especially if the women are well acquainted or of similar ages, the women regroup and visit in a spatially distinct setting. Hildred Geertz describes this pattern for the Central Javanese households she observed: "In most Modjokuto houses the father receives male visitors, inviting them to sit with him at a table in the front room. The women visitors go to one side of the main front room if there is space, or out back with the women of the house" (H. Geertz 1961:62-63). "Out back" probably refers to the backyard—possibly sheltered by a short extension of the roof. Apart from the front room, the typical house in Java includes only one or two sleeping rooms (Jay 1969: 49-50), which are not used for receiving visitors other than household intimates.

8.3.1 Schematic Space

In ordinary social interaction the "marked" term of the front-region/back-region dichotomy is thus the front region, the "stage" of social interaction, as opposed to the back-region domain of intimate family life. The front/back dichotomy subsumes the structure of oppositions summarized in figure 8.3

In this ideal conception, the front room of the house is the locus of activity that is *social* (rather than pragmatic), *formal* (rather than informal), and *male* (rather than female). The back region, in this conception, is residually defined as pragmatic, informal, and female.

Such an ideal model is far too simple, however, to describe the realities of social life. The most obvious departure is the case just described, in which the back region of the house (probably the backyard) is called into service for an activity that is *social* rather than pragmatic—the visit of a married woman accompanied by her husband—and that may be conducted on rather *formal* terms, as reflected in the use of polite speech styles. The ideal schema is adequate to describe only the case in which visitors are exclusively male or in which male visitors are the husbands of kinswomen of the female househead. In the latter case, the women may comfortably occupy any back-region space in informal and more or less pragmatic activities while their husbands visit formally with the male househead. In all other cases, women guests must be received more or less formally, even if they must be received in the backyard.

By thus conflating several oppositions into a single spatial dichotomy, the ideal model poses a problem of social choreography. The front/back dichotomy presents a picture in which all formal social functions are conducted by males and, conversely, all male social functions are formal. The inaccuracy of both parts of this ideal conception necessitates functional and sometimes architectural adaptations.

A more realistic picture of Javanese domestic space requires recognition of a second, crosscutting spatial dimension: *inside/outside*. The back region of the house is not a unitary region but consists of an inside area (the sleeping rooms) and an outside area (the backyard and, in Suriname houses, the kitchen). Only the outside portion of the back region is available for formal social activities; the house itself is best described as comprising not a front and a back region but rather a front region and an inside region—a public face and a private interior.

Figure 8.3 The ideal structure.

	Front	Back
social	+	−
formal	+	−
male	+	−

8.3.2 Expanded Structures

The minimal domestic structure, then, consists of a front room, a sleeping area, and a backyard. Many rural Javanese households (and most Suriname-Javanese households) are larger and more complexly structured than this. The enlargement and subdivision of household space can be described in part as a process of articulating the inside/outside dimension.

If space allows, the front room is likely to be functionally subdivided to accommodate a women's visit alongside the men's formal visit, so that the "back region" of women's social interaction enters spatially into the front region in what I term the "side visiting area." (The backyard, no longer called into use for formal visiting, is now simply a pragmatic and informal area.)

A more elaborate spatial adaptation is reported by Jay (1969) for the larger households he observed in rural Java. A second structure is constructed in the backyard consisting of front and back rooms. The entire unit partakes of the informal character of back-region space, so that its front room serves as what Jay calls an "inner living room." As a front room imaging the main visiting area, this room serves as a male social setting; as a back or inside space, however, it is reserved for informal rather than formal uses.

Both the front region and the back region can be subdivided, then, in such a way as to provide for all the possible uses of social space implicitly disregarded in the original schema (fig. 8.3). There are now four areas that have social functions: 1a, 1b, 2b, and 2c. Taken together they represent all the possible combinations of the two factors ± formal and ± male (all, of course, are social).

This subdivision of the front and back regions serves to resolve the problem of social choreography posed by the simple dichotomy of social space represented in figure 8.3 The three additional visiting areas—the side visiting area, the backyard, and the inner visiting area—accommodate social interaction that is informal (− formal) or that involves women rather than men (− male). This expansion of

Figure 8.4 Expanded structure.

	1a	1b	2b	2c
formal	+	+	−	−
male	+	−	−	+
	main visiting area	side visiting area	backyard	inner visiting area

social space clearly illustrates the working of a crosscutting spatial dimension, inside/outside.

8.3.3 Summary

The best way to map a floor plan accommodating the layered model of domestic space (fig. 8.2) is to diagram the minimal Javanese house as it is used—that is, reserving the back room of the house for nonsocial uses as an inside region and defining the backyard of the house as the appropriate setting for informal social interaction.

There is a subtle but important distinction between the layered model, derived from the semantics of social activity, and the floor plan just described. This is the purely conceptual distinction of valuative focus: the layered model gives chief emphasis to the inside region and thus to the inside/outside dimension; the floor-plan model begins with a primary focus on the front region, that is, the front/back division. This conceptual distinction is diagramed in figure 8.5, with the focal region shaded in each case. (Interestingly, the floor plan of fig. 8.5b is duplicated in a line drawing of an [evidently aristocratic] "Javanese house from the Yogyakarta region," in which the wall dividing the interior house space from the exterior cuts across the surrounding yard space as well [Dumarcay 1987:44].)

8.4 COMPARATIVE SPATIAL STRUCTURE

These spatial dimensions—front/back, inside/outside—are not unique to the Javanese case. Their significance is possibly universal, and together with a third spatial dimension (high/low) they perhaps serve to structure all social interaction in space.[3] Some comparative material will show, however, that the combination of perspectives I describe for Javanese domestic interaction is far from universal. Meaningful distinctions among cultures may be drawn according to the relative weight the cultures place on each of these two basic spatial dimensions. The case is most simply made by examining the Yakan house, whose physical structure nearly duplicates that of the Javanese house but whose structure of social meanings contrasts sharply.

8.4.1 Javanese and Yakan Houses: A Conceptual Comparison

Frake (1975:29-33), employing an interactional approach, reports for the Yakan a conception of the house as a layered enclosure—strikingly similar to that of the Javanese—with boundaries established by a hierarchy of verbal invitations. The Yakan inhabit the island of Basilan, in the extreme southwestern portion of the Philippines. (The termi-

Figure 8.5 Two perspectives of domestic space.

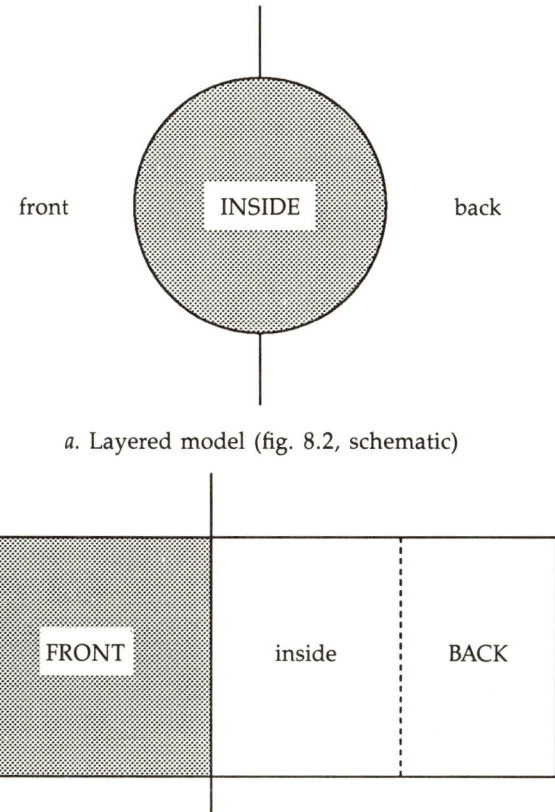

a. Layered model (fig. 8.2, schematic)

b. Floor plan (schematic)

nology and greetings reported by Frake show a striking kinship to Malay [Indonesian] in both grammatical structure and root forms and to Javanese in grammatical structure.) Like the Javanese, they are Moslems and agriculturists, their villages compounded of nuclear family households.

As the floor plans of figure 8.6 illustrate, the Yakan and Javanese houses are virtually identical in their physical layout. In each case there is a porch area that gives onto a first room, with a second room lying behind the first. In both cases the kitchen is a separate structure housed in a simple shed or lean-to. The only major difference between the physical structures is the fact that the Yakan house is elevated, requiring

Figure 8.6 Javanese and Yakan house plans.

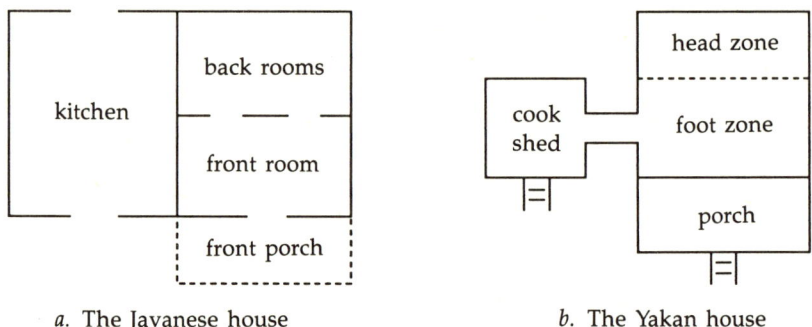

a. The Javanese house   b. The Yakan house

Sources: Jay (1969:46–50); Frake (1975:28).

use of a ladder for access, whereas the Javanese house is built directly on the ground.

Conceptually, however, there is a striking difference between the two cases that goes to the heart of the analysis. Whereas for the Javanese the doorway and the porch outside define the front of the house—the locus of formal social interaction—for the Yakan *there is no front door:* the front (or "head") of the house is the area *farthest* from the porch and entryway, the "blind" wall most clearly "inside" the house: "The head wall, not the entrance wall, defines the 'front' of the house facing 'up-slope' [i.e., towards the midline of the island]. From the perspective of a person inside the house, someone on the porch is 'in back' (*si bukut*). This means that one enters a Yakan house through what is conceptually the back door, there being no entrance in front" (Frake 1975:29).

Yakan domestic social interaction exhibits a clearly layered pattern—but without the dual Javanese regions of "front" and "back" social activity. For the Yakan this layered character of domestic space is the defining framework of interaction: "One can characterize a social encounter between householder and outsider by the degree of penetration of household settings achieved by the outsider, penetration being measured by the number of moves across setting boundaries required to reach a given position" (ibid.). The most formal social interaction takes place in the "head zone"—the area the Javanese consider a private back region; conversely, the porch, which features so prominently in the formal social interaction of Javanese men, is for the Yakan a marginal and informal social arena. Thus, on ritual occasions the Yakan must invite their guests, "move by move," into the innermost part of the house; the Javanese, by contrast, transform the outside space into a formal reception area and reserve the inside space (now including the front room itself) for the private ritual preliminaries (see Wolfowitz [forthcoming]). At night the Yakan home becomes a fully private and nonsocial region; the head zone is transformed into the sleeping area. This transformation may be only one of the necessary shifts between fully informal insider activity and fully formal social interaction, both of which are identified in Yakan terms with the inside region (head zone) of the house.

In their valuation of public and private social spaces, then, the Yakan and Javanese cases present a clearly contrastive set of meanings. The Javanese designate the public and private zones of the house respectively as its front and back, placing definite emphasis on the front room as the focus of social significance. For the Yakan the house is divided not into front and back regions but into a head zone and a foot zone—the private and public areas, respectively. That is, the interior of the house—which for the Javanese is the residual back region—is for the Yakan its head, the locus of ritual as well as formal social activity.

Such a clear case of contrasting perceptions exemplifies, again, what Hymes calls "negative pattern." The social sciences, he observes, commonly arrive at generalizations through a process of "positive patterning"—the accumulation of evidence to yield categories and distinctions. Equally legitimate, however, is the evidence of specifically contrastive pairs of cases, or "negative patterning." The juxtaposition of the Javanese and Yakan cases clearly illustrates both the symbolic significance and the variability of spatial values.

8.4.2 Village Spatial Structure

Domestic space is probably never completely self-contained. In "traditional" cultures, the domestic sphere is defined in relation to (and perhaps in opposition to) a wider social framework, whether of lineage or community organization.

Hall's (1969) proxemic analyses delineate some connections between domestic and community spatial organization. Similar connections are demonstrated by other writers (Geertz and Geertz 1975; Gregor 1977). Rapoport (1960:66-73) relates a desire for privacy in domestic architecture (an "inward" facing house) to the character of the community (whether dispersed or concentrated, emphasizing private or communal life). Without adopting Rapoport's somewhat narrow conception of privacy as relating to attitudes toward sex and to the position of women, we can accept his focus on the physical and social "separation of domains"—of domestic and public life—as the heart of the issue of social space.

8.4.3 The Javanese *Barisan*

The Javanese village plan roughly resembles a grid. A commonly used term for "neighborhood," Jay reports, is *barisan*, literally "line"; the underlying concept is a line of houses oriented in the same direction, fronting onto the street, without any physical barriers either between individual houses or between one such line and the next. Jay (1969:229-30) suggests that this conception denies any residential subgrouping below the level of the village (although such subdivisions do exist).

In this conception, the street itself constitutes a social-spatial focus. Indeed, the simple act of accompanying another person—met by chance—along the street is a mark of shared village membership and a minimal requirement of conventional courtesy. The street in front of the house is treated as part of its social space in that anyone sitting in the front region of the house will exchange greetings with a casual passerby. Moreover, the street serves as a gathering place for young men, who are expected to participate in peer groups rather than domestic groups but cannot afford their elders' style of coffee shop socializing. (Jay 1969:35-36, 200.)

We can schematize this arrangement of houses as forming a line of front rooms oriented toward the street, literally attached to a line of back rooms oriented toward the cooking area and the kitchen garden. Not only the life of the household but also the life of the community itself is patterned by this spatial division. Figure 8.7 illustrates this schematic conception.

If we juxtapose once again the Javanese and the Yakan house plans, a difference of focus again becomes obvious. The Javanese front room is the space opening onto the porch and the street beyond; it faces outward toward the community and toward the locus of communal social life. In contrast, the Yakan head zone is the space farthest from the door, the porch, and the street; it faces not the community but the (conventionally defined) center of the island. Unlike the Javanese house, the Yakan house is defined not by its public face but by an individual, sacred relation to the island itself.

When the house is viewed in its relation to the community and to its surroundings, the force of the spatial dimensions identified above—FRONT/back, outside/INSIDE—becomes fully apparent. The Javanese emphasis on the FRONT/back axis is, very clearly, an outward-facing orientation; the Yakan house embodies an inward orientation, away from community life.

Figure 8.7 The Javanese *barisan* (schematic representation).

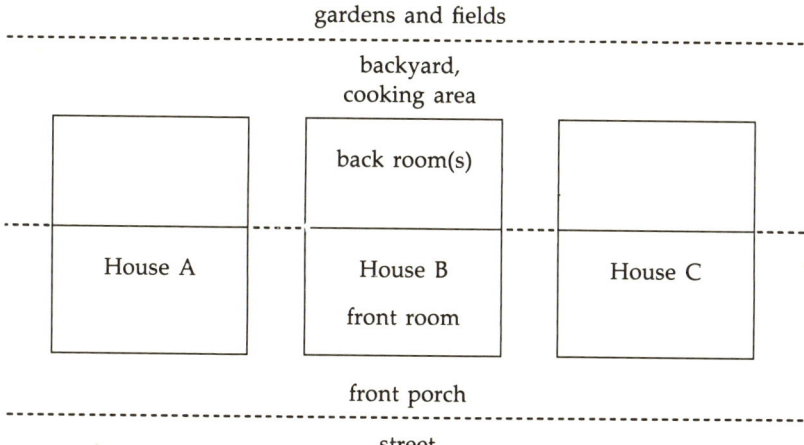

8.4.4 Conceptual Ambiguity in Atoni Domestic Space

The kind of shifting perspective I have presented for Javanese domestic space (fig. 8.6) is strikingly paralleled in the ethnographic literature of another Indonesian cultural group, the Atoni. In his analysis of Atoni domestic space, Cunningham (1964) discerns a fundamental ambiguity in the valuation of interior versus exterior space; spatial values, he finds, are a function of particular social contexts.

Atoni social structure has little in common with the Javanese village. The Atoni (of the island of Timor, the largest island of the chain to the east of Java) are organized into patrilineal descent groups, which play a major role in ritual and social life. There is "a minimum of economic cooperation between households" (Cunningham 1964:204-5). Like the Javanese village, however, the Atoni have no communal houses or other structures; the house itself is the locus of ritual and social activity.

The essential pattern discerned by Cunningham is a complex arrangement of inner and outer space. *Enclosure* is the dominant theme:

> The wall and roof ... mark the unity of a house and the social groups it comprises, and the house, viewed from without, is an almost solid circle and dome with no windows and one small entrance. Viewed from within, however, the house is a constant web of intersecting sections and beams, all symbolized as complementary, appropriate to the Atoni view of any structured social or political grouping in which the premise of inequality is pervasive.

The patterns of concentricity and intersection in the "order" of the house continually concern *what spheres, or groupings, are to be included or excluded.* (Cunningham 1964:232; emphasis added)

Specifically, the *inner* section of the Atoni house is restricted to agnatic kin, and guests are permitted only in the *outer* part of the house. Conceptually, this division is quite different from the Javanese use of the front room to receive guests, even though in both cases there is an outer guest area and an inner region reserved for insiders. In the Atoni house only the inner area has ritual weight—symbolized, for example, in the height of the central house posts—whereas for Javanese the outer, front region has its own ritual value. For the Javanese villager, the inner, back region is not the place of male kin, who in fact practice a degree of mutual avoidance as well as a general avoidance of the domestic back region (H. Geertz 1961:45, 121); rather, it is customarily the place of women and children (but see Errington [1988:37] for a *priyayi* analogue to Atoni usage). Among the Atoni, a wife must be initiated into her husband's descent group ritual before she may enter the inner section of his parents' house (Cunningham 1964:208-9).

Here again is a case of "negative patterning," a contrastive pair of structures that illustrates a conceptual distinction. In this case, the physical structures are not identical, but the functional division of space in both cases presents a definite parallel: the outer and inner regions of the house are assigned, respectively, to outsiders and insiders. The crucial difference concerns the valuative weight assigned to the two regions. The spatial division of the house is most aptly described for the Atoni as an outside/INSIDE boundary, but for the Javanese as a FRONT/back boundary.

However dramatic the Atoni emphasis on the primacy of "inside" space, Cunningham nevertheless reports a competing conception, which is enacted on social occasions: "[The] seating pattern expresses covertly the importance, unity, and closeness of those [the agnates] nearer the 'house center.' However, respect to guests is mandatory, and the hosts must strive to reverse this primacy of the 'house center' by stressing the *nanan* [inner section] as subordinate 'inner' opposed to outer, rather than superordinate 'center' opposed to periphery" (Cunningham 1964:227-28). That is to say, the evident inner/outer spatial division may be given a valuation opposite to the implied superiority of center space. To adapt Goffman's terminology, the inner section of the household may be presented, insofar as possible, as merely a back region rather than an inner sanctum. This redefinition of space is accomplished by means of a politeness code: "The hosts must abase themselves, remain at the left or in bowed positions, and serve others. They claim that their food and gifts are inadequate in quantity and quality. ... The claims about the poor food are particularly important in this reversal, since feeding is pre-eminently an obligation of a superior to an inferior" (Cunningham 1964:228). Etiquette in this case serves as a kind of compensatory ritual, asserting a counterpoint to the dominant message of enclosure, conveyed in seating arrangement and architectural symbolism, as well as to the sociopolitical reality of insider group membership. Cunningham's analysis of Atoni social space thus yields the same sort of kaleidoscopic conception as I describe for Javanese. Depending on context, inner space (and insider relationships) may be given either positive or negative emphasis—in Cunningham's terms, either superordinate or subordinate value.

8.4.5 Public and Private Domains

The ambiguity of domestic social function is perhaps inherent in the situation—common to both Atoni and Javanese—in which the house, in the absence of such communal or kin-group forums as plazas, temples, or men's houses, is virtually the only setting of social interaction. The Javanese village has no central plaza and, often, no public architecture. For the villages described most fully in the literature, there is no community meetinghouse of any kind; the headman's house serves as a meeting place or polling place when the need arises, and the coffee shop provides an informal gathering place for adult males. The village graveyard serves as a stage of community activity at the time of funerals (particularly those of prominent villagers), as well as on the annual day of "cleaning the graves," when households individually visit the graves of their deceased. The village shrine (*punden*) becomes a communal focus at the annual "cleaning the village" observance, but here again households participate as individual units (Jay 1969:323-30, 384). In the *santri* (orthodox Muslim) villages there is, of course, a communal gathering place—the mosque itself—and at least one Suriname-Javanese community used a public recreation hall for such events as shadow-puppet performances, which were hosted by individual households. Javanese tradition nevertheless implicitly assumes that the domestic household provides an adequate setting for the ongoing business of community participation, including casual or formal visiting, public ritual observances, celebrations, and meetings.

Such an assumption contrasts sharply with the social conventions described for some other traditional societies. A detailed account of a contrastively structured village is provided by Gregor (1977), writing about the Brazilian Mehinaku, a horticultural tribal group. For Mehinaku, "women, trash yard [i.e., backyard] men, secular events, and private activities are contrasted with men, good citizens, rituals, and public conduct" (Gregor 1977:54). Except on certain ceremonial occasions, a guest never goes beyond the doorway of the Mehinaku house.[4] One might say that the traditional Javanese emphasis on public participation, together with the lack of public spatial settings, relocates the public/private spatial boundary from the threshold of the house (as in the Mehinaku case) to an interior front/back boundary or partition. But if the front portion of the Javanese house is to a degree preempted for formal male social life, the back region of the house becomes not merely a private setting but a women's domain. On the one hand, the plaza has been internalized to the household structure; on the other hand, the men of the household have, conversely, been more or less excluded from the domestic interior.

It is this wholesale entry of public life into the private domestic household that imposes on participants the necessity to shift perspectives as the occasion requires—to redefine according to social context the function and value of domestic space. On those occasions when the house serves as a setting for formal or public ritual activity, the public/private boundary may be shifted from the front door to the interior, while at the same time, the interior is redefined as merely back region rather than inside. The precisely adaptable system of Javanese speech style is admirably suited to this shifting spatial framework.

8.5 Social Space and Interaction Codes

In the absence of a public social forum, the traditional map of household space is also the map of social interaction in general. The system of speech styles for Javanese speakers in Suriname presents a map of social interaction that essentially duplicates the map of domestic social space. The key semantic dimension may be summarized as "openness" versus "enclosure."

8.5.1 Spatial and Stylistic Maps

The map of Javanese speech style presented in chapter 2 is a three-way model—formal style, respect style, and ordinary style. As a first approximation, this three-way model can be mapped onto the three basic regions of household space (front, inside, and back), as diagramed in figure 8.8. (The underlying spatial model is presented in fig. 8.2.) Formal politeness (polite lexicon, complete syntax, monotone intonation) is associated with front-region interaction. Ordinary style (expressive vocabulary, punctuate syntax, dramatic intonation) is associ-

Domestic Space

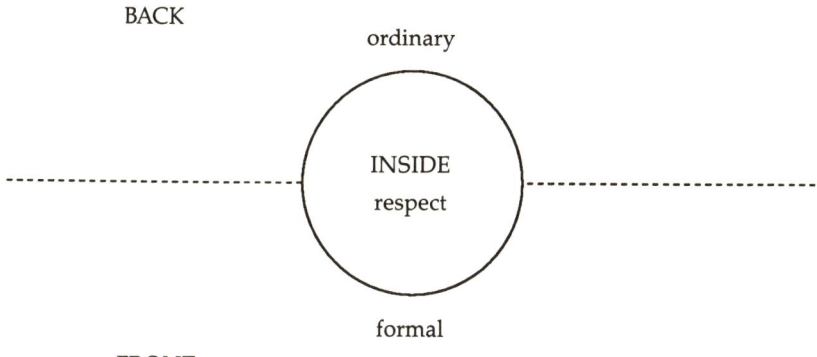

Figure 8.8 A speech style map.

ated with back-region interaction. Respect style (kin-term vocatives, crooning intonation) is associated with the inside region. (This map shows only the *stylized* interaction repertoire; unstylized, or uncritiqued, speech occurs both in the inside region, as familial speech, and in the outside region, as "public" speech.[5])

There is nothing rigid about this association between spatial and stylistic categories; it is certainly not the case that, for example, formal style is used only in front-region settings. The practical value of the stylistic code may well be its flexibility of application: to use formal speech style is to signal to the listener, "this is a front-region interaction"—wherever the interaction is taking place. The association of a particular interaction style with a particular social space is thus not prescriptive but emblematic or even definitive: ordinary style *is* back-region style, even when the participants are sitting on the front porch (as they may well be if no formal activity is going on at the time). Insofar as interpersonal relationships are conceived of as an adjunct of household relationships, the association of speech style with a particular domestic region is the core of the system. To adopt an appropriate interaction style is to take, figuratively speaking, *an appropriate place* in relation to the household of the person addressed. Speech style literally establishes social position—not so much, in this case, on a ladder of status relationships as in a world of front porches and backyards. *Interaction codes may thus be thought of as a kind of portable structuring of social space.* The use of the appropriate style instantly places any acquaintance within the appropriate region of domestic life, so that a young woman meeting a senior aunt in the market will use a style of respectful politeness that conveys an insider relationship. The categories enacted daily in the use of the house as a social arena are projected onto extradomestic interaction in the use of distinct speech styles.

This representation of the workings of the style system implies that it is impossible for the observer to interpret the Javanese use of styles without having some idea of the spatial map of domestic interaction. The argument is very much like the one presented by Radcliffe-Brown ([1940] 1965:90ff.) in his classic analysis of joking relationships: the interpretation of the interaction code (in that case, joking versus avoidance) rests firmly on a map of kinship and affinal relationships. In the Javanese case, where the links of kinship and affinity are by no means as structured as they are in South Africa, the relevant map is not genealogical but spatial. The community, the neighborhood, and what Jay (1969:216ff.) calls the "principle of proximity" are central in structuring social expectations.

8.5.2 Open and Closed Interaction Styles

The Javanese pattern of interaction codes may be partially summed up in terms of "open" and "closed" social space. The front of the Javanese village house is a markedly open arena. Front doors are rarely closed, except in the evening or possibly for midday siesta (S. Kuhns, personal communication). Conversation is expected and even obligatory between porch sitters and passersby. Men in particular are more or less publicly available during the active day, spending leisure moments on the front porch or visiting with friends (Jay 1969:199; H. Geertz 1961:126-27). And in the use of the front room itself there is (in Suriname) a marked tendency for casual visiting to take place not in the interior of the room but in the marginal space between the porch and the front room, the doorway area, which I term the "porch extension" (chap. 9).

The central image identified by C. Geertz (1960:255) for Javanese speech style—the walls of politeness constructed by the speaker—contrasts sharply with the complete absence of walls, gates, or other spatial obstructions in the approach from the street to the house. (This physical openness is regarded by Suriname Javanese as a key distinguishing feature between Javanese and Hindustani homes.) The maintenance of social distance between neighbors is accomplished not by physical boundaries but by the observance of more or less formal interaction norms.

It may be precisely this spatial and conventional emphasis on openness that fosters a compensatory sensitivity to intrusion. Where spatial design offers no firm boundaries for interaction, stylistic norms serve to pattern social life and make it safely predictable. Thus, even though the front door stands open, it is incumbent on visitors who are not insiders to announce themselves in good time with a formulaic *Kula nuwun* ("I ask") and to refrain from crossing the threshold until specifically invited.

There is more, perhaps, to the use of formal speech style than merely the maintenance of safe distance between neighbors. In principle, formal style seems to be identified as a men's language (though by no means rigidly so). Formal speech thus serves as an emblem of men's participation in their own social sphere—public but nevertheless esoteric—and their common avoidance of the domestic sphere. As the language of public interaction in a publicly oriented tradition, *formal speech style is a sign of common membership in the (male) corporate community*. It affirms the participants' mutual respect as joint managers of a delicately structured social equilibirum. The element of social distance expressed in formal style is thus, in its own way, a strongly positive message and not adequately characterized as "negative politeness."

If formal style expresses the involvement of the front region within the larger (male) community, ordinary style expresses the openness of the back region of the house and its involvement within the (female) community. Recall the double line of front rooms and backyards—the *barisan*. The elliptical drama of ordinary style, along with the close-polite exchange of interrogative greetings, communicates that a visitor is "as if" an insider to the household. The two aspects of the Javanese style system are complementary: ordinary style is a gesture of openness that reiterates the absence of spatial boundaries; the use of formal style is the emblem of a more structured involvement that at the same time expresses a compensatory sensitivity to intrusion. (Hymes's observation is relevant here: "the particular [stylistic] trait may be directly expressive, or it may be compensatory"—and there is "no general rule to decide between them in advance" [Hymes 1974:114].)

The discriminations of social closeness and social distance enacted in Javanese style are less interpersonal than they are household-centered. The household has its own social persona, requiring appropriate recognition from other community members in the form of both neighborly involvement and neighborly distance.

NOTES

1. The Javanese community in Suriname is less than a hundred years old. It should not be surprising that the categories of household space as well as

of language style closely resemble those of the relevant areas of Java, even though usage diverges in detail. I have, accordingly, incorporated (with clear identification) material from the literature on the Javanese house.

2. For an account of ritual space see Wolfowitz (forthcoming).

3. Domestic space and the conceptual framework it reflects are topics that appear only sporadically in the ethnographic literature, but there are nevertheless several detailed and suggestive analyses. For other references see Wolfowitz (in press).

4. I am grateful to Kathleen Ryan for bringing this study to my attention.

5. "Public" speech style, following Bernstein ([1958] 1974), is the perfunctory and uncritiqued form of speaking allowable where no social relationship, actual or potential, is assumed to exist. Such a style is observable, for example, in Java from audience members to street performers and in Suriname Javanese to address Creoles who speak a minimal form of market Javanese. If included in the stylistic map, public speech style would constitute a further layer of outsider relationship beyond the formal-polite (front-region) style and the close-polite (back-region) style, but its use is quite marginal.

CHAPTER 9

Functional Adaptation in Suriname-Javanese Households

9.1 INTRODUCTION

Suriname-Javanese houses are substantially modified from the simple house plan presented in the previous chapter. Only in the older homes of first-generation immigrants is the cooking performed entirely outside the house, in a lean-to equipped with a charcoal or gas-cylinder burner. Even very modest houses of more recent construction—whether rural or urban—include an indoor kitchen equipped with a gas-cylinder burner or stove. However small, the kitchens have some seating space and, if possible, a Western-style kitchen table. The kitchen has thus become a setting for informal visiting, particularly but not exclusively for women; it is now fully a part of the social life of the household.

The sleeping space, too, is arranged somewhat differently from the basic Javanese model. Only the oldest houses have a sleeping platform in the front room (such as Jay [1969] describes as typical for rural Java) designed to accommodate overnight guests; visitors may share the sleeping rooms of family members. (Possibly, however, the bedroom of the head of the household remains a private region, not used for extra sleeping accommodation.) Spatially, then, an overnight guest becomes a member of the family. What was clearly a private region in the rural Javanese house—the back or inside region—is in the Suriname-Javanese house rather an informal social area: a place for receiving casual visitors (in the kitchen) and for housing overnight guests (in the sleeping rooms).

The functional distinction between front and back regions has by no means completely disappeared; it emerges most clearly on ceremonial occasions. For a large *slametan*, the front yard and sometimes the side yard as well are converted for the entertainment of guests, with rented tables and folding chairs set out under the shelter of a temporary roof. The back region remains a pragmatic setting, dominated by the women preparing food with the assistance of male kin in certain tasks. In the more traditional *slametan*, only men are seated in front as guests and the boundary between the front and back regions is rigidly observed: one or two young men act as servers, mediating between the back region and the front, and women do not enter the front yard even to serve the food. The entire house, however, now becomes an inside region, and the women of the family may be seen sitting in the front room of the house watching the proceedings from the front door or window.

This functional distinction between front and back space is adapted to a wide variety of architectural structures. Many Suriname houses are elevated over a groundlevel "basement" room; an outside stairway leads from the cement yard up to the house itself, with its elevated porch. For such a house, a *slametan* requires transforming a normally back-region space—the cement yard—into the setting for a front-region celebration by means of rented tables and chairs, decorations, and music.

On nonceremonial occasions, however, the functional boundary between front and back regions virtually disappears in many Suriname-Javanese households. Women participate in front-room visits along with their husbands—in some cases with equal formality of speech style and with no spatial separation such as the side seating area of the Javanese house. Conversely, I have observed men assisting occasionally with such back-region chores as cooking and laundry, and once with marketing as well (however, such participation is subject to comment). Although there are indeed occasions when a front-room visit is restricted to male participation, the women on these occasions are just as likely to occupy the front porch as the backyard for their own socializing. Conversely, women may carry an essentially formal front-region interaction out into the kitchen or backyard when convenient (though I have not seen men do this). When no formal guests are present the entire house becomes a back-region or inside space, to the extent that laundry may be seen hanging out on the front porch.

While Suriname-Javanese interaction is by no means rigid or rule governed, the use of space nevertheless shows a constant awareness of its semantic properties as analyzed in the previous chapter. Some examples of this awareness and of general spatial adaptation follow.

9.2 FUNCTIONAL DISTINCTIONS WITHOUT BOUNDARIES

Three nonarchitectural features of household space illustrate a definite cultural awareness of the semantics of social space. The "porch chair" is a niche within the front room distinctly associated with outsider participation, a front porch substitute. The "kitchen extension" is, conversely, an extension of the back region or kitchen setting into the front room. And the "sleeping platform" arguably has the character of an insider setting within the front room. In each of these cases, the front room is adapted to accommodate functions that according to the ideal schema are inappropriate to it. Such "inappropriate" functions may readily co-occur with other social uses by this device of functional demarcation without physical boundaries—a form of stylistic compartmentalization.

9.2.1 The Porch Chair

In all but the oldest and humblest of Suriname-Javanese homes, the living room (or front room) seating is arranged on the European model. Even in the most minimal wooden dwelling there is usually a set of Western-style furniture consisting at least of a metal-frame, vinyl-covered sofa, a formica-topped coffee table, and perhaps one or two armchairs to match the sofa. (Almost as predictable is some kind of shelving, often a cabinet with glass doors, to display prized or decorative objects.) In wealthier homes, the furniture is of better quality, with wooden rather than metal frames and fabric rather than vinyl coverings. There may also be an older, less comfortable set of furniture, which, instead of being discarded, is arranged at the side of the room to provide a secondary seating area.

Even in homes that are thus amply provided with living room furniture, there is often an extra seat that I call the porch chair. This is not an easy chair but a kitchen chair, straight backed and with a higher seat; it is placed, whether permanently or for the occasion, just inside the front door, which opens out to the front porch or porch area. (The porch may be nothing more than a slight overhang of the roof over the dirt yard, but it has functional reality nevertheless.)

The porch chair serves to bring the social functions of the front porch inside the house itself. Whereas the front room is associated with formal social visits—from distant kin, for example—the front porch is the place best suited to receive those formal visitors who have a purely business connection with the household, who are outsiders to its social and familial functions. For example, in one village household, a long-absent nephew was received rather formally in the front room; a contingent of city politicians, by contrast, met with the head of the household (himself a village official) on the front porch. While there was no strict rule against receiving familial visitors on the front porch, to usher business visitors inside would have established an unusual degree of personal involvement and perhaps suggested an inappropriately private rather than public, or open, character of business.

The porch chair, then, allows a formal visitor to enter the house on being invited while maintaining a posture of noninvolvement—of outsider rather than insider status. Selecting the porch chair signals a brief and businesslike visit.

For example, the treasurer-secretary of the funeral association would pay a brief call at each member's home on the occasion of the death of one of the group. This was purely a business visit, aimed at collecting the stipulated sum that served as burial insurance for members of the group. His visit was never unexpected; the Javanese radio station was prompt in broadcasting death notices. On one occasion, I was sitting idly in the front room of the Paramaribo household along with the grandfather, Ba Pèn, and one or two children. Hearing the approaching motorbike of the funeral society official, Ba Pèn reached over from his seat to brush the sand off the porch chair—in this case, a schoolroom chair—and to set it straight in its position near the front door. When the visitor entered, Ba Pèn was again settled back to receive him with appropriate dignity. The official, without a moment's hesitation, sat with equal dignity in the porch chair, as he clearly had been expected to do. The easy chair across from Ba Pèn remained empty. An American visitor would have expected to be shown to that chair rather than the little straight-backed chair; lacking a direct invitation, the American visitor would probably have remained standing—an impossibility for a Javanese, who would thereby tower arrogantly above the host.

To sit in the porch chair, then, is a gestural statement of separation from the domestic context, in which one's presence might otherwise be felt as an intrusion. It is perhaps the nonverbal equivalent of the English assurance "I won't stay a minute"—a refusal, in advance, of any offer of refreshment and an acknowledgment of other claims on the host's (and the visitor's) time and attention. In this example, the visitor entered as briefly as possible to conclude a definite piece of business, a frequent necessity in a community without telephones. The style of speech was consistently formal, in keeping with the serious subject matter and the official status of the visitor, as well as the absence of a close relationship between the two men. The official visitor sat stiffly, hat in hand (it was the traditional black *pici*, the men's headgear popularized in Indonesia by former President Sukarno), and he took his leave, quite formally, only a few minutes after his entrance.

On another occasion, Ba Pèn created a porch chair when he evidently felt the lack of one. On this occasion, I had accompanied him on a courtesy visit to a friend's home. On the way back we paid a call at another friend's house, the home of a woman who had virtually an honorary daughter-in-law relationship to Ba Pèn. (Ba Pèn and his wife had provided childcare for one of the woman's children for several years; the boy was treated as their grandchild, and his mother —never as close as a foster daughter—seemed to fit into the category of "mother of the grandchild," or daughter-in-law.)

The courtesy visit that had been the primary object of the outing had taken place, predictably, in the main seating area of the host's front room. I therefore unthinkingly allowed myself, when we stopped at the "daughter-in-law's" house, to be ushered to the front-room sofa. This evidently created a problem for Ba Pèn, who had not intended to launch a full-scale social visit. He indicated the front porch instead, but there was only a single chair there. To resolve the dilemma, the hostess's son fetched a straight-backed chair from the kitchen and placed it, as we all waited in suspended animation, toward the middle of the front room and only a few feet from the front door, in effect creating a porch chair. Then, as if to make his reluctance perfectly clear, Ba Pèn picked up the chair and moved it a foot or so closer to the front door. Only then did he sit down, his "daughter-in-law" taking her place in the easy chair opposite me. She and I thus entered, spatially, into a full social visit, while Ba Pèn spatially declared his marginal relationship to the domestic and social context. For whatever reason, Ba Pèn clearly wished to keep this visit within the category of "stopping" (*mampir*) and well short of "entering" (*mlebu*). No doubt he understood that the event would be reported on, and he did not want it to take on undue significance.

9.2.2 The Sleeping Platform

If the porch chair suggests a certain aloofness from the domestic scene, the sleeping platform, though it is situated similarly just inside the front door, creates a different sort of niche expressive not of formality but of a diffident familiarity. The sleeping platform—a wide, wooden bench built onto the wall next to the front door—is not an extension of the front-porch setting but rather an incursion of the back region into the front room.[1] Visitors who are fully insiders (close kin, school-age friends) may lounge comfortably on the sleeping platform as they chat with householders. In the following example, a rare visit by my friend Sita to her maternal "grandparents" (discussed also in sec. 6.2.2), the sleeping platform provided a marginal niche for a nonparticipant alongside a more ceremonial use of the front room.

The background of kin relationships in this case (as in the case of many of the families I met) is a bit complicated. Sita, the twenty-one-year-old foster daughter of the elderly couple who were my hosts in Paramaribo, had been given up in adoption by her mother in infancy. Sita nevertheless retained a place in her natural family, in accordance with Javanese tradition and customary law. The "grandparents" she was visiting on this occasion were an elderly couple in her biological mother's natal village. Though not in fact kin of that family, the old man—as "boat-mate" (*djadji*) of Sita's mother's father and a highly respected ritual expert—stood as grandfather to the entire extended family after the actual grandfather's death.

Sita had recently turned twenty-one. Because the old couple were unable to travel to attend the birthday celebration, it was necessary for Sita to mark the occasion—a transition to adulthood—by visiting them to pay her respects and receive their blessing. I was privileged to accompany Sita on her trip to the village, in part, I assume, because of the felt impropriety of a young woman traveling alone. Our first stop was Sita's mother's house, a quarter of a mile beyond the grandparents' house. After a leisurely visit with Sita's mother, stepfather, and her two younger half-sisters, the stepfather, Hasan, escorted the two of us to the tiny, dilapidated one-room house in which the revered grandparents lived.

Hasan was no stranger to the elderly couple, but neither was he fully part of the family circle, being an affine rather than (for example) a maternal uncle. As an adult male, his participation would have changed the character of the visit to a more formal one. Perhaps it was for these reasons that he chose to remain outside the house instead of accompanying Sita and me into the front room. At first he simply walked up and down in the front yard, as I could see through the open door. Eventually, he sat down on the bench just in front of the door, where a son-in-law was sitting, similarly passing the time while his wife did a few chores in the back of the house. The two men made polite, evidently slightly formal conversation (judging from their gestural and intonational style).

Just before he took his seat on the bench, however, Hasan made a brief appearance in the front room, sitting for only a minute or so on the sleeping platform. I was surprised to note that he did so without a verbal greeting of any kind.[2] It is impossible that he intended any offense by this omission. It must rather be the case that, although in entering the house he became a participant in the social interaction, both the seat he chose and the omission of a greeting identified his position as peripheral, claiming no special attention such as being served tea (which Sita and I had been served). Hasan exchanged no words with the grandfather but instead conversed briefly and informally with the grandmother before returning outside to take his seat on the bench.

My interpretation at the time was that Hasan had not intended to "enter" the house at all (see sec. 8.2.3) but had expected to wait outside until the visit was concluded. The bench, however, was already occupied, and not by a close friend with whom he might have welcomed a chat. He had tired of pacing the yard in the hot sun: it was either enter the house or share the bench. After first choosing the former option he resigned himself to the latter, possibly feeling awkward in the marginal niche he occupied in the front room.

Only now does it occur to me that Hasan might have felt it necessary to "announce" himself, if only to the grandmother, before parking himself on the bench outside the front door. In general, Javanese visiting proceeds by "entering" and then "sitting"; to pace up and down the yard is one thing, but to sit on the porch is perhaps another. Hasan had to make the transition from nonparticipant to marginal participant, and he did so by "entering" as briefly as possible, by way of the sleeping platform. If Hasan had chosen to sit in the porch chair instead of the sleeping platform (and this modest home had both, in addition to the vinyl-covered sofa and easy chair), he would undoubtedly have felt obliged to greet the grandfather and thus become a full participant.

The porch chair provides an outsider niche within the front room, an extension of the front-porch setting; the sleeping platform provides a back-region niche in the front room. These niches are spatial subdivisions, but perhaps it is more useful to think of them as the spatial representations of the stylistic compartmentalization of social interaction. As physical boundaries, these spatial niches are almost negligible. It is as tokens of distinct interactional categories that they have definite significance. Just as the selection of speech style signals the performer's intended category of social participation, the position he or she takes within the spatial setting signals his or her intended role. Normally, the two signals are mutually reinforcing (i.e., redundant). Occasionally, however, the signals may conflict, creating a mixed message.

Hasan's behavior nicely indicates the importance of the spatial and stylistic compartmentalization of social activity in Suriname-Javanese life. Whatever his actual concerns were on that occasion, his full participation would have created a very real difficulty. As an adult male visitor he would have had to conduct a formal visit with the grandfather, not only taking attention away from Sita but in effect taking precedence over her. Sita herself would have become, no doubt, a back-region participant, compartmentalized into virtual invisibility as she chatted on the sidelines with the grandmother. Hasan's apparently determined unobtrusiveness was thus quite necessary to permit the relatively informal and affectionate reunion between Sita and her grandparents. (My own presence posed less of a problem simply because I was identified as Sita's girlfriend and a member, however temporarily, of her household: as the former, a back-region participant, and as the latter, already an insider where she was concerned. No adjustment of speech style was made to accommodate my marginal role, except in specifically offering me a glass of tea in polite style.) In choosing the sleeping platform as his momentary perch, then, Hasan made clear his refusal to transform the ongoing inside interaction into a front-region one. His failure to address even a greeting to the grandfather may be interpreted along the same lines. In this case, a spatial message was allowed to take the place of the normally expected verbal greeting.

9.2.3 The Kitchen Extension: Sharing Rice Meals

In addition to the porch chair and the sleeping platform, the front room has another fairly consistent spatial subdivision I call the kitchen extension. This is the area at the margin of the front room adjacent to the kitchen or rear passageway, not marked by any sort of furniture but used in predictable ways to demarcate front-room activities, as in the following example.

Ba Pèn and Ba Nom, my hosts in Paramaribo, were frequently visited by others of their generation, particularly Ba Nom's women friends. These visits often took place on a Saturday or Sunday in the late morning, and the midday meal would be eaten with the guest(s).

Sharing a meal is not the same social activity in a Javanese household as in Western cultures, where it serves as the central event or even the purpose of a visit and entails rituals of its own (setting places, offering seats, passing dishes, and so forth). Jay makes this clear in his discussion of mealtimes:

> No space is set aside specifically for dining, since among the villagers family members do not join for daily meals. Each returns to the family hearth for food, especially in the middle of the day when the main meal is served, but comes in his own time, collects a plate of food, and retires alone to eat it. The wife usually eats as she has time in the kitchen; the children, each by himself, also eat in the kitchen or in a corner of the front room, while the father usually eats alone at the table in the front room (though I have often seen men also eating off to one side in the kitchen). Eating is felt to be a highly personal act requiring privacy. At a dinner party, where people do eat together, each guest being served ex-

cuses himself to those on either side of him and, turning to one side, eats straight through as though temporarily absent from the company. (Jay 1969:50)

In Suriname the Western approach to mealtime is quite familiar to the Javanese, and this emphasis on privacy is attenuated. Nevertheless, the elderly couple in my Paramaribo household did follow the Javanese pattern, while the foster daughters and their friends followed the Western pattern. The two girls had their supper sitting together at the kitchen table, where I was invariably instructed to join them; the grandfather occasionally ate at the kitchen table after they had finished their meal or carried his dinner to his sleeping room. Possibly as a response to my presence, he almost never ate a meal in the front room but preferred to eat so inconspicuously that I was not aware he had taken a meal until he brought the empty plate out to the backyard. The grandmother ate very little in general and took her supper as it occurred to her in the course of her other kitchen activities. Her teeth were not good, and her chief staples seemed to be the glasses of dark tea and hand-rolled twists of tobacco favored by her generation.

It is of interest in this context to see how the presence of mealtime guests was accommodated. This depended crucially on the type of meal being served. On Sunday, Ba Nom frequently prepared a special dish as a variation from the usual rice, fish, and vegetable. Such dishes included the substantial chicken soup known as *saoto;* the sautéed Chinese-noodle dish, *bamie;* and a sweet stew of cassava, plantains, and coconut milk. Any of these special dishes could serve as a snack or party food, and there was no embarrassment in eating such foods among company, sitting in the front room as if no food were involved and chatting casually or commenting about the food. When Ba Nom served one of these dishes to her Sunday visitors, no one—not even Ba Pèn—moved from his or her chair, except briefly to help with the serving.

The sense of mealtime privacy made itself felt only in the case of "eating rice." The ordinary meals of a Javanese household consist largely of rice, accompanied by vegetable, fish, and sometimes poultry side dishes and a hot pepper sauce. When the food offered to guests was this sort of home-style rice meal rather than the special snack foods described above, eating became a compartmentalized activity rather than an integral part of the social visit. Whereas a snack food would be served in individual portions to each guest where he or she sat, a rice meal was invariably "self-service." At the grandmother's invitation, the visitors and family members would go one by one to the kitchen to help themselves from the pots and dishes on the stove and then find a spot to sit and eat. I never noticed anyone return to his or her original seat to eat a plate of rice.

Serving a rice meal thus dispersed the social gathering instead of, as in the Western model, bringing people together for a shared activity. To be more precise, the serving of rice seemed to divide the social gathering into male and female groups. This, however, is a very tentative observation: all the mealtime visitors to this household happened to be women; the grandfather—the only male present—would retire from view to eat the rice meal alone. Whether he would have gathered with other male guests or family members is impossible for me to say. The women, however, including the grandmother, did form a new sort of group. Instead of returning to their chairs they would squat on the floor holding their bowls, in traditional Javanese style. They sat closer together than they did in their chairs, not in the main seating area of the front room but on its margin.

Like other social matters, mealtime allowed considerable latitude for individual style. One of the women visitors always sat in a chair, even to eat a rice meal, but on these occasions she would choose the chair closest to where the other women were sitting on the floor. On one occasion, Ba Nom herself sat in a chair to eat a rice meal, but she squatted on it in the traditional floor-sitting posture. If there was a rule in operation, it seemed to be simply that eating rice was not properly a front-room function. Either the eaters located themselves apart from the main sitting area, or else the dispersal of the company perhaps redefined the front room as an informal setting. (Even in an informal setting, however, male and female family members in many households would avoid eating together.)

Spatially, there were two marginal areas in the front room that the women normally used in regrouping to share a rice meal. If they were the only occupants of the front room, they would sit on the floor in the front doorway (which opened onto the front porch); the room itself became a back region in that case, and the front door marked the boundary with the front region (the front porch). More often, however, the women arranged themselves next to the wall leading back to the kitchen. (The kitchen itself was too small to accommodate floor sitting.) Again, the women grouped themselves on the margin between the front and back regions, but now the front room retained its proper character, and the door to the kitchen marked the boundary between back and front regions.

This marginal area along the side wall in effect provided a back-region niche within the front room. I observed a similar use of space in other households: at a gathering such as the *jagongan* before a funeral, any passageway between the kitchen and the front room would be filled with women sitting on the floor. I use the term "kitchen extension" to refer to such a space, whether bounded (as a hallway) or undefined, as in the Paramaribo household just described. Like the porch chair, the kitchen extension shows how the definition of space may be adapted to accommodate more than one social activity at a given time.

Floor sitting may indeed be an integral part of this social-spatial niche, so that in mapping the social uses of the house one must perhaps specify the *level* as part of the floor plan. For example, the women grouping themselves on the floor just inside the front door are in fact occupying the same spatial area as the porch chair, but by sitting on the floor they are defining it quite differently. The official visitor would not use the space this way: to sit on the floor would contradict his self-definition as an outsider and a formal visitor.[3] By sitting on the floor and by directing their focus outside, the women identify themselves as insiders occupying a back-region space rather than as outsiders briefly visiting in the front region.

9.2.4 Back Door and Front Door

The clear sense of a semantic dimension to household space is illustrated also in the different associations attached to the front and back doors. Certainly, entering another person's home through the back door suggests definite insider relationship. More interesting, however, is the following evidence of differential use of an individual's own front and back doors.

In the Paramaribo household, the grandmother, Ba Nom, took charge of all food purchases. She seemed to regard her market expeditions as a kind of public appearance: she would wear her best-quality *jarik* and *kebaya* (traditional wrapped skirt and long-sleeved blouse), and she always went to those market stands where she felt some social relationship to the seller. For her, these trips had the character of revisiting old haunts, since she had, some years before, held a stall in the marketplace.

In setting out for the market, Ba Nom always left by the front door, dressed in her best and carrying empty shopping bags. On her return, however, laden with purchases, she always took the slightly longer route to the *back* door. On other errands, by contrast, she would leave and return by the same door, usually the front door, whether it was to visit a neighbor or to take a child to school. It seemed to be the function of handling food supplies that suggested the propriety of the back door entrance. There was no sense of a corresponding boundary within the house, between the front and back regions, that could not be transgressed by food preparation functions: peanuts might be shelled in the front room, or a friend might enter by the front door bringing a bag of soup greens. It nevertheless seemed clear that Ba Nom distinguished semantically between front door and back door functions, even in the absence of any social interaction. (I am assuming that my presence, either working in the house or helping with the marketing, was not sufficient, by this time, to constitute a special social situation.) Marketing in its social aspect—setting out in one's good clothes—was a *front door* function; in its pragmatic aspect—returning with food items—it was a *back door* function.

9.2.5 Summary

The front region of the house presents an assortment of niches, allowing far more flexibility of social interaction than the ideal schema suggests. The porch—which may be marked only by a slight overhang of the roof above the dirt yard—may function as a formal social setting for some sorts of interaction. Within the front room itself, the main seating area is supplemented by at least two marginal seating areas. The area just inside the front door may be called the porch extension; it accommodates marginal floor sitting and is also the niche for the straight-backed porch chair, which provides a temporary seat for a formal visitor who intends only a brief visit. There may be also, or instead, a simple wooden sleeping platform built against the front wall that provides seating for informal guests who thereby "make themselves at home" rather than enter as guests to be entertained. Figure 9.1 diagrams the previously described subdivisions for the house in which I stayed in Paramaribo.

9.3 Functional Flexibility

The spatial subdivisions described in the preceding section are evidence of a generally pronounced awareness of spatial semantics. Although none of these subdivisions is marked by a physical barrier, each is more or less clearly demarcated in terms of function.

It would be inaccurate, however, to infer from these observations a rigid or invariant set of rules governing the use of space, even given the complex subdivision. Personal styles, even among the older generation of Suriname Javanese, vary dramatically. Moreover, a particular space may be adapted almost instantaneously from one social use to a very different one. Just as striking as the evidence of spatial awareness

Figure 9.1 Paramaribo house floor plan (not to scale).

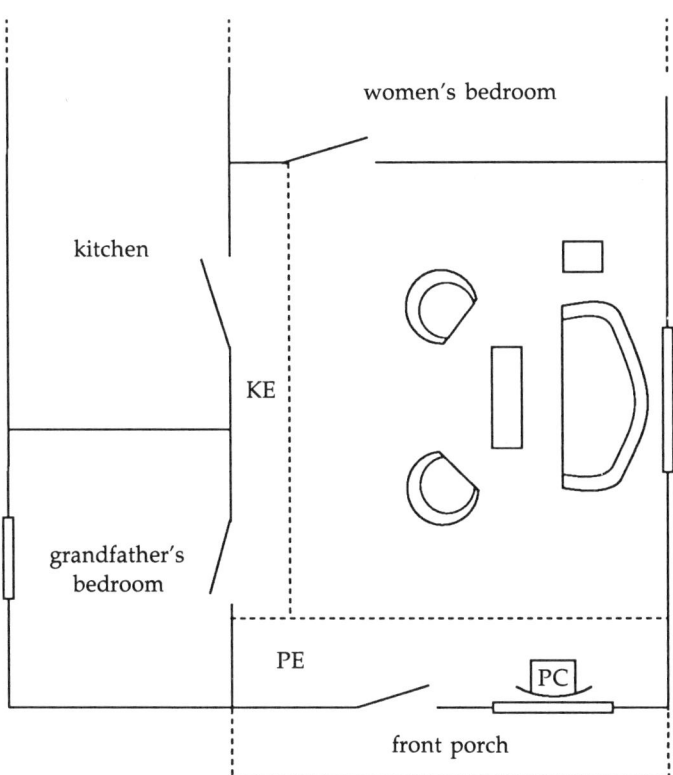

KE = kitchen extension
PE = porch extension
PC = porch chair

on the part of the Suriname Javanese is their ability and willingness to adapt to changing social situations.

9.3.1 Adaptability

When only insiders are present, the domestic life of the household extends indiscriminately throughout the avilable space. There is nothing separate or sacred about the front room or its furnishings, which become the vehicles of children's games or napping places for their elders. At any moment, however, a visitor may announce himself or herself with a completely formal social purpose—a formal invitation to a *slametan,* a ritual presentation of cooked food, or the collection of dues for the funeral society or contributions for the mosque construction project. At the moment of the guest's appearance, the domestic space is reoriented to present its properly public aspect. The front room becomes more formal, as children and women retreat to its margins or to the back region. The presiding househead rearranges his posture or changes his seat to receive his visitor. The visitor may stay only a few moments, but for the duration of the visit the space has a completely changed character.

As seen in the example of Sita's visit to her maternal "grandparents," the front room can also become another kind of social setting—the setting of an informal and yet ceremonial insider visit. Sita's visit to her grandparents did indeed have a ritual overtone, though no ritual invocation was uttered; it was perhaps a variant of the parental blessing that is the invariable private prelude to the public life-cycle celebrations (circumcision, marriage). In this case, the insider interaction was not to be transformed by the entrance of an outside party, as Hasan's brief appearance made clear. Rather, the front room was allowed to retain its inside character, and the almost nonexistent front porch accommodated the necessarily formal outsider interaction. In other circumstances the spaces may be differently defined: the front room may be the setting of a formal male visit, while the front porch is used for informal visiting by the women. In this case, the front porch is absorbed into the general category of outside space, associated more closely with the surrounding yard than with the front of the house. This functional flexibility illustrates the kaleidoscopic nature of the participants' model of domestic space: either the inside/outside dimension or the front/back dimension can have primary relevance on any given occasion or for any particular spatial division.

9.3.2 Personal Styles

As noted above, one of the women visitors to the Paramaribo household—Ba Siji—never sat on the floor with the other women. Even she, however, would make some gestural acknowledgment of the transformed social setting entailed in floor sitting. On one occasion, as Ba Nom and two other women visitors sat and talked in the front doorway, Ba Siji participated in the conversation from her nearby easy chair by turning her entire body toward the conversation, though the chair itself remained facing the center of the room. Another of the regular women visitors, Ba Loro, presented a dramatically contrasting style. She, too, sometimes conveyed a sense of distance from the ongoing social interaction, but at the expense of her own dignity. On one occasion, after helping the grandmother serve a meal of *saoto* (soup), she ate her own portion alone at the kitchen table—that is, in the back region rather than the front. If it had been a rice meal, this might have been a matter of eating privately; but to eat a nonrice meal alone suggested rather the position of a child or servant, one not fully part of the front-region proceedings. On another occasion, after a rice meal, Ba Loro fetched the broom and began to sweep the porch and the doorway area—the act of a young woman visitor or household insider rather than an elderly guest. Again, Ba Loro was the only visitor I observed who would enter the house without announcement and simply wait, squatting on the floor near the front door until the grandmother or grandfather took note of her presence. Her demeanor in these instances resembled that of a household dependent, an invisible insider; indeed, she was regarded by the grandmother as a consistent "asker of favors," including monetary assistance. (Entering and squatting may also have signaled that a favor was going to be asked.) Her linguistic style also contrasted sharply with that of Ba Siji, indicating a difference of social origins and education: whereas Ba Siji almost invariably used some degree of polite vocabulary (madya), Ba Loro consistently used familiar style (ngoko), even when others present were speaking more formally. Ba Loro did on occasion use the porch chair, when she was the only visitor present, but never adopted the formal style of interaction that other porch chair visitors used. For her, the porch chair seemed to serve as a marginal niche in the front room that was more comfortable than the floor.

9.4 ARCHITECTURAL ADAPTATION: THE NARDI HOUSE

The examples cited so far in this chapter illustrate the complex use of severely limited household space. I was fortunate to spend some time also in a far larger house, which had been built by the househead himself, a carpenter. This house was located in a village—almost a "bedroom suburb"—across the river from Paramaribo and about ten miles down the highway. The family—whom I will call the Nardis—had an extensive kin network on both the husband's and wife's sides. Pak Nardi, the husband and househead, was a prominent participant in the local conservative mosque and served as assistant headman of the village. The household was not large: the couple's only son was attending medical school in the Netherlands, and only their nine-year-old foster daughter, Rini, lived in the house with them. But the couple's community and business activities—not only his construction business but also her roadside food stand, which stood in front of the house—made good use of the substantial domestic space they had constructed.

The house was set only fifteen or twenty yards from the major east-west highway, which connects Paramaribo with the capitals of neighboring French Guiana and Guyana and with Venezuela beyond. Houses in this area were widely separated; it was about as far to the nearest neighbor on the north side of the street as it was across the highway to the neighbor on the south. At the edge of the road, in front of the house, was the small wooden *warung*, the produce and snacks stand Bu Nardi maintained.[4]

9.4.1 Floor Plan

The house space itself began with a fenced-in, raised concrete porch extending across the front and partway around the west side of the house (see fig. 9.2). The front porch—(*a*) on the diagram—was used for both formal and informal visiting. The side porch (*b*) served as a play area for children when no formal visit was in progress.

The front door led directly from the front porch into the Western-style living room. The living room was large enough to contain both a formally arranged seating area (*c*) and a secondary seating area (*d*) just inside the front door. This second seating area apparently served some of the purposes of the porch chair as well as occasionally substituting for the kitchen extension.

At the rear of the living room were doors to the two bedrooms (*e*) occupied by the family. A third bedroom (*f*), on the front (southeast) corner of the house, was used as a guest room and workroom. This room opened not onto the living room but onto a small parlor/storeroom (*g*) off the living room.

This connecting room (*g*) had a somewhat indeterminate character but served several important functions. It led out to a kitchen addition that had recently been built at the back of the house and thus mediated, so to speak, between front and back regions: to go from the living room to the kitchen or backyard one had to pass through the parlor. The parlor provided informal seating space—two easy chairs—and housed Bu Nardi's sewing machine. Before the addition of the modern kitchen, this room had been used also for food storage, the actual food preparation being performed outside in the backyard. This room served as the inside space for the ritual food apportioning before the *slametan*, an important women's activity (see Wolfowitz [forthcoming]). And on occasion, the connecting parlor became a women's front room; for example, on my second visit I was received in this parlor by Bu Nardi and a woman neighbor.

Figure 9.2 Nardi house floor plan (not to scale).

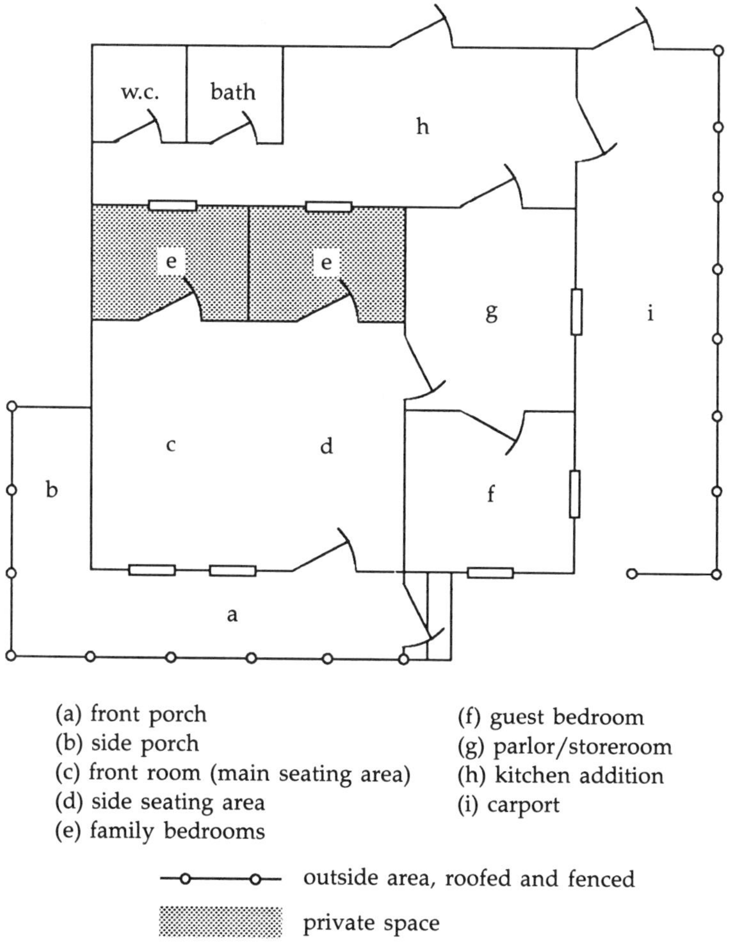

(a) front porch
(b) side porch
(c) front room (main seating area)
(d) side seating area
(e) family bedrooms
(f) guest bedroom
(g) parlor/storeroom
(h) kitchen addition
(i) carport

—o——o— outside area, roofed and fenced

▓▓▓▓▓ private space

Along the entire width of the house, in back, was the kitchen addition (*h*). The addition included not only the kitchen, with a table and two chairs, but also a toilet and a bathing room. (The water supply for all three came from rainwater storage barrels, elaborately channeled from roof to faucets.) The kitchen table was used for some meals: Rini and her father ate their breakfasts there together; Pak Nardi ate his lunch there when he was at home; and they both ate supper there, though rarely together. Bu Nardi never ate a meal sitting at the kitchen table.

Whether she ate with her family or later by herself, she always pulled a chair up to the kitchen counter instead of sitting at the table.

The kitchen table and the counter were relatively recent innovations, and I have no very clear idea how meals had been handled before the addition took shape.[5] Evidently, the space at the side of the house—now the carport—had been used far more extensively than it was at present. Pak Nardi still sometimes had a meal at the small desk that stood there, and Rini or her mother might eat a meal sitting on one of the benches against the carport walls. Guests who were insiders might be served a rice meal, which they either ate at the kitchen table or carried out to the carport.

Behind the kitchen addition was the backyard, populated by chickens, a turkey, and an obstreperous goose. A few yards in back was the latrine and an outdoor bathing enclosure, which were still much in use at the time of my visit. A laundry tub and a dish-washing tub were located here as well, supplied with water from the rain barrels.

The carport itself (*i*), on the east side of the house, was reached through the side door out of the kitchen addition and was fenced and gated against the poultry. Eventually it housed a secondhand car, which still left ample room for the benches, desk and chair, and wash lines. The carport provided informal visiting space for such back-region functions as buying and selling, picking up and delivering produce, or negotiating an order for construction work. The kitchen served similar informal functions in cases where there was a personal relationship between Bu Nardi and the visitor.

The architectural modifications of the Nardi house followed an essentially Western pattern. The large living room and the porch were specifically social settings, whereas the rest of the space was designed to serve rather utilitarian purposes. What had once been a large surrounding yard had been given over to pragmatic functions: domestic fowl had the run of the backyard, which was considerably diminished by the addition of kitchen and carport. The comfortable front porch—furnished with four cushioned wicker armchairs and a small table—was the only architectural feature that suggested a specifically Javanese social context, the formal front-porch visit.

It seems likely nevertheless that an important consideration behind the architectural layout was precisely the flexibility of spatial functioning that characterizes Javanese domestic life. Construction of kitchen and carport had apparently been planned for completion in time for the long-awaited visit of the Nardis' son and his fiancee, to take place on their vacation from school in the Netherlands, and the culmination of that visit would be the large *slametan* marking the couple's departure.

The adaptation of household space to host the *slametan* had certainly been envisioned in undertaking the construction of the two Western-style additions.

The carport became the setting of the *slametan* ritual itself. It was larger than the front porch and already roofed; indeed, its proportions were more suited to hosting a *slametan* than to housing a car, which when it arrived took up scarcely a quarter of the space. The backyard was reclaimed from those chickens that survived the wholesale "cutting" required by the feast, and cooking fires were constructed there to handle the vast quantities of rice, chicken, and fried snacks to be prepared. The kitchen itself served merely as a staging area and command headquarters.

This architectural expansion of the Nardi household space—by no means atypical of Suriname-Javanese villagers—had definite consequences for the use of domestic space in everyday social interaction. As the following section suggests, these additions circumvented the rigidities of the ideal Javanese model without violating or ignoring the traditional logic. The Nardis themselves, indeed, were more old-fashioned in their interactional styles than were most of the Suriname Javanese I knew; Pak Nardi was generally regarded as a model of traditional formality. These innovative spaces allowed them to accommodate to modern social requirements without dramatically altering their own gestural repertoires.

9.4.2 Analysis: The Suriname Context

The ideal model of the Javanese house, discussed in the previous chapter, is oriented around a simple front/back division that subsumes three functional distinctions: male/female, social/pragmatic, formal/informal. In the Suriname context both the spatial division and the associated functional distinctions are substantially modified. The male/female distinction in particular receives relatively little emphasis, except on ritual occasions, and in place of the front/back division, the most salient spatial dimension seems to be the separation of *inside* and *outside* regions.

The distinction between insider and outsider participation underlies most of the adaptations described in this chapter: the porch chair, the sleeping platform, and the Nardis' kitchen addition and carport. The layered character of domestic space, suggested in the preceding chapter, here has physical as well as verbal reality. To sit on the porch is a first-stage entrance; to occupy the porch chair is a second stage; to occupy the main sofa is a third stage; and to eat a rice meal is an important fourth stage, marked by a physical change of location. For the Nardis, the addition of kitchen and carport provided a useful intermediate region—a buffer zone, so to speak—between outside and inside.

The Nardi house clearly provided far more interior space for social interaction than does the minimal rural Javanese dwelling. The only strictly private regions were the two family bedrooms. The parlor/storeroom served on occasion as a second front room specifically for women visitors; at other times, it was a completely informal insider setting. The kitchen, as in most modern Suriname houses, provided informal visiting space, occasionally for men but more often for women who were insiders or who had pragmatic business to transact. The kitchen of this modern Suriname house circumvented the rigidities of the ideal Javanese spatial schema by providing a setting that was part of the back region but nevertheless inside the house and that, unlike the sleeping rooms, was available for social interaction.

The carport most dramatically blurred the front/back division of domestic social space. In everyday use the carport served as a setting for casual socializing for both men and women, sometimes together.[6] Whereas for women the carport was simply a backyard equivalent, for men it constituted a substantial innovation as an alternative to the front porch. Passersby, perhaps waiting for the bus or the rice-truck delivery, might sit on a bench in the carport without entering into the Nardis' domestic space and even without any social interaction or acknowledgment. For most visitors, the carport was a completely marginal, outside region with none of the insider connotations of the kitchen and backyard. This was a more public setting than the traditional Javanese house affords—analogous, perhaps, to the verandah of the larger houses of rural India (cf. Srinivas 1976 and see sec. 9.5.2).

As in any sign system, the addition of an extra signal or option alters the character of existing signs or options. The availability of the carport as a male social context probably gave a more marked character to the act of entering the front porch. The half-wall and gate enclosing the Nardis' front porch and the two or three steps that led up to it provided a corresponding physical demarcation unusual in more traditional Javanese homes. In essence, the porch took on a more clearly inside character, in contrast to the carport.

The male/female distinction in social participation still existed. Bu Nardi did not participate in formal male gatherings, except to serve refreshments; Pak Nardi only rarely participated in the kitchen visits with casual outsider visitors and never participated in parlor visits. In spatial terms, the back region was perhaps a more exclusively female domain than the front region was a male domain—a difference that may be true also of rural Javanese homes. The front porch was used as much for women's visits as for men's, whereas the parlor was used strictly for women's visits.

The front room, too, was affected by the innovation. Entering onto the front porch took on some of the meaning of being received into the house itself; the porch was used for a range of social visits, including those by kinsmen who were not on insider footing. Accordingly, entering the front room indicated some degree of insider status, some private relation to the household. The Nardis' son and his fiancee were received there, along with an attendant crowd of close kin; in his absence, one of his close friends was entertained there. Official visitors, however, convened on the front porch. I suggest that the front room for the Nardis was less a male-oriented, formal social setting than a family-oriented, informal region. The addition of the carport on the one hand provided a neutral outside region (neither front nor back) and on the other hand enhanced the inside character of both the porch and the front room.

The two architectural adaptations just described for the Nardi household, the indoor kitchen and the carport, are standard features of recently built, larger houses in Suriname. As in this case, the carport becomes the setting for any large social gathering, such as a *slametan*. Many houses are built on stilts, so to speak: pillars and a cinderblock utility room on ground level support the main structure of the house. In this case, the concrete carport extends beneath the house itself, and the front/back distinction completely disappears with respect to outside yard space.

9.5 THE COMMUNITY CONTEXT AND INTERACTION STYLES

It is not merely the design of houses but also the character of the community that shapes social interaction. The statement of community integration expressed so clearly in the "line" of houses in rural Java is almost completely absent from the layered space of the Suriname house. Fences and gates are still very rare, in marked contrast to the houses of other Surinamers, including those of Hindustani families, but there is no longer the implicit assumption that the community consists chiefly of two categories of people—men and women—each integrated into a more or less homogeneous social world. More prominently reflected in domestic architecture are, rather, the alternative categories of insiders and outsiders. To put it another way, the statement of the Javanese neighborhood line (*barisan*) is, as Jay points out, the absence of divisions between households and even between neighborhoods; the term "insider" thus refers ideally only to the entire village community and its membership rather than to the privileged associates of the individual family dwelling. In the Suriname context, contrastingly, each household defines its own circle of insiders.

9.5.1 Corporate versus Network Organization

The distinction is, at bottom, the difference between a corporate conception of community and a network conception. In the rural Javanese setting, male social interaction is perceived as defined principally by the boundaries of community membership. Male social life, particularly as it utilizes domestic space, carries the full weight of household representation in the community of households. The stylistic emphasis on proper distance, as opposed to positive interpersonal involvement, reflects such a conception. The Suriname context, on the other hand, is closer to a Western social model of social integration, defined not by corporate membership of individuals or households but rather by individual- or household-centered networks of graduated social involvement. (It makes no difference here whether such a network is based on relations of kinship, neighborship, or other forms of social involvement.) *Stylistically, this network pattern places greater emphasis on gestures of positive involvement than on those of polite distance.* The maintenance of proper social distance is no longer the central motif of male social life but rather provides the background against which the gestures of positive, insider involvement take on their significance.

9.5.2 Class versus Ethnic Awareness

Another aspect of Suriname community organization also has an effect on the stylistic sign system. In Java, the rural community occupies a position that is defined in contrast to urban Javanese society, with its traditional aristocratic culture. The gestures of formality that serve to maintain proper social distance among the male village community are, realistically enough, viewed as the humble country version of the more refined formal styles of urban politesse. In Suriname, however, the elevated urban model is absent from the scene—except insofar as it is preserved in an occasional Javanese recording and in written texts of ritual invocations; the Suriname-Javanese community, moreover, defines itself in immediate contrast not to a Javanese hierarchy but rather to a collection of other ethnicities. Whatever their position on the ladder of socioeconomic success, in their interethnic dealings, the Suriname Javanese—particularly the older generation—maintain a sense of a superior cultural tradition. Only the occasional visitor from Indonesia and the few remaining Dutch nationals are perceived as unquestionably superior in culture and social standing.

This radical alteration of cultural context has its effects on the style system. In the absence of any local model of refined formal style, current formal usage appears to exhibit substantial drift from the Javanese norm (although directly comparable data from rural Javanese districts are lacking).[7] But if a highly valued and accessible model of correct usage is missing, there is instead an enhanced sense of the cultural value of the community's own speech forms. Not only the codes of formal politeness but indeed all of Javanese speech-style repertoire become an emblem of ethnic membership and, possibly, a hallmark of culturally "superior" identity.

A gathering of non-Javanese officials at the Nardis'—possibly having some bearing on the local construction business, though this is only conjecture—provided an illustration of the cultural gulf between Javanese and other ethnic groups, in this case, Creole. The gathering presumably had some official purpose, but it was the only such meeting I observed to take place in the carport rather than on the front porch. The meeting was unbusinesslike in the extreme: in marked contrast to the formal restraint of male Javanese interaction, the style was casual and loud; in place of the customary round of tea or soft drinks, liquor was made available in self-service fashion. Pak Nardi drank nothing and stayed only as long as the business required, leaving his visitors to entertain themselves long after he had departed the scene. Bu Nardi made no gesture of participation, but commented to me that these were people who don't work but like to "play" all day (*dolan*, "play, visit"). In a word, these were ethnic outsiders.

The carport in this instance (and several others) was not only a neutral male/female and formal/informal space, but was also a conveniently *outside* space, more removed from the house even than the front porch. As such it could mediate, when necessary, between the Javanese community and the surrounding cultures. The use of the outsiders' language, Sranang, stylistically expressed the sense of social distance without formality. The simple social distance evidenced in the carport setting, the use of Sranang, and the early departure of the host are a far cry from the kind of formal social distance so scrupulously maintained within the Javanese male community.

The interethnic context provides a countervailing influence against the tendency in the network community setting to devalue the forms of social distance and emphasize the forms of closeness. That is, the necessary interaction with non-Javanese outsiders establishes an alternative language of simple distance, Sranang, which is indeed used among Javanese speakers in a variety of settings. Formal Javanese speech style retains, to some extent, its function of signaling shared community membership, even in the absence of the strong corporate village.

Nevertheless, the overall tendency in Suriname-Javanese usage is probably a shift in emphasis away from the front/back constellation of social distinctions, with its focus on formal male social interaction, and toward the inside/outside perspective, with its emphasis on the kinship network centering on the household. The close-polite forms of speech style, expressive both of respect and connectedness, begin to represent the dominant, positively valued stylistic alternative for men as well as for women. In Brown and Gilman's terms, the solidarity semantic begins to dominate stylistic choices.

NOTES

1. In Suriname, only the oldest frame houses have such a sleeping platform. Jay (1969:50) reports it as a customary feature of rural Javanese homes, used to accommodate overnight guests—there, built of bamboo.

2. Presumably, the form *"Kula nuwun"* would have marked his entrance too obtrusively, claiming social recognition from the househead (the grandfather). The domestic greeting formulas would have been too familiar. I would have expected him to use the everyday greeting *"Wilujeng"* (the krama form of *"Slamet"*).

3. In ritual contexts, floor sitting has a completely different meaning and is fully part of the formal ceremonial.

4. *Pak* and *Bu* are informal titles, abbreviated forms, respectively, of *bapak* ("father") and *ibu* ("mother").

5. Bu Nardi had rather a quelling manner in dealing with questions generally, responding with either a penetrating gaze that suggested some hidden motive behind the question or else an expression of frank amazement at the lack of common sense it betrayed. I felt that our relationship might have been easier if my topic of interest had been an area in which expertise was more commonly recognized, so that my questions could have been more readily accepted as those of a novice seeking instruction. (See the discussion of interrogative usage in chap. 4.) There was no question of my conversing with Pak Nardi in a casual fashion, particularly about domestic or personal arrangements; our relationship was thoroughly distant and formal.

6. In many cases, especially between men, carport interaction has a stiffly formal character, expressive of the distance between outsiders. This distant-polite interaction, while not informal, is casual in the sense of having no specific purpose—not even that of socializing, since it is completely incidental to more pragmatic objectives, such as boarding a bus.

7. In some ways, the Suriname speech style is probably more conservative

than that heard in Java, where education in both Indonesian and Javanese have had substantial effects on rural usage. In the semirural area studied by Bax (1974), the younger generation were better versed in the forms of high Javanese than were their elders.

CHAPTER 10

Stylization and Social Context

10.1 SURINAME-JAVANESE SPEECH STYLES

The picture of Suriname-Javanese speech style presented here differs in several ways from other accounts of Javanese. The focus here is largely on the stylistic expression not of social distance but of social closeness (or connectedness). Close-polite stylistic elements include not only the distinctive characteristics of ordinary speech style and the stereotypic formulas of domestic politeness but also, importantly, the special category of respect politeness.

Respect style must be regarded as a style of pure deference, without any implied element of social distance. For Suriname-Javanese speakers (and perhaps for non-elite Javanese as well), this close but asymmetrical relationship is encoded using prosodic elements alone, without the use of formal lexicon. (Respect style that employs formal lexical elements may be viewed as a mixed style, formal-respect.) The overall picture is summed up in the basic three-way model of *ordinary, formal,* and *respect* styles. These three basic styles cannot be assigned a uniform ranking; there is no sense in which formal style is "more polite" than respect style, although it is indeed more distant.

Each of the three styles has its own, correspondingly contrastive, contextual associations. The asymmetry of respect style is rooted in the peculiarly close grandparent-grandchild relationship. The formulas of ordinary style take place within the culturally prescribed agenda of domestic routine. Formal style is epitomized in the formal visits between men who are members of the same (local or religious) community and who thus encode the distinctive male responsibility—and privilege—of coparticipation in its ritual and social life. If respect style expresses a mediated closeness, formal style expresses a collegial social distance.

10.1.1 The Background of Unstylized Interaction

All three of these distinct styles—ordinary, formal, and respect—emerge against the background of what I have termed the unstylized (familial) speech of domestic interaction, which is characterized by its laconicity and by the strongly directional character of task-oriented utterances.[1] The working assumption in household relationships is that of seniority, which implies the prerogative of unquestioned authority in the delegation of everyday tasks. Such authority may indeed be resisted, most effectively by simple inaction; the stylistic assumption, however, is that a senior need only command, without elaboration or mediation.

This unstylized asymmetry has its stylized echo as well as its counterpoint in the three speech-style categories. The emphatic bossiness of ordinary speech style, in which invitations are issued as imperatives and greetings are interrogations, mimics the senior-junior asymmetry of kinship relations. Stylization here takes the form of exaggeration: dramatic intonation, expressive interjections, and reiterated vocatives. Respect style, too, dramatizes the asymmetry of family life, but with mediating elements: intonation takes the form of a placating or indulgent croon, with or without dramatic exaggeration, and some term of address is obligatory.

Formal speech style also takes account of the sharp asymmetry in intrafamilial relationships, but by stylistically negating rather than dramatizing or mediating the directional element. The shift to formal lexical style, particularly of the most frequent markers—"yes," "no," "who," and so on—eliminates the echo of the abrupt domestic interrogatives, imperatives, and responses. Similarly, it is perhaps the association of personal pronouns with the home context of familial interaction that necessitates their stylistic shift or replacement in formal style. The background of unstylized interaction is thus implicitly assumed as an underpinning to the values and forms of stylized interaction.

10.1.2 The Consciousness of Style

The laconicity of familial or unstylized speech is significant as an index of the effort routinely required of Javanese speakers in close-polite as well as distant-polite contexts. As discussed in chapter 4, the hallmark of unstylized interaction is the minimization of interactional effort—moving, speaking, interpreting—especially on the part of the senior party to the interaction. The kind of performing energy routinely expended in every other sphere of social interaction is seemingly begrudged in extra-social (familial) contexts. For Javanese speakers—unlike, perhaps, the British—there is no myth of effortlessly correct speech. To labor at cultivating the best British accent is somewhat to invalidate the performance, since the essential stylistic message has to do with "breeding." To cultivate proper Javanese, on the other hand, is regarded as a life's work and is respected as such; the effort of suppressing the familial ngoko style (to use Siegel's terms) is an expected part of the process. There exists for every speaker a comfortable and uncritiqued manner of speech, available for occasional retreat from the effort of polite interaction. This familial speech style is expected and normal within its own domain. (To this extent the speech system resembles a system of diglossia, but see the discussion of sec. 10.2.5.)

The case of Javanese stylistics—including the Suriname version reported here—presents in general a picture of extraordinary linguistic consciousness. All of the stylistic devices I describe are present to some extent in the awareness of individual speakers. The clearest evidence of this linguistic awareness was provided by the unceasing efforts of informants to instruct me in the appropriate use of style, including the subtleties of close-polite stylization. Seven-year-old Lan on one occasion coached me in the appropriate crooning response to the grandmother's invitation to eat:

1. Iyaa, wis maangan!
"Yees, I've eeaten!"

On another occasion, the grandfather provided a more complete leave-taking announcement in place of my own, as I attempted to demonstrate to my husband how to say goodbye. Instead of the everyday

2a. Aku budal, mbah.
"I'm going, grandfather."

he suggested the slightly more submissive

2b. Aku arep dolan, mbah!
"I want to go visiting, grandfather!"

Most revealing of the conceptualization of style was the approving comment of one woman, on hearing me greet a neighbor correctly:

3. Wis inter "mbah"!
"(She) can already (say) 'grandfather.'"

This was precisely the same formulation as the standard critique of a youngster's competence in formal lexicon:

4. Wis inter basa.
"(He) already knows polite language."

For this speaker at least, the use of the vocative "grandfather" established a stylistic competence analogous to the mastery of polite lexicon (*basa*). The word *basa*—literally, "language"—is used to refer strictly to formal lexical style. It is clear, nevertheless, that there are other, contrastive components of polite stylization in Javanese that speakers actively cultivate and as readily criticize.

The concept of stylistic repertoire, as a participants' model, itself represents quite a sophisticated understanding of personal interactional style. In ritual and cultural performance (music, dance, etc.) the awareness of stylistic repertoire is probably quite widespread, if not necessarily articulated: wherever there coexist, for example, "high" and "low" forms of theater or primary and secondary forms of ritual activity, one may speak of the culture as exhibiting a repertoire of styles even though individual participants (performers) may be committed to a single genre.

In the matter of interactive performance, however, the notion of stylistic repertoire may go against more simplistic assumptions. In English, the concept of "personality," like that of "character," presents style as an attribute of the person rather than of the situation. Individuals' inevitable situational adaptations of personal style run up against a conceptual preference for consistency: sincerity is understood less as a situational than a personal attribute. A too-rapid shift from one style to another is seen as undercutting the speaker's performance, as belying one or the other stylistic statement.

That these are culturally specific assumptions is clear from their inapplicability in other cultural contexts. The Javanese concept of person evidently allows the elements of personal style to function as repertoire. Only in *wayang* (shadow theater) are individual characters associated with immutable stylistic attributes: Arjuna is always refined, Bima is always direct in manner. Actual persons, though they may vary in their degree of control over behavioral style, are nonetheless expected to behave differently in different contexts, and the definition of context can shift literally instantaneously with a shift in focus of attention.[2]

10.2 The Compartmental Model and the Stylistic Map

Two diagrammatic approaches are used in this work to represent the compartmental model of speech style. In chapter 3, a general model is presented in which the style system is compartmentalized into context A and context B, each with its particular value paradigm and its corresponding style paradigm. The respective paradigms of context A and context B are opposed: the positively valued pole of paradigm A is negatively valued in paradigm B. Figure 3.1 is here adapted as figure 10.1.

Figure 10.1 Compartmental model of politeness styles.
(Dominant value is capitalized.)

Social context:	CONTEXT A	CONTEXT B
Social value:	CLOSENESS	DISTANCE
Politeness style:	CLOSE / distant	close / DISTANT

In chapter 8, a similar shift of valuative perspective is presented in the form of a conceptual map of domestic space. From one point of view, the front region of the house presents a highly valued public face, whereas the back region is merely a private and residual zone; from an alternative perspective, however, the inner region is a privileged ritual domain, and the front region is merely an outsiders' area. Both perspectives may be sustained in a given event, for different participants or different purposes. Figure 8.8 is redrawn here as figure 10.2.

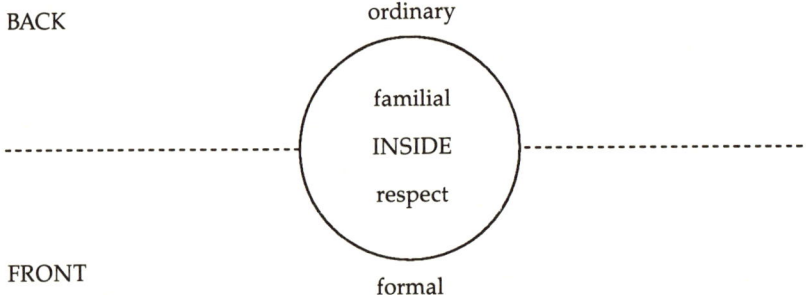

Figure 10.2 A style map of Suriname Javanese.

These two schematic representations are two different ways of describing the same basic phenomenon—the kaleidoscopic shift of perspective that potentially or actually occurs in a compartmental style system. Context A corresponds to the insider's perspective, in which marks of closeness are a valued affirmation of the relationship; context B corresponds to the outsider's perspective, which identifies closeness as a form of intrusion and therefore calls for the affirmation of distance. The spatial representation is a special case of the general compartmental model, which may of course focus on values other than interpersonal closeness and distance and which can as easily model nonlinguistic stylistic elements.

This way of representing the style system—as the product of cross-cutting contextual distinctions—is not the way it was presented to me by any informant and is probably not the way any native speaker sees the system. At most two of the four styles are recognized as such by Javanese speakers—the formal and respect styles. (Even the latter, though it is explicitly taught to children, is not generally recognized as a verbal skill in the same way that formal style is recognized.) What I have labeled back-region styles (ordinary and familial) are taken for granted as background by native speakers. Nevertheless, the spatial image is not merely a metaphor but serves almost as an anchor for the style system. The use of space is closely coordinated with verbal style, whether in compensation for verbal inadequacies, as stylistic reinforcement, or, conceivably, as a signal of ambivalence that undercuts the stylistic message. From this point of view, social space is more than merely the (invariant) setting of interaction. Space itself may be manipulated as an element of the speech-style system, as, for example, in the case of interaction taking place outside the domestic setting, which can be mapped along lines that mimic the use of household space. I once observed a family taking the ferry from the rural district across the river to Paramaribo. The entire family was seated on one of the long wooden benches that ranged down the center of the enclosed deck. The father sat at the end of the bench, and when several acquaintances approached for a formal-style conversation, he reoriented himself (a bit awkwardly) at a ninety-degree angle for the duration of the crossing. In so doing he transformed the aisle of the ferry into a front-region space, where his interlocutors clustered, and the bench became (apart from his own place on it) the back region. He rejoined his family only to disembark.

10.2.1 Close and Distant Politeness: A Kaleidoscopic Perspective

For the Javanese of Suriname, the affirmation of closeness entails, stylistically speaking, a consistent negation of social distance. It is not simply that impositions are tolerated between close friends that would be resented by strangers; rather, *some level of imposition must be routinely enacted as a kind of demonstration of closeness.* The characteristic domestic greeting takes the form of a somewhat personal inquiry, affirming not only the speaker's interest in the hearer's affairs but also his or her right to intrude. Such questions are inappropriate between relative strangers or from subordinate to superior, where negative or distant politeness prevails, but they are obligatory between close acquaintances, as if the affirmation of closeness requires a systematic transgression of the distant-polite negative face boundaries (to use Goffman's formulation). For example, a neighbor will offer as greeting, "What are you doing?" or "Have you finished cooking?" or "What did you buy?" These greetings are more a gesture than an actual imposition, since they do not in fact require an answer: the response may be a return question or even silence. Such questions might best be described as a statement of willingness to suffer mutual imposition, a waiver of the polite claims of mutual distance in favor of the polite claims of mutual connectedness. If, as Brown and Levinson (1978) suggest, the avoidance of imposition is a universal theme of (distant) politeness, then the affirmation of mutual imposition may be a universal feature of close politeness.

Goffman makes this point more generally, regarding positive and negative ritual: "In suggesting that there are things that must be said and done to a recipient, and things that must not be said and done, it should be plain that there is an inherent opposition between these two forms of deference" (1967:72). Stylistic distinctions are inherently invidious. To label one verbal form "appropriate" is to label the alternative forms "inappropriate"; and, unlike a rule of grammar, a stylistic rule implicitly assumes the availability and intelligibility of *inappropriate* alternative forms.[3] Before framing an utterance the speaker must *choose between alternative codes*—that is, identify the social context as either close or distant. The dominant value of one context is specifically disvalued in the other.

Analytically, then, there are two oppositions at work here instead of one. Even though in both cases the speaker has to make the choice between close and distant styles of politeness, the choice is quite different in context A than in context B (as diagramed in fig. 10.1). In context A (close interaction), the speaker must choose between a positively valued (appropriate) gesture of closeness and a negatively valued (inappropriate) gesture of distance; in context B, the values are reversed. The compartmental model is a way of emphasizing that stylistic choices are not neutral and that the speaker must shift perspectives as he or she shifts between contexts.

The speech-style map of figure 10.2 diagrams this shifting perspective by permitting an alternation of focus between the inside region and the front region. The latter reading is the conventionally dominant one, as reflected in the cultural emphasis on formal speech style as the only recognized politeness form (*tata krama*). In this conventional perspective, no distinction is made between formal style and respect style; the latter is assumed to comprise all the hallmarks of formal style. Similarly (as in Siegel's analysis), no distinction is made, conventionally, between close-polite and familial speech styles, which are lumped together as Ngoko. (This simple binary perspective is the basis of the conventional ladder model of speech style, described in chap. 2.)

An alternative reading of the speech-style map of figure 10.1 would focus on the inside region as positively valued. From this point of view, the stylization of formal (distant-polite) speech is a function of social exclusion, similar to the deferential treatment accorded to guests in the Atoni house, who are nevertheless kept outside the sacred inner area of the house. Stylized interaction from this point of view has a compensatory function coexisting with its more conventional function of showing consideration or deference.

10.2.2 A Kaleidoscopic Map of Style Alternation

There is a subtlety about this sort of shifting perspective that is difficult to capture in any analytic model; the kaleidoscopic map of figure 10.3 is a way of representing the alternation of contexts within a spatial framework.[4] Context A, in which close politeness is dominant, is mapped as a pair of concentric circles indicating inner and outer

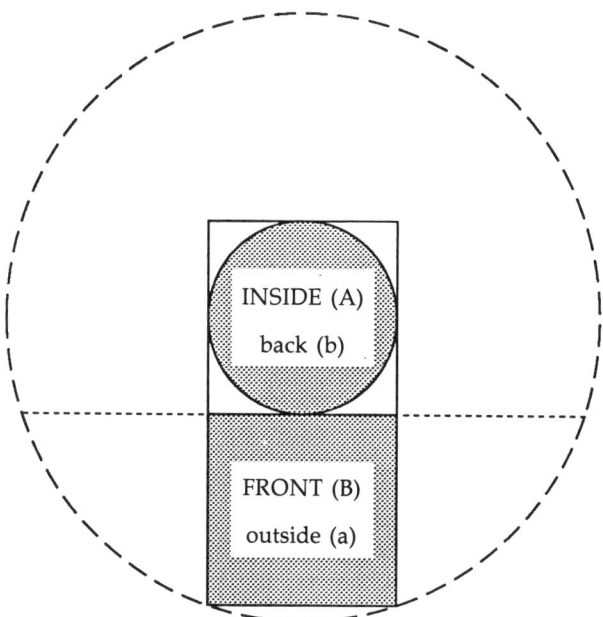

Figure 10.3 A kaleidoscopic map.

(domestic) regions. Context B, in which distant politeness is the dominant value, is mapped as the front and back regions of a (superimposed) rectangular space. As the participant's perspective shifts from one to the other framework, so does the focal region of the model: the focal inside region of context A is identical to the residual back region of context B, and conversely, the focal front region of context B overlaps the residual outside region of context A. A key feature of the model is that neither framework ever disappears from awareness. With regard to speech style, significance within the intended framework is always colored by a latent, unintended interpretation; dispreferred readings inevitably resonate.

10.2.3 Paradigm Shift

The social force of stylistic rules is especially marked in the circumstance of shifting political paradigms. Brown and Gilman (1960) describe such a shift for European pronominal usage, discussed in chapter 7 of this book. Peacock (1968) identifies a secular shift in the themes of Javanese proletarian drama (*ludruk*), in which stylistic changes reflect substantive changes in relationships of authority. Once an alternative political or social paradigm becomes available in a particular culture, any breach of traditional stylistic norms takes on the character of an ideological challenge rather than a simple lapse of social or verbal competence.[5]

The case of Suriname Javanese presents a less self-conscious form of paradigm shift, reflecting the reality of social structural realignments. In comparison to village social life in rural Java, the traditional hierarchical and corporate institutions—especially those of patronage and village membership—play a diminished or nonexistent role. Only the mosque remains as a compelling institutional forum of (male) formal interaction. Rather, informal household-centered networks of kin and quasi-kin play a dominant role in structuring Suriname-Javanese society. From this point of view, a shift of perspective away from the conventional front-oriented model and toward an insider orientation seems logical, accompanied by a shift in speech style away from formal politeness and toward ordinary and respect politeness styles.

10.2.4 Compartmentalization and Diglossia

Value compartmentalization fundamentally distinguishes the Javanese speech-style system from the diglossic model. In the literature on diglossia, the high speech form is *in all contexts* accorded higher value than the low form (Fasold 1984: chap. 2). In a compartmentalized style system, however, the selection of a low form corresponds to a contextual shift of values, such that the high form is dispreferred not just as inappropriate but as insufficiently emblematic of the relevant contextual value (e.g., closeness). Diglossic systems may perhaps be viewed as a special case of compartmental stylistic repertoire, in which an ideological construct overrides the set of values associated with what comes to be viewed as the low form of speech. The case of Javanese illustrates a different tendency, one toward stylistic contrast and the articulation of distinct social codes with minimal ideological override of the "lower" set of values.

In Javanese, whether in Java or in Suriname, the contextual values evoked by the use of the low style (Ngoko) are not restricted to the social values of interpersonal closeness or even liveliness (*ramé*). The use of Ngoko to express downward respect plays an important role in establishing the low style as culturally valued. For example, the rich repertoire of proverbs in Javanese is invariably rendered in Ngoko: proverbs are regarded as utterances of the ancestors directed toward the current generation. Many classical Javanese texts are written in Ngoko, as representing a teacher's communication to his students. This dimension of Ngoko valuation is nicely illustrated in the widespread coverage accorded in the Indonesian press (Aug. 1, 1988) to the reported last words of the late mother-in-law of President Soeharto. The national newspapers are published entirely in either Bahasa Indonesia or English but on this occasion the reported utterance, a solemn injunction to continue living in harmony, was invariably given in the original Javanese. The fact that the utterance was, quite properly, phrased in Ngoko — the low style, appropriate in senior-junior kin relationships — in no way detracted from the dignity of either the reported event or the utterance, as it would in a conventionally diglossic language system.

10.3 Stylistics: Theoretical Considerations

The study of stylistic phenomena has at present no accepted place in either anthropology or linguistics. As is often the case in ethnographic analysis, the choice of focus here was suggested by the ethnographic material itself: stylistic phenomena for Suriname Javanese constitute a highly salient and explicitly attended element of observed social interaction. The analysis of style undoubtedly has broader relevance, however, and some consideration must be given to questions of definition and scope.

The larger intention of this work is to bring to serious attention the phenomenon of stylistic discrimination as a universally recognized system of establishing and maintaining social categories or boundaries. It is no more possible, by now, for anthropologists to use a phrase such as "empty ritual" than it would be for a linguistic philosopher to use the phrase "merely semantic." Style, however, retains the common-language implication of standing in opposition to "substance," as an essentially meaningless and nonessential aspect of what people do.

Stylistic distinctions are more accurately regarded as an integral and significant element of human activity. Whatever other functions are served by such cultural forms as language, ritual, and artistic production, at some level the *style* of performance serves to set apart—sometimes with far-reaching sociopolitical implications—one category of practitioner from another. A theory of performance in any of these areas must include systematic attention to the stylistic aspect; similarly, an analysis of political process might have to take into account the dynamics of stylistic compartmentalization and paradigm alternation.

10.3.1 A Definition of Style

Several points suggest themselves as minimal requirements of a theoretical treatment of stylistic repertoire. First, a theory must provide for two distinct levels of decision making on the part of the speaker/performer: at the conceptual level, the speaker defines the social context of the particular interaction in terms of the specific cultural values to be expressed; at the performance level, the speaker articulates those values in a culturally intelligible way. The performance can accordingly be challenged at either level, either as an inappropriate definition of social context (the "appropriateness test") or as an inadequate expression of the intended cultural values (the "adequacy test").

Second, any treatment of stylistic repertoire must do justice to performers' perceptions of stylistic choices. Not only do speakers have command of a repertoire of options, but they may also have strong feelings about the importance of appropriate style selection and articulation. Individual participants (critics as well as performers) may place differing relative emphasis on the appropriateness test and the adequacy test.

A theoretical treatment of stylistics might begin with the following two-part working definition. *Style*, as the socially significant qualitative aspect of performance, is the element of performer activity that (a) signals the intended category of performance, or *genre*, and (b) is subject to a culturally directed *critique* with reference to that performance category. (The definition might be broadened to include nonactive features of performance, such as participants' clothing.) Performance need not be understood as limited to interactive performance; "staged" performance, including ritual, may also be analyzed stylistically from this beginning point.

Viewed as a signal of the category of performance—part (a) of the working definition—stylistic elements may be analyzed much like other elements of communication. Viewed as a critiqued aspect of performance, however—part (b)—stylistic elements must be understood on their own terms; the critical function goes beyond the normal decoding and interpretive functions inherent in successful communication.

10.3.2 Style versus Manner

An initial distinction may be drawn between *style* and what might be termed *manner*. If style is understood as the socially significant qualitative aspect of performance, the term "manner" may refer to any qualitative aspect of performance that is incidental rather than socially significant, that is regarded by participants as either idiosyncratic or universal within the particular culture.

Manner is thus a qualitative aspect of performance that is unsignaled (not selected from among a repertoire of genres) and uncritiqued (no cultural standards of performance are applicable). For example, in American interaction physical posture is for the most part extrastylistic; a characteristic stoop of the shoulders or an overly long stride may be noted as an idiosyncratic feature of manner but not marked as a stylistic genre. For Javanese, however, a very broad array of postural elements are treated as stylistically significant, often with resonances of *wayang* (shadow theater) characterization and with a specialized descriptive vocabulary. Idiosyncratic personal style is a topic of great interest for Javanese, not only in discussions of staged performance (e.g., of the *wayang* characters) but also in observing and commenting on interactive performance. In a culture that regards self-control, inner and outer, as an aspect of religious observance, it is arguable that aesthetic comment is indistinguishable from moral criticism and that no area of observed behavior is exempt from stylistic critique and classification. Since virtually all personal style is subject to such critique in Javanese culture, the distinction between manner and style thus tends to collapse.[6]

10.3.3 Stylistic Intelligibility and Adequacy

What distinguishes the stylistic element of performance is the level of mastery required, which may be far more demanding than the sort of competence entailed in simple communication. It is precisely the problem of stylistic mastery that creates the scope for a critical judgment of performance as "intelligible but inadequate"—intelligible, that is, as a signal of the stylistic category but inadequate as a performed representation of the clearly intended style.

The importance of stylistic markers may be understood as reflecting this problem of mastery. Style markers are communicative features that are no more demanding in terms of performance than any other element of communication and that serve precisely to signal the intended style category. In Suriname Javanese, stylistic performance is in many cases limited to stylistic marking, and in the Suriname-Javanese style system, the judgment of intelligibility in general supersedes questions of stylistic adequacy: an intelligible performance is generally considered to be adequate, though a greater degree of mastery, in any of the three basic styles, is nevertheless recognized and appreciated. (Suriname Javanese do, however, customarily critique their own formal speech style as generally inadequate with reference to the standard of the Javanese language as spoken in Java.)

The potential gap between intelligibility and adequacy has special relevance for the place of stylistic analysis within the broader study of interaction phenomena. Levinson (1983:16) calls attention to a fundamental insight of the philosopher Grice that "communication is a complex kind of intention that is achieved or satisfied just by being recognized." This observation clearly points to the difference between stylistic phenomena and other forms of communication: only part (a) of the working definition—the signaling function—is achieved simply by virtue of being recognized as an intention. Part (b), by introducing the concept of a cultural critique, identifies style as an element (the element?) of performance that is *not* adequately achieved simply by communication of the performer's intention.[7]

Not only the performance as a whole but also the particular stylistic marker may adequately fulfill (a) but not (b): it may successfully signal the intended category of performance but nevertheless be critiqued as an inadequate exemplar of that category. An example from Javanese (as spoken and critiqued in Central Java) is the use of hypercorrect lexical forms, which are derived from the correct krama form by the superaddition of a standard phonetic "kramafication" feature (e.g., hypercorrect *sedanten* for krama *sedoyo*). These forms are clearly intelligible as signaling the performer's intention to speak Krama but are subject to standard cultural critique as inadequate performance of Krama speech style.

A critical function is implied not only by part (b) of the working definition but by part (a) as well. Whereas part (b) is subject to critical validation of stylistic adequacy, part (a) is subject to critical validation of *appropriateness* of the signaled style category. It is not enough for the performance to be successfully "read" (decoded) as a signal of the intended style category or even for it to be accepted as an adequate representation of the intended style. A matter of primary concern is that the signaled style category be critically validated as the *appropriate* category for the performance as situated; that is, the critic's definition of the social context must agree with that of the speaker (the appropriateness test).

10.3.4 Performer and Critic

Part (a) of the working definition implicitly assumes a repertorial paradigm of relevant stylistic categories and their associated values (diagramed in fig. 10.1). This paradigm is assumed to be largely shared by performer and critics, as coparticipants in a particular stylistic code. Part (b) permits a somewhat different relationship between performer and critic, who may have sharply diverging assessments of particular stylistic features. Nevertheless, the role of criticism in the functioning of a style system is essentially collaborative: the critique is part of the performance, in the sense that stylistic elements have significance and efficacy only by virtue of critical appreciation.[8] Felicitous stylistic performance rests on a felicitous critique; communication of style is a bilateral process, in that successful communication requires the message to be not merely received and decoded but also validated by critical acceptance.

The performer similarly monitors the performance, to some extent serving as a self-critic. In the case of virtuoso performance, the performer may be the most adequate (i.e., stylistically most educated) critic, presenting the paradox of a performance that by its virtuosity critiques its audience as inadequate critics. In Western art forms such a reverse critique is almost a standard; indeed, it is an accepted function of the Western artist to enlarge the critical paradigm, not merely through virtuoso technical performance but also through the construction of an alternative stylistic code or paradigm. (Nevertheless, innovation is, strictly speaking, a function of criticism rather than of performance; the innovative performer acts as critic of the existing paradigm.) Even in a traditional style system—one in which the construction of new stylistic codes is not an institutionalized part of performance—stylistic paradigms may be subject to expansion or shift, as adaptations in performance are ratified by cultural critique and as critics impose shifting stylistic standards on performance. (See S. Price [1984] for a study of style change within a genre.)

In the case of style-inflected language, all speakers are necessarily also interpreters of a stylistic code. Conversely, all speakers are also critics of speech-style performance. Many observers have noted the pervasiveness of an aesthetic critique in Javanese culture: there is a correct way to perform most routine tasks, quite apart from the interactive decorum imposed by politeness norms.

In interactive (as opposed to staged) performance, there is a special relation between performance and critique. Speech performance is normally directed to a principal hearer or group of hearers (or better, interpreters); there may be other, marginal or incidental hearers/interpreters as well. The stylistic element of speech performance is similarly specifically directed to a principal critic, who is usually the addressee. In a style-inflected language, many or most stylistic features (both stylemics and honorifics) are oriented specifically to the addressee and tailored to the speaker-hearer relationship. The critic judges not merely a stylistic performance but, in essence, a performed interpretation of the social relationship between critic and performer. There is thus not merely the risk of inadequate performance but also the graver risk of giving offense, since the performance addresses the critic's personal face as well as his or her aesthetic standards.

The interactive character of speech performance is especially complex because the critique may itself be embedded in a reciprocal speech performance. That is, the critic in turn offers a performance that responds stylistically as well as substantively to the initial performance. In spoken Javanese, the choice of style is broadly affected not only by the social context but also by the speaker's evaluation of the stylistic competence of the hearer. The critic incorporates a critique of the performer's stylistic competence in selecting (or constructing) a speech style to frame a response.

The performer, too, takes into account an estimate of the hearer's stylistic competence in the initial stylistic presentation, in a form of reverse critique. Errington (1985) gives examples of this process in discussing how elite speakers addressing non-elite speaker use Madya styles as a form of stylistic compromise reflecting the speaker's estimation of the hearer's limited stylistic competence. The elite speaker's personal face is potentially placed in jeopardy by any lack of competence on the part of a coparticipant, and to speak "down" in this way serves as a form of preemptive defense.

10.3.5 Summary

Stylization may be summarized as a two-level selection process in which the performer (a) selects an appropriate genre of performance style from a culturally framed repertoire of alternative styles, and (b) encodes the intended genre (along with any referential elements of communication) by selecting and performing particular performance elements associated with that genre and, importantly, by avoiding the use of elements associated with alternative genres. A performance structured in this way may be spoken of as "stylized," as are those performance elements that are clearly and exclusively associated with a particular genre of performance style. It is perhaps possible to speak of degrees of stylization of performance as reflecting the overall pattern of genre exclusivity of performance elements—that is, the proportion of performed gestures that may be identified with a specific stylistic category. I have occasionally used the term "unstylized" to represent a category of performance in which the performer is free to disregard stylistic expectations; a better term is "uncritiqued."

A separate issue is the specific meaning of particular stylistic elements. It is possible to design a style system in which the contrastive signals have no meaning apart from the simple fact of stylistic contrast—that is, a stylistic code made up of arbitrary and unmotivated words and gestures. More usual, probably, is the style system in which at least some of the significant elements carry meaningful resonance, as in the case of the close-polite features discussed in chapter 4. Additionally, stylistic elements may have mimetic meaning; that is, they may be interpreted as behavioral manifestations of a valued inner state or of specific character traits (e.g., refinement or benevolence, intelligence or courage, competence or nonconformity). Finally, elements of politeness style, verbal and nonverbal, may have specific referential or practical implications of positive or negative politeness, such as the conventional gesture of holding open a door (as a gesture of inclusion as well as of effort sparing).

10.4 STYLISTIC AND SOCIAL DISTINCTIONS

A basic function of stylistic markers is to register culturally important distinctions between categories of participation, relative to the addressee (close/distant, in-group/out-group) and to the event (front region/back region, male/female). It is quite possible, as Lakoff (1973) suggests, that there is a universal logic to the association of social distance with "avoidance of imposition" and of social closeness with making the other "feel good." However, I suggest that the primary function of stylistic rules is not the substantive one of making participants feel either "good" or "safe from imposition" but rather the formal one of signaling and maintaining clear categories of social relationship.

There are specific, socially meaningful styles to be avoided wherever stylistic rules operate. There is thus the implicit possibility of turning the social order on its head by deliberately violating a stylistic standard—for example, by choosing the familiar rather than the deferential form or vice versa; by introducing intimate usage into a formal setting; by using women's rather than men's verbal forms; or by crossing an ethnic or class boundary of verbal style. In each case, the socially accepted definition of "we" versus "they" can be stylistically negated by the misuse of appropriateness rules whose primary function may well be the maintenance of just such social distinctions. That is, for the dominant "we"/they" paradigm of a particular culture (whether hierarchical, familial, sexual, or ethnic), there exists an alternative paradigm that, if it should surface in behavior, would challenge the established divisions. If no such alternative paradigm were conceivable, there would be no force to the style system. The "rules" of style are social and not grammatical: in every case there is a meaningful (though not necessarily "acceptable") option of violating the appropriateness rule.[9]

The choice of politeness strategy cannot, then, be treated as yet another series of transformational rules, operating at a level beyond syntax and hence farther removed from the level of semantic formation (the Chomskian deep structure). Rather, the basic choice of overall style (close or distant, positive or negative) must occur at the presyntactic level, in the process of shaping the content of the utterance itself. (This is the argument made by Suharno [1974] for the selection of pronominal variant in Javanese and, by implication, for Javanese lexical alternation in general.) The mutually contradictory rules of stylistic performance require as their logical context a structure of relatively sharp social discriminations, distinguishing stylistically between classes of participation, categories of relationship, social settings, or even topics of conversation. Stylistic elements, far from representing a superficial adornment or an incidental social message, reflect a basic communicative choice—including, in some cases, a stylistically motivated choice between speech and silence.

NOTES

1. The concept of stylization developed in section 10.3 allows room for modes of interaction that are "unstylized," that is, that are not informed by a critical standard of performance. This is the sense in which the term is used here.

2. The seminal discussion of the concept of "person" as a negotiated construct is Geertz (1973). For an insightful discussion of the Javanese conception of self and performance, see Keeler (1987).

3. Grammatical rules may, of course, take on stylistic significance, as when a particular usage signals membership in a particular social or regional class.

4. I am indebted to Clifford Geertz for focusing my attention on the mutual "coloration" of stylistic contrasts and so prompting this version of the model.

5. There are many instances in the anthropological literature of synchronic paradigm shift: see Ardener (1975) for a case of male versus female paradigms and the associated shift in perspective; Bateson (1958) is the classic exploration of the paradigm shift associated with ritual inversion.

6. C. Geertz (personal communiction) has suggested that facial expression may be an example of a feature that, conversely, has stylistic meaning for American culture and is merely manner for Javanese.

7. A complex question is what it is exactly that the speaker achieves with a stylistically successful performance. An answer requires a very thorough knowledge of the social system within which the performance takes place. As a form of shorthand, however, we may speak of stylistic "efficacy" as well as adequacy.

8. In the case where the performer's and critic's paradigms are widely divergent it may make sense to speak of distinct style systems. This sort of critique, directed from a vantage point outside the performer's style system, is no longer collaborative; it is an extraneous critique, distinct from the essential critique implied in the concept of performed style.

9. Note that the criterion of stylistic acceptability imposes a *narrower* standard than the criterion of meaningfulness. This contrasts with grammatical acceptability, which is a broader standard than meaningfulness, as illustrated by Chomsky's well-known examples of grammatically acceptable but meaningless constructions, such as "colorless green ideas sleep furiously."

References

Anderson, Benedict. 1972. The idea of power in Java. In *Culture and politics in Indonesia*, ed. Holt, Anderson, and Siegel. Ithaca: Cornell University Press.
Ardener, Edwin. 1975. Belief and the problem of women. In *Perceiving women*, ed. Shirley Ardener. New York: J. Wiley.
Bateson, G. 1958. *Naven*. 2d ed. Stanford, Calif.: Stanford University Press.
Bax, Gerald W. 1974. Language and social structure in a Javanese village. Ph.D. diss., Tulane University, New Orleans.
Bernstein, Basil. 1958. Some sociological determinants of perception. Reprinted in Bernstein. 1974. *Class, codes, and control: Theoretical studies toward a sociology of language*. New York: Schocken.
Bloch, Maurice. 1975. *Political language and oratory in traditional society*. New York: Academic Press.
Blom, J. P., and J. J. Gumperz. 1972. Social meaning in linguistic structures: code-switching in Norway. In *Directions in sociolinguistics*, ed. J. J. Gumperz and D. Hymes. New York: Holt, Rinehart and Winston.
Brown, Penelope, and Stephen Levinson. 1978. Universals in language usage: Politeness phenomena. In *Questions and politeness*, ed. Esther N. Goody. Cambridge: Cambridge University Press.
―――. 1987. *Politeness: Some universals in language usage*. Cambridge: Cambridge University Press.
Brown, Roger, and A. Gilman. 1960. The pronouns of power and solidarity. In *Style in language*, ed. T. A. Sebeok. Cambridge: M.I.T. Press.
Burling, Robbins. 1970. *Man's many voices: Language in its cultural context*. New York: Holt, Rinehart and Winston.
Cooke, J. R. 1970. *The pronominal systems of Thai, Burmese, and Vietnamese*. Berkeley: University of California Publications in Linguistics no. 52.
Coulthard, Malcolm. 1985. *An introduction to discourse analysis*. London: Longman.
Cunningham, Clark E. 1964. Order in the Atoni house. Reprinted in R. Needham, ed. 1973. *Right and left*. Chicago: University of Chicago Press.
Derveld, F. E. R. 1982. *Politieke mobilisatie en integratie van de Javanen in Suriname*. Groningen: Bouma's Boekhuis.
Dewey, Alice. 1960. *Peasant marketing in Java*. New York: Free Press of Glencoe.

Dumarcay, Jacques. 1987. *The house in south-east Asia*. Trans. and ed. by Michael Smithies. Singapore: Oxford University Press.
Errington, James Joseph. 1982. Changing speech levels among a traditional Javanese elite group. Ph.D. diss., University of Chicago, Chicago.
———. 1985. *Language and social change in Java: Linguistic reflexes of modernization in a traditional royal polity*. Athens, Ohio: Ohio University Center for International Studies.
———. 1988. *Structure and style in Javanese: A semiotic view of linguistic ettiquette*. Philadelphia: University of Pennsylvania Press.
Ervin-Tripp, S. 1964. An analysis of the interaction of language, topic, and listener. In *The ethnography of communication*, ed. Gumperz and Hymes, pp. 86-102.
———. 1972. On sociolinguistic rules: Alternation and co-occurrence. In *Directions in sociolinguistics*, ed. J. Gumperz and D. Hymes. New York: Holt, Rinehart, and Winston.
———. 1976a. Speech acts and social learning. In *Meaning in anthropology*, ed. Keith H. Basso and Henry A. Selby. Albuquerque: University of New Mexico Press.
———. 1976b. Is Sybil there? The structure of some American English directives. *Language in Society* 5, no. 1.
Evans-Pritchard, E. E. 1937. *Witchcraft, oracles and magic among the Azande*. Oxford: Clarendon Press.
Fasold, Ralph. 1984. *The sociolinguistics of society*. Oxford: Blackwell.
Ferguson, Charles A. 1959. Diglossia. *Word* 15.
———. 1976. The structure and use of politeness formulas. *Language in Society* 5, no. 2.
———. 1977. Linguistics as anthropology. In *Georgetown University round table on languages and linguistics*, ed. Muriel Saville-Troike. Georgetown: Georgetown University Press.
Firth, Raymond. 1972. Verbal and bodily rituals of greeting and parting. In *Interpretation of ritual*, ed. J. LaFontaine. Cambridge: Cambridge University Press.
Fishman, Joshua A. 1967. Bilingualism with and without diglossia; diglossia with and without bilingualism. *Journal of Social Issues* 23, no. 2.
———, ed. 1968. *Readings in the sociology of language*. The Hague: Mouton.
———. 1970. *Sociolinguistics*. Rowley, Mass.: Newbury House.
———. 1972. Domains and the relationship between micro- and macrosociolinguistics. In *Directions in sociolinguistics*, ed. Gumperz and Hymes.
———. 1983. Levels of analysis in sociolinguistic explanation. *International Journal of the Sociology of Language* 39.
Fishman, Joshua, et al. 1986. *The Fergusonian impact: In honor of Charles A. Ferguson on the occasion of his 65th birthday*. Berlin: Mouton de Gruyter.
Frake, Charles O. 1975. How to enter a Yakan house. In *Sociocultural dimensions of language use*, ed. Sanchez and Blount. New York: Academic Press.
Friedrich, Paul. 1979. Russian pronominal usage. *Language, context, and the imagination*. Stanford, Calif.: Stanford University Press.

Gal, Susan. 1979. *Language shift: Social determinants of linguistic change in bilingual Austria.* New York: Academic Press.

———. 1988. The political economy of code choice. In *Codeswitching*, ed. Heller. Berlin: Mouton de Gruyter.

Geertz, Clifford. 1960. *The religion of Java.* Glencoe: Free Press.

———. 1968. *Agricultural involution.* Berkeley: University of California Press.

Geertz, Hildred. 1961. *The Javanese family.* Glencoe: Free Press.

Geertz, Hildred, and Clifford Geertz. 1975. *Kinship in Bali.* Chicago: University of Chicago Press.

Goffman, Erving. 1967. *Interaction ritual.* New York: Anchor.

———. 1971. *Relations in public: Microstudies of the public order.* New York: Harper.

———. 1976. Replies and responses. *Language in Society* 5, no. 3.

Goody, Esther. 1972. "Greeting," "begging," and the presentation of respect. In *Interpretation of ritual*, ed. J. LaFontaine. Cambridge: Cambridge University Press.

———. 1978. *Questions and politeness.* Cambridge: Cambridge University Press.

Gregor, Thomas. 1977. *Mehinaku: The drama of daily life in a Brazilian Indian village.* Chicago: University of Chicago Press.

Gumperz, John J. 1964. Bilingualism, bidialectalism and classroom interaction. In *Functions of language in the classroom*, ed. C. Cazden, V. John, and D. Hymes. New York: Teachers College.

———. 1970. Verbal strategies in multilingual communication. *Monograph Series on Language and Linguistics No. 23*, 21st annual roundtable. Washington D.C.: Georgetown University.

———. 1971. *Language in social groups.* Stanford: University of California Press.

———. 1976. The sociolinguistic significance of conversational code-switching. In *Papers on language and context*, ed. J. Cook-Gumperz and J. J. Gumperz. Berkeley: University of California Press.

———. 1982. *Discourse Strategies.* Cambridge: Cambridge Univerity Press.

Gumperz, J. J., and D. Hymes, eds. 1964. The ethnography of communication. *American Anthropologist* 66: vi, pt. 2, special publication.

———. 1972. *Directions in sociolinguistics.* New York: Holt, Rinehart and Winston.

Hall, Edward T. 1966. *The hidden dimension.* New York: Doubleday.

Heine-Geldern, Robert. 1942. Conceptions of state and kingship in south east Asia. *Far Eastern Quarterly* (November).

Heller, Monica, ed. 1988. *Codeswitching: Anthropological and sociolinguistic perspectives.* Berlin: Mouton de Gruyter.

Horne, Elinor C. 1961. *Beginning Javanese.* New Haven: Yale University Press.

———. 1974. *Javanese-English dictionary.* New Haven: Yale University Press.

Hymes, Dell, ed. 1964. *Language in culture and society.* New York: Harper and Row.

———. 1967. Models of the interaction of language and social setting. *Journal of Social Issues* 23, no. 2.

———. 1974. *Foundations in sociolinguistics*. Philadelphia: University of Pennsylvania Press.

———. 1971. *On communicative competence*. Philadelphia: University of Pennsylvania Press.

———. 1980. Foreword to Sankoff (1980).

Irvine, Judith T. 1974. Strategies of status manipulation in the Wolof greeting. In *Explorations in the ethnography of speaking*, ed. R. Bauman and J. Sherzer. London: Cambridge University Press.

———. 1979. Formality and informality in communicative events. *American Anthropologist* 81.

Jain, Dhanesh K. 1969. Verbalization of respect in Hindi. *Anthropological Linguistics* 11, no. 3.

Jay, Robert R. 1969. *Javanese villagers*. Cambridge: M.I.T. Press.

Keeler, Ward. 1984. *Javanese: A cultural approach*. Athens, Ohio: Ohio University Press.

———. 1987. *Javanese shadow plays, Javanese selves*. Princeton: Princeton University Press.

Keesing, Roger M. 1971. *Cultural anthropology: A contemporary perspective*. New York: Holt, Rinehart and Winston.

Labov, William. 1970. The study of language in its social context. *Studium Generale* 23.

Lakoff, Robin. 1973. The logic of politeness; or, minding your p's and q's. *Papers from the Ninth Regional Meeting of the Chicago Linguistic Society*. Chicago: Chicago Linguistic Society.

———. 1976. *Language and woman's place*. New York: Octagon.

Levinson, Stephen C. 1983. *Pragmatics*. Cambridge: Cambridge University Press.

Lockard, Craig A. 1971. The Javanese as emigrant: observations on the development of Javanese settlements overseas. *Indonesia* 11.

Malefijt, Annemarie de Waal. 1963. *The Javanese in Suriname: Segment of a plural society*. The Hague: Van Gorcum.

Martin, S. 1964. Speech levels in Japan and Korea. In *Language in culture and society*, ed. Hymes. New York: Harper and Row.

Mintz, Sidney W., and Richard Price. 1976. *An anthropological approach to the Afro-American past: A Caribbean perspective*. Philadelphia: Institute for the Study of Human Issues.

Moerman, Michael. 1969. A little knowledge. In *Cognitive anthropology*, ed. Stephen A. Tyler. New York: Holt, Rinehart and Winston.

Parkin, David J. 1974. Language switching in Nairobi. In *Language in Kenya*, ed. W. H. Whiteley. Nairobi: Oxford University Press.

———. 1983. Comment. In Fishman, ed. (1983).

Peacock, James L. 1968. *Rites of modernization*. Chicago: University of Chicago Press.

Poedjosoedarmo, G. 1977. *Thematization and information structure in Javanese*. NUSA: Miscellaneous Studies in Indonesian and Languages of Indonesia, pt. 2. Jakarta: Badan Penyelenggara Seri NUSA.

Poedjosoedarmo, Soepomo. 1968. Javanese speech levels. *Indonesia* 7.
Price, Sally. 1984. *Co-wives and calabashes.* Ann Arbor: University of Michigan Press.
Pride, J. B. 1979. A transactional view of speech functions and codeswitching. In *Language and society: Anthropological issues,* ed. William C. McCormack and Stephen A. Wurm. The Hague: Mouton.
Pride, J. B., and J. Holmes. 1972. *Sociolinguistics.* Harmondsworth: Penguin.
Radcliffe-Brown, A. R. 1940. On joking relationships. *Africa* 13, no. 3. Reprinted in A. R. Radcliffe-Brown. *Structure and function in primitive society.* New York: The Free Press.
Rapoport, Amos. 1960. *House form and culture.* Englewood Cliffs, N.J.: Prentice-Hall.
Rosaldo, Michelle. 1973. I have nothing to hide; the language of Ilongot oratory. *Language in Society* 2.
———. 1982. The things we do with words: Ilongot speech acts and speech act theory in philosophy. *Language in Society* 2.
Rubin, Joan. 1968. *National bilingualism in Paraguay.* The Hague: Mouton.
Sankoff, Gillian. 1971. Language use in multilingual societies: Some alternate approaches. Reprinted in Sankoff (1980).
———. 1980. *The social life of language.* Philadelphia: University of Pennsylvania Press.
Schegloff, Emmanuel, and Harvey Sacks. 1973. Opening up closings. Reprinted in Roy Turner, ed. 1974. *Ethnomethodology.* Middlesex: Penguin.
Scherer, Klaus R., and Howard Giles, eds. 1979. *Social markers in speech.* London: Cambridge University Press.
Schiffman, Harold. 1986. Deferential speech acts and the pragmatics of politeness in Tamil: From case to aspect. In Fishman et al., *The Fergusonian impact,* vol. 2. Berlin: Mouton de Gruyter.
Scotton, C. M. 1986. Diglossia and code-switching. In Joshua Fishman et. al., *The Fergusonian impact: In honor of Charles A. Ferguson on his 65th birthday.* Berlin: Mouton de Gruyter.
———. 1988. Code switching as indexical of social negotiation. In *Codeswitching,* ed. Heller. Berlin: Mouton de Gruyter.
Scotton, C. M., and W. Ury, 1977. Bilingual strategies: The social functions of codeswitching. *International Journal of the Sociology of Language* 13.
Siegel, James T. 1986. *Solo in the new order: Language and hierarchy in an Indonesian city.* Princeton: Princeton University Press.
Silverstein, Michael. 1976. Shifters, linguistic categories, and cultural descriptions. In *Meaning in anthropology,* ed. Keith H. Basso and Henry A. Selby. Albuquerque: University of New Mexico.
———. 1979. Language structure and linguistic ideology. In *The elements: A parasession,* ed. Paul R. Clyne, William F. Hanks, and Carol L. Hofbauer. Chicago: Chicago Linguistic Society.
Smith-Hefner, N. 1981. To level or not to level: codes of politeness and prestige in rural Java. *Chicago Linguistic Society: Papers from the Parasession on Language and Behavior.* Chicago: Chicago Linguistic Society.

Srinivas, M. 1976. *The remembered village.* Berkeley: University of California Press.
Suharno, Ignatius. 1974. Grammatical and Communicative Aspects of Javanese. Ph.D. diss., Georgetown University, Washington, D.C.
Suparlan, Parsudi. 1976. The Javanese of Suriname. Ph.D. diss., University of Illinois, Urbana.
Tannen, Deborah. 1986. *That's not what I meant! How conversational style makes or breaks relationships.* New York: Ballantine Books.
Uhlenbeck, E. M. 1950. *De tegenstelling krama: ngoko: Haar positie in het Javaanse taalsysteem.* Groningen: J. B. Wolters. Reprinted in English in Uhlenbeck (1978).
——. 1970. The use of respect forms in Javanese. In *Pacific Linguistic Studies in Honour of Arthur Capell,* ed. S. A. Wurm and D. C. Laycock. Australian National University Pacific Linguistic Series C, no. 13. Reprinted in Uhlenbeck (1978).
——. 1978. *Studies in Javanese morphology.* The Hague: Martinus Nijhoff.
Wolff, John, and Dede Utomo. 1986. *Beginning Indonesian through self-instruction.* Ithaca, N.Y.: Cornell University Southeast Asia Program.
Wolff, John, and Soepomo Poedjosoedarmo. 1982. *Communicative codes in central Java.* Ithaca, N.Y.: Cornell University Southeast Asia Program, Linguistic Series 8, Data Paper 116.
Wolfowitz, Clare. Forthcoming. Ritual Space in an Overseas Javanese Community.
Yamanishi, Masa-aki. 1974. On minding your p's and q's in Japanese: A case study from honorifics. In *Papers from the Tenth Regional Meeting of the Chicago Linguistic Society.* Chicago: Chicago Linguistic Society.

Index

Affirmative response, 44, 73, 75, 105, 109-13, 118n, 125, 144, 150, 155, 162, 177
Agenda, 20, 33, 90, 107-15, 183-84, 236
Aku (first-person familiar pronoun), 44, 49, 57, 106, 112-16, 123, 149, 151, 165-67, 173-83 (passim), 186n, 193, 194, 238
Alternative stylistic values, 4, 11, 33n, 78-82, 191, 195, 231, 234, 240-44, 249, 250, 252
Anderson, B., 13
Announcement, 41, 54, 109, 112-16, 180-81, 225, 238
Ardener, E., 253n
"As-if" interaction, 16-18, 39, 50, 80, 85, 98, 106-12 (passim), 116, 117, 132, 151-53, 209
Asymmetrical interaction, 6, 37, 63n, 75, 118n, 154, 172-73
Atoni, 203-5, 243
Avoidance (interaction or speech style), 10, 15, 22, 38, 62, 75-77, 80, 114-17, 171, 174, 176-78, 184-85, 204, 208, 209

Back door, 200, 221
Back region, 6-7, 11, 12, 97, 190-97, 200, 204-9, 210n, 211-21, 224, 225, 228, 230, 240, 241, 243, 251
Bahasa Indonesia, 63n, 70, 137n, 245
Basa (polite speech), 60, 62, 79, 137n, 135, 139, 238, 239
Bateson, G., 253n
Bax, G., 121, 126, 137n, 169n, 235n
Bernstein, B., 60-61, 210n
Bloch, M., 8

Blom, J. P., 12, 192
Brown, P., 85n, 169n
Brown, P., and S. Levinson, 7, 10, 15, 16, 19, 34n, 97, 100, 105, 136n, 242
Brown, R., and A. Gilman, 6, 18, 64n, 122, 131, 134, 171-72, 174, 234, 244
Burling, R., 120

Ceremonial interaction, 33n, 38, 51, 55, 88, 96, 119n, 163, 166, 167, 191, 193, 194, 206, 211, 212, 215, 224, 234n. *See also* Ritual.
Children, interaction involving, 15-16, 38, 40, 47, 50, 74, 76, 83, 88, 89, 91-99 (passim), 106, 108-15, 118n, 143, 151, 166, 175, 178, 180, 186n
Closeness, 6, 16, 18, 32, 37, 46, 50, 80, 83-85, 90, 100, 109-18 (passim), 134, 150, 178-80, 204, 209, 233, 236, 240-42, 245, 251
Coda, 39, 40, 63n, 115, 150, 158, 159, 162, 169n, 177-80, 184
Codeswitching, 7-9, 12, 16, 34n
Compartmental model, 4, 8, 9, 11, 14-16, 33n, 37, 62, 80-83, 191, 239, 240, 242, 244
Co-occurrence, 9, 125, 126, 128, 133, 141, 142, 145, 147, 148, 169n, 176
Cooke, J. R., 120
Corporate social organization, 11, 209, 232, 234, 244
Correction, stylistic, 40, 48, 167
Coulthard, M., 7
Critic, vs. performer, 248-50, 253n
Critique, stylistic, 83, 86n, 238, 246-50, 253n
Cunningham, C., 203-5

Derveld, F., 28, 30
Dewey, A., 29
Diglossia, 33n, 137n, 238, 244
Directional interaction, 23, 46, 47, 54, 63n, 75, 87, 88, 91, 94-98, 100-101, 107-8, 111, 117, 156, 179, 237
Discursive syntax, 54, 70, 71, 75, 77, 99, 101, 142-44, 150, 151, 158-66 (passim)
Distance, stylistic, 64-65n, 84, 151, 152
Distance, social, 6, 13, 16, 24, 32, 37, 50, 61, 64-65n, 70, 79-80, 85, 100-101, 106, 117, 122, 127, 129, 131-34, 151, 166, 172-79, 184, 208, 209, 224, 232-33, 234n, 236, 240-42, 251
Distant-politeness, 18-22, 24, 33n, 37, 48, 72, 75, 87, 104-6, 108, 110, 114, 117, 118n, 143, 147, 150, 152, 174, 182, 184, 234n, 237, 241, 244
Djadji (boat-mate), 110, 141, 148, 163, 216
Domestic politeness, 85, 87, 107, 108, 116, 150, 236
Downward respect, 92, 175, 245
Dumarcay, J., 198
Durkheim, E., 6, 8, 15
Dutch (language), 6, 21, 31, 36, 41-42, 45, 79, 137n, 147, 157, 168, 233

Eating, 31, 108-11, 115, 180, 183-84, 195, 218-20, 225
Elite speech style, 5, 21, 69-70, 82, 121, 122, 128-36, 138n, 173-75, 186n
Ellipsis, 38-39, 70-72, 78, 83, 97-101 (passim), 107, 113, 114, 118n, 119n, 140, 176, 179, 185n
English, 21, 22, 36, 76, 93, 96, 100, 103-5, 109, 113, 114, 122, 124, 178, 181, 186n, 214, 239, 245
Errington, J., 37, 63n, 82, 121, 123, 129, 131, 133, 137n, 138n, 169n, 170n, 186n, 250
Ervin-Tripp, S., 3, 97, 105, 107, 169n
Ethnic interaction, 4, 6, 11, 18, 27-29, 31, 232, 233, 252

Face, personal, 11, 241, 250
Familial speech style, 40, 64n, 72, 79, 83, 84, 87, 92, 94-97, 100, 101, 138n, 144, 181, 184, 185, 194, 207, 213, 237, 238, 240-42, 252

Fasold, R., 244
Ferguson, C., 97, 107
First-person pronoun, 17, 103, 114-16, 123, 151, 152, 162, 171, 173, 175-85, 185n, 186n
Firth, R., 107
Fishman, J., 11, 12, 120
Formal speech style, 5, 6, 8, 12, 13, 17-25 (passim), 28, 33n, 34n, 37-62 (passim), 63n, 69-90, 93-98, 101, 109-12, 117-18, 118n, 121-27, 136, 137n, 138n, 139-53 (passim), 157-68, 169n, 171-85 (passim), 189, 191, 192, 195-97, 200, 201, 205-9, 210n, 212-17 (passim), 221-26, 228-34, 234n, 236-44, 248, 252
Foster kin, 17, 43, 46, 48, 84, 91, 94-96, 141, 168, 215, 216, 219, 225
Frake, C., 198-200
Front door, 22, 95, 192, 200, 206, 209, 212-15, 217, 220-22, 225, 226
Front porch, 193, 194, 200, 203, 207, 208, 212, 213, 215, 217, 220, 223, 224, 226-31, 233
Front region, 6-7, 11, 12, 97-98, 189-98, 202, 204, 206-7, 209, 212, 218, 220-22, 225, 230, 240-41, 244, 251

Gal, S., 8
Geertz, C., 5, 38, 58, 59, 64n, 69, 80, 86n, 120, 121, 138n, 173, 201, 208, 252n, 253n
Geertz, H., 21, 23, 50, 58, 64n, 84, 98, 111, 118n, 195, 204, 208
Gilman, A., 6, 18, 122, 131, 134, 171, 172, 174, 234, 244
Goffman, E., 6-12 (passim), 15-17, 20, 33n, 34n, 64n, 80, 97, 107, 190, 204, 241, 242
Goody, E., 85n, 97, 107
Grandparent-grandchild relationship, 48, 50, 95, 215, 236
Greetings, 10, 14-16, 20, 32, 70-71, 75, 80, 88, 90, 107-11, 113, 114, 117, 118n, 141, 144, 153, 154, 157, 162, 167, 168, 190, 216, 218, 234n, 242
Gregor, T., 201, 205, 206
Grice, H. P., 248
Gumperz, J., 3, 12, 192

Hall, E., 201, 205

Heine-Geldern, R., 13
Heller, M., 7-9
Honorific lexicon, 21, 36, 64n, 76, 119n, 122-36 (passim), 138n, 142, 157, 170n, 172-77, 185n
Horne, E., 76, 78, 86n, 119n
Hymes, D., 3, 7, 88, 201, 209

Imperative verb form, 89, 95-113 (passim), 118n, 119n
Imposition, 17-24, 34n, 241, 242, 251
Indexicality (meaning), 34n
Indexicals (deictics), 8, 38, 72, 74, 83, 99, 118n, 145, 164, 166
Indirection, 14, 22, 61, 97, 98, 105
Indonesian language, 19-21, 36, 106, 171, 178, 179, 199, 235n, 245. *See also* Bahasa Indonesia.
Inequality, 23, 38, 91, 100, 108, 117, 127, 172-75, 179, 198, 203, 232
Interaction, 3, 5-7, 9-22, 37-48, 56-62, 69, 72-76, 80, 83-117, 121, 122, 129-35, 138n, 139-41, 144, 147-67 (passim), 172-85 (passim), 189-201 (passim), 205-9, 212, 216-18, 222-25, 229-34, 234n, 236-48
Interrogatives, 18, 20, 22, 24, 42, 44, 70-75, 80, 87, 95, 97, 100-110, 112-14, 118n, 143, 144, 148, 150, 153-55, 157, 159, 162, 209
Intonation, 4, 8, 18, 24, 38-56, 61, 62n, 63n, 69-72, 74-76, 80, 84, 85n, 88, 106-13, 146-47, 150, 158, 168, 179, 206, 207, 237
Invitation, 21, 33n, 39, 42, 91, 92, 100, 104, 107, 114, 115, 143, 166, 192, 193, 214, 219, 223, 238
Irvine, J., 8, 37

Jain, D., 120
Jay, R., 23, 35n, 50, 51, 58, 64n, 76, 84, 85, 195, 197, 200, 202, 205, 208, 211, 218, 219, 231, 234n
Junior-senior interaction, 34n, 39, 40, 46, 49, 51, 55, 58, 72, 74, 85n, 89, 92-96, 99, 106, 108, 111-17 (passim), 118n

Keeler, W., 13, 14, 19-21, 34n, 38, 58-59, 62, 76, 77, 85, 85n, 86n, 119n, 121, 137n, 252n

Keesing, R., 120
Kinship terms, 4, 23, 32, 38-40, 43-46, 50-55, 62, 63n, 83, 94, 98-100, 105-6, 112, 114, 118n, 146, 147, 150, 152-57, 159, 174-77, 179, 184-85, 185n, 207
Kowé (second-person familiar pronoun), 137n, 147, 173, 174, 177-80, 182, 183, 185, 186n
Krama, 24, 36, 37, 38, 41-43, 48, 51, 63n, 77, 78, 82, 83, 86n, 123-36 (passim), 137n, 138n, 139, 142, 144, 150, 157, 159, 163, 169n, 170n, 171, 181, 182, 186n, 234n, 242, 248
Kula (first-person formal pronoun), 17, 54, 56, 57, 123, 142, 146, 149, 154, 160, 162, 165, 173, 175-77, 186n, 209, 234n

Labov, W., 3
Lakoff, R., 8, 9, 33n, 251
Leave-taking, 97, 100, 105, 112, 151, 152, 166, 238. See also *Pamitan*.
Levinson, S., 7, 10, 15, 16, 19, 34n, 242, 248
Lévi-Strauss, C., 24
Lexical style (see also *ngoko, madya, krama*, honorifics, neutral lexicon, subfamiliar lexicon), 3, 8, 18, 21-24, 32, 34n, 36-52 (passim), 55, 56, 61, 63n, 64n, 69, 74-77, 82, 89, 95, 97-101, 104, 106, 118n, 119n, 120, 122-27, 133, 136, 139-59 (passim), 163-68, 169n, 170n, 171, 173, 176, 177, 182, 184, 206, 236-39; shift in, 19, 23, 24, 34n, 37, 49, 74, 75, 77, 88-89, 93-96, 101, 106-8, 112, 125, 144, 147, 150, 158, 164-68, 169n, 171, 176, 178, 181, 206, 237, 239, 244
Lockard, C., 28

Madya, 21, 22, 36, 38, 63n, 82, 86n, 125-35 (passim), 137n, 138n, 139, 144, 159, 166, 167, 169n, 225, 250
Male-female interaction, 165, 220, 230, 233
Malefijt, A., 28
Manner, 238, 239, 247, 253n
Markedness, 9-10, 101, 103-5, 147, 171, 173, 176, 178-80, 190, 192, 195, 230, 247

Marker, stylistic, 41, 80, 99, 105, 144-50, 161, 166, 169n, 248
Market, 30, 31, 74, 98, 181, 207, 210n, 221
Mbah (grandparent), 35n, 39-46, 49, 54-57, 62, 100, 104, 108, 111, 113, 115, 118n, 147, 153-59, 162, 167, 169, 180, 238
Men, interaction among, 25, 139, 141, 168, 192-98, 200, 202, 204-9, 212, 214, 216-18, 224, 230-34, 234n, 236, 244, 251
Metaphor, 12, 16, 24, 80, 106, 108, 114
Metaphor model, 171-75 (passim)
Mintz, S., 28

Negative face, 11
Negative interaction ritual, 6, 15, 34n
Negative politeness, 6, 16-17, 34n, 84, 209, 241, 251-52
Negative utterance, 24, 41, 72, 80, 93, 105, 118n, 150, 158, 161, 162, 164-66, 168
Neighborhood, 26, 47, 88-90, 92, 95-96, 98-101, 202, 208, 231
Network, 11, 57, 84, 169n, 225, 232-34
Neutral lexicon, 123-25, 128, 134, 135, 140, 231, 233, 242
Ngoko, 21, 22, 24, 33n, 36-38, 60, 62, 63n, 64n, 77, 82, 83, 85, 86n, 98-99, 123-36 (passim), 137n, 138n, 144, 163-66, 168, 169n, 171, 181, 225, 238, 243, 245
Non-elite speech style, 37, 69, 70, 78, 121, 122, 128-36, 137n, 138n, 147, 174, 175, 236, 250

Openness, 208, 209
Ordinary speech style, 12, 24, 37, 41, 43, 46, 48, 51-62, 69-72, 75-84, 87, 123-126, 132, 133, 136, 142, 148, 150, 151, 158, 163-66, 169n, 171, 177, 181, 184, 191, 195, 206, 207, 209, 236, 237, 240, 241, 244

Pamitan, 41, 44, 54, 91, 100-101, 104, 112-14. *See also* Leave-taking.
Paradigm, 3-4, 32, 33n, 78, 80-82, 123, 124, 126, 127, 169n, 173-75, 184, 189, 192, 239, 240, 244, 246, 249, 253n

Paramaribo, 22, 23, 25, 26, 29, 30, 43, 46-48, 140, 145, 166, 214, 216, 218, 219, 221-26, 241
Parkin, D., 9
Particle, expressive or syntatic, 44, 70-71, 100-102, 107, 115, 143, 150, 163, 164, 177
Passive verb forms, 151, 152, 179, 180, 182, 183
Peacock, J., 69, 244
Phonology, 72, 76, 77, 78, 86n, 119n, 158
Poedjosoedarmo, G., 62n
Poedjosoedarmo, S., 77, 121, 124, 125, 128, 129, 132-35, 138n
Politeness, as a speech style, 4, 8, 14-24 (passim), 36-48, 50-57, 59, 61, 69, 72-85, 87, 90, 95, 98-117 (passim), 122-26, 128-30, 132, 135, 136, 137n, 139, 141-68, 171-85 (passim), 196, 206, 209, 210n, 216, 218, 225, 232, 234, 236-39, 241-43, 248, 251
Politeness formulas, 40, 70, 104-6, 108-16, 118, 151, 169n, 180
Positive politeness, 15-17, 32, 34n, 90
Pragmatics, 7
Price, R., 27, 28, 31
Price, S., 249
Pride, J. B., 120, 165
Private vs. public spheres of action, 80, 190, 195, 196, 200, 201, 205, 206, 211, 214, 224, 227, 230, 231, 240
Priyayi (aristocracy), 5, 58, 120, 129, 131, 136n, 138n
Pronoun replacement, 118, 171, 173, 174, 177, 179, 180, 186n
Pronouns, 4, 17, 18, 32, 64n, 122-23, 131-32, 134, 137n, 138n, 143, 147, 150, 152, 154, 162, 164, 166, 171-85, 185n-86n, 244, 252
Prosody, 136, 141, 147, 159, 236
Public spheres of action, 30, 38, 61, 89, 93-97, 102-17 (passim), 190-92, 195, 196, 201, 202, 205-7, 209, 210n, 214, 221, 224, 230, 240
Punctuate syntax, 43, 53, 70, 71, 142, 147, 150, 153, 206

Questions, 70, 71, 75, 80, 85n, 97-98, 143, 154, 168, 169n, 182, 183, 234n, 242

Quotation, 49-50, 85n, 167-68

Radcliffe-Brown, R., 6, 8, 10, 208
Ramé (liveliness), 37, 62, 79-82, 86n, 191, 245
Redress, 14
Regions, socially significant, 6-7, 11-12, 34n, 189-209 (passim), 210n, 211-13, 215, 217, 218, 220-22, 224, 225, 228, 230, 231, 240-44, 251
Remediation, 14, 20, 21, 24, 34n
Repertoire, 4-6, 9, 10, 34n, 76, 78, 85, 87, 126, 131, 133-35, 143, 144, 147, 167, 189, 207, 233, 239, 244-46, 250
Respect, 204, 209, 234
Respect style, 4, 6, 8-10, 12, 21-22, 36-58, 60-62, 63n, 64n, 65n, 69, 72, 79, 81-83, 87, 92-100, 106, 114-17, 118n, 126, 129, 131-34, 136, 138n, 139-45 (passim), 150-60, 163, 167-68, 169n, 171, 173, 175-79, 181, 184-85, 191, 206, 207, 236, 237, 240-42, 244, 245
Response, 22, 23, 73, 74, 80, 118n, 125, 142-44, 150, 154-56, 158-63, 167, 169n, 219, 238, 242, 250. *See also* Affirmative response.
Rice meal, 89, 93, 98, 110, 219, 220, 225, 228, 229
Ritual, 6, 9, 14-17, 20, 21, 28, 32, 33-34n, 38, 55, 58, 59, 62, 80, 140, 191, 200, 201, 203-6, 210n, 216, 224, 226, 229, 232, 234n, 236, 239, 240, 242, 246

Sampéyan (second-person formal pronoun), 48, 142, 143, 146, 149, 150, 155, 160, 161, 173-77
Schiffman, H., 7, 120
Scotton, C., 9, 10, 34n
Second-person pronoun, 32, 89, 98, 104-7, 109, 114-17, 118n, 122, 126, 128-35, 137n, 138n, 147, 150, 170n, 172-85, 185n
Setting of interaction, 3, 10-12, 21, 26, 32-33, 37, 45, 58, 83, 107, 122, 157-58, 165, 189-91, 195, 197, 211-13, 215, 217, 218, 220-22, 224, 229-33, 241, 252
Siegel, J., 14, 19, 51, 59-62, 82, 84, 85, 137n, 238, 243

Silence, 88, 93, 94, 96, 101, 118n, 242, 252
Silverstein, M., 120, 121, 172
Slametan (ritual), 33n, 38, 56, 58, 152, 163, 166, 181, 194, 211, 212, 223, 226, 228, 229, 231
Smith-Hefner, N., 33n, 121
Social boundaries, 8, 10, 11, 15, 16, 57-58
Sociolinguistics, 3, 5-7, 18, 120
Speech act, 7, 21, 34n
Sranang (Suriname creole), 31, 41, 45-48, 86n, 137n, 168, 233
Srinivas, M., 230
Stylistics, 245-51; stylistic adequacy, 246-48, 253n; stylistic alternation, 3-12, 18-26, 32, 33, 36-39, 47-62, 69, 72-84 (passim), 86n, 87, 97, 103-8, 113-17, 171-85 (passim), 185n, 236-52, 252n; stylistic appropriateness, 11, 20, 45, 80, 131, 246, 248, 249, 252; stylistic boundaries, 131-36; stylistic competence, 5, 7, 33, 38, 47, 95, 117, 133, 139, 166, 238, 244, 247, 250, 251; stylistic meaning, 3-4, 8, 12, 18, 26, 32-33, 34n, 78, 120, 127, 132, 185, 193, 231, 251, 253n; stylistic norms, 9, 11, 147, 208; stylistic perspectives, 3, 7-9, 13, 24, 26, 59, 83, 191, 200, 203, 234, 240-44, 253n; stylistic structure, 189-91, 206, 207, 210n; stylistic values, 37, 51, 58-62, 69, 78-82, 86n, 191, 204-7, 232-34, 239-44; stylization, 24, 37, 57-61 (passim), 70, 72, 75, 78-80, 83-90, 97-107 (passim), 115-17, 178, 236-39, 243, 250, 251, 252n
Subdivisions, spatial, 197, 212-22
Subfamiliar lexicon, 161
Suharno, I., 64n, 121, 125, 252
Suparlan, P., 35n, 137n
Syntax, 3, 20, 32, 38, 43, 52, 54-56, 62n, 69-72, 78, 84n, 86n, 93, 98, 101, 114, 127, 142, 146, 147, 150, 151, 154, 159, 176, 178, 206, 252. *See also* Discursive syntax and Punctuate syntax.

Task-oriented language, 71, 83, 87-102 (passim), 106-17 (passim), 118n, 150, 154-56, 169n, 237
Topic, 3, 19, 20, 24-26, 33n, 76, 139, 150, 163, 247

Uhlenbeck, E. M., 62n, 78, 121, 123-25, 127, 137n, 138n
Urban interaction, 5, 10, 15, 20, 28, 31, 38, 45, 121, 137n, 138n, 139, 145, 157, 211, 232

Village, 10, 25, 28, 30, 31, 35n, 57, 85, 152, 167, 192, 201-3, 205, 208, 213, 216, 225, 232, 234, 244
Visiting, 17, 18, 21-26 (passim), 45, 88-90, 93-94, 98, 101, 105-15 (passim), 117, 141, 145, 148, 150-52, 156, 158, 163-66, 168, 190, 209, 211-28, 230-33, 236, 192-97 (passim), 205, 208, 211, 216, 217, 221, 224, 226, 228, 230, 238

Wayang (shadow theater), 239, 247
Wolff, J., 70, 121
Women, interaction among, 10, 11, 21, 25, 30, 193-98, 201, 204-6, 211-12, 218-26 (passim), 230-31, 234

A Note on the Author

CLARE WOLFOWITZ earned an M.Phil. in 1971 from the London School of Economics and Political Science, where she was a Marshall Scholar, and her Ph.D. in 1984 from Johns Hopkins University. She has been Professorial Lecturer at the Johns Hopkins School of Advanced International Studies since 1985 and served from 1986 to 1989 as wife of the American ambassador to Indonesia. She currently serves on the Board of Trustees of Deep Springs College (Deep Springs, California) and on the Board of Advisors of the Smithsonian Institution's Office of Folklife Studies.